# NES

# Middle Grades Social Science

# SECRETS

## Study Guide

Your Key to Exam Success

NES Test Review for the
National Evaluation Series Tests

Dear Future Exam Success Story:

Congratulations on your purchase of our study guide. Our goal in writing our study guide was to cover the content on the test, as well as provide insight into typical test taking mistakes and how to overcome them.

Standardized tests are a key component of being successful, which only increases the importance of doing well in the high-pressure high-stakes environment of test day. How well you do on this test will have a significant impact on your future, and we have the research and practical advice to help you execute on test day.

The product you're reading now is designed to exploit weaknesses in the test itself, and help you avoid the most common errors test takers frequently make.

**How to use this study guide**

We don't want to waste your time. Our study guide is fast-paced and fluff-free. We suggest going through it a number of times, as repetition is an important part of learning new information and concepts.

First, read through the study guide completely to get a feel for the content and organization. Read the general success strategies first, and then proceed to the content sections. Each tip has been carefully selected for its effectiveness.

Second, read through the study guide again, and take notes in the margins and highlight those sections where you may have a particular weakness.

Finally, bring the manual with you on test day and study it before the exam begins.

**Your success is our success**

We would be delighted to hear about your success. Send us an email and tell us your story. Thanks for your business and we wish you continued success.

Sincerely,

Mometrix Test Preparation Team

**Need more help? Check out our flashcards at: http://mometrixflashcards.com/NESINC**


Written and edited by the Mometrix Exam Secrets Test Prep Team
Printed in the United States of America

## TABLE OF CONTENTS

# Top 20 Test Taking Tips

1. Carefully follow all the test registration procedures
2. Know the test directions, duration, topics, question types, how many questions
3. Setup a flexible study schedule at least 3-4 weeks before test day
4. Study during the time of day you are most alert, relaxed, and stress free
5. Maximize your learning style; visual learner use visual study aids, auditory learner use auditory study aids
6. Focus on your weakest knowledge base
7. Find a study partner to review with and help clarify questions
8. Practice, practice, practice
9. Get a good night's sleep; don't try to cram the night before the test
10. Eat a well balanced meal
11. Know the exact physical location of the testing site; drive the route to the site prior to test day
12. Bring a set of ear plugs; the testing center could be noisy
13. Wear comfortable, loose fitting, layered clothing to the testing center; prepare for it to be either cold or hot during the test
14. Bring at least 2 current forms of ID to the testing center
15. Arrive to the test early; be prepared to wait and be patient
16. Eliminate the obviously wrong answer choices, then guess the first remaining choice
17. Pace yourself; don't rush, but keep working and move on if you get stuck
18. Maintain a positive attitude even if the test is going poorly
19. Keep your first answer unless you are positive it is wrong
20. Check your work, don't make a careless mistake

# History

## United States History

### Well-known Native Americans

The following are five well-known Native Americans and their roles in early US history:

- Squanto, an Algonquian, helped early English settlers survive the hard winter by teaching them the native methods of planting corn, squash, and pumpkins.
- Pocahontas, also Algonquian, became famous as a liaison with John Smith's Jamestown colony in 1607.
- Sacagawea, a Shoshone, served a vital role in the Lewis and Clark expedition when the two explorers hired her as their guide in 1805.
- Crazy Horse and Sitting Bull led Sioux and Cheyenne troops in the Battle of the Little Bighorn in 1876, soundly defeating George Armstrong Custer.
- Chief Joseph, a leader of the Nez Perce who supported peaceful interaction with white settlers, attempted to relocate his tribe to Canada rather than move them to a reservation.

### Native American groups

The major regional Native American groups and the major traits of each are as follows:

- The Algonquians in the eastern part of the United States lived in wigwams. The northern tribes subsisted on hunting and gathering, while those who were farther south grew crops such as corn.
- The Iroquois, also an east coast tribe, spoke a different language from the Algonquians, and lived in rectangular longhouses.
- The Plains tribes lived between the Mississippi River and the Rocky Mountains. These nomadic tribes lived in teepees and followed the buffalo herds. Plains tribes included the Sioux, Cheyenne, Comanche and Blackfoot.
- Pueblo tribes included the Zuni, Hopi, and Acoma. They lived in the Southwest deserts in homes made of stone or adobe. They domesticated animals and cultivated corn and beans.
- On the Pacific coast, tribes such as the Tlingit, Chinook and Salish lived on fish as well as deer, native berries and roots. Their rectangular homes housed large family groups, and they used totem poles.
- In the far north, the Aleuts and Inuit lived in skin tents or igloos. Talented fishermen, they built kayaks and umiaks and also hunted caribou, seals, whales and walrus.

## Age of Exploration

The Age of Exploration is also called the Age of Discovery. It is generally considered to have begun in the early fifteenth century and continued into the seventeenth century. Major developments of the Age of Exploration included technological advances in navigation, mapmaking and shipbuilding. These advances led to expanded European exploration of the rest of the world. Explorers set out from several European countries, including Portugal, Spain, France and England, seeking new routes to Asia. These efforts led to the discovery of new lands, as well as colonization in India, Asia, Africa, and North America.

> ➢ **Review Video:** Age of Exploration
> *Visit **mometrix.com/academy** and enter **Code:*** **167264**

## Advancements in navigation and seafaring tools

For long ocean journeys, it was important for sailors to be able to find their way home even when their vessels sailed far out to sea. A variety of navigational tools enabled them to launch ambitious journeys over long distances. The compass and astrolabe were particularly important advancements. The magnetic compass was used by Chinese navigators from approximately 200 B.C.E., and knowledge of the astrolabe came to Europe from Arab navigators and traders who had refined designs developed by the ancient Greeks. The Portuguese developed a ship called a caravel in the 1400s that incorporated navigational advancements with the ability to make long sea journeys. Equipped with this advanced vessel, the Portuguese achieved a major goal of the Age of Exploration by discovering a sea route from Europe to Asia in 1498.

## Voyage of Christopher Columbus

In 1492, Columbus, a Genoan explorer, obtained financial backing from King Ferdinand and Queen Isabella of Spain to seek a sea route to Asia. He sought a trade route with the Asian Indies to the west. With three ships, the *Niña*, the *Pinta* and the *Santa Maria*, he eventually landed in the West Indies. While Columbus failed in his effort to discover a western route to Asia, he is credited with the discovery of the Americas.

> ➢ **Review Video:** Christopher Columbus
> *Visit **mometrix.com/academy** and enter **Code:*** **765231**

## Colonization of the Americas

France, Spain, the Netherlands, and England each had specific goals in the colonization of the Americas:

- Initial French colonies were focused on expanding the fur trade. Later, French colonization led to the growth of plantations in Louisiana which brought numerous African slaves to the New World.
- Spanish colonists came to look for wealth, and to convert the natives to Christianity. For some, the desire for gold led to mining in the New World, while others established large ranches.

- The Dutch were also involved in the fur trade, and imported slaves as the need for laborers increased.
- British colonists arrived with various goals. Some were simply looking for additional income, while others were fleeing Britain to escape religious persecution.

New England colonies

The New England colonies were New Hampshire, Connecticut, Rhode Island and Massachusetts. These colonies were founded largely to escape religious persecution in England. The beliefs of the Puritans, who migrated to America in the 1600s, significantly influenced the development of these colonies. Situated in the northeast coastal areas of America, the New England colonies featured numerous harbors as well as dense forests. The soil, however, was rocky and had a very short growing season, so was not well suited for agriculture. The economy of New England during the colonial period centered around fishing, shipbuilding and trade along with some small farms and lumber mills. Although some groups congregated in small farms, life centered mainly in towns and cities where merchants largely controlled the trade economy. Coastal cities such as Boston grew and thrived.

Middle or Middle Atlantic Colonies

The Middle or Middle Atlantic Colonies were New York, New Jersey, Pennsylvania and Delaware. Unlike the New England colonies, where most colonists were from England and Scotland, the Middle Colonies founders were from various countries including the Netherlands and Sweden. Various factors led these colonists to America. More fertile than New England, the Middle Colonies became major producers of crops including rye, oats, potatoes, wheat, and barley. Some particularly wealthy inhabitants owned large farms and/or businesses. Farmers in general were able to produce enough to have a surplus to sell. Tenant farmers also rented land from larger land owners.

Southern Colonies

The Southern Colonies were Maryland, Virginia, North Carolina, South Carolina and Georgia. Of the Southern Colonies, Virginia was the first permanent English colony and Georgia the last. The warm climate and rich soil of the south encouraged agriculture, and the growing season was long. As a result, economy in the south was based largely on labor-intensive plantations. Crops included tobacco, rice and indigo, all of which became valuable cash crops. Most land in the south was controlled by wealthy plantation owners and farmers. Labor on the farms came in the form of indentured servants and African slaves. The first of these African slaves arrived in Virginia in 1619.

## French and Indian Wars

The British defeat of the Spanish Armada in 1588 led to the decline of Spanish power in Europe. This in turn led the British and French into battle several times between 1689 and 1748. These wars were:

- King William's War, or the Nine Years War, 1689-1697. This war was fought largely in Flanders.
- The War of Spanish Succession, or Queen Anne's War, 1702-1713
- War of Austrian Succession, or King George's War, 1740-1748

The fourth and final war, the French and Indian War (1754-1763), was fought largely in the North American territory, and resulted in the end of France's reign as a colonial power in

North America. Although the French held many advantages, including more cooperative colonists and numerous Indian allies, the strong leadership of William Pitt eventually led the British to victory. Costs incurred during the wars eventually led to discontent in the colonies and helped spark the American Revolution.

### Navigation Acts

The Navigation Acts, enacted in 1651, were an attempt by Britain to dominate international trade. Aimed largely at the Dutch, the Acts banned foreign ships from transporting goods to the British colonies, and from transporting goods to Britain from elsewhere in Europe. While the restrictions on trade angered some colonists, these Acts were helpful to other American colonists who, as members of the British Empire, were legally able to provide ships for Britain's growing trade interests and use the ships for their own trading ventures. By the time the French and Indian War had ended, one-third of British merchant ships were built in the American colonies. Many colonists amassed fortunes in the shipbuilding trade.

### Higher taxes after the French and Indian War

The French and Indian War created circumstances for which the British desperately needed more revenue. These needs included:

- Paying off the war debt
- Defending the expanding empire
- Governing Britain's 33 far-flung colonies, including the American colonies

To meet these needs, the British passed additional laws, increasing revenues from the colonies. Because they had spent so much money to defend the American colonies, the British felt it was appropriate to collect considerably higher taxes from them. The colonists felt this was unfair, and many were led to protest the increasing taxes. Eventually, protest led to violence.

### Triangular trade

Triangular trade began in the Colonies with ships setting off for Africa, carrying rum. In Africa, the rum was traded for gold or slaves. Ships then went from Africa to the West Indies, trading slaves for sugar, molasses, or money. To complete the triangle, the ships returned to the colonies with sugar or molasses to make more rum, as well as stores of gold and silver. This trade triangle violated the Molasses Act of 1733, which required the colonists to pay high duties to Britain on molasses acquired from French, Dutch, and Spanish colonies. The colonists ignored these duties, and the British government adopted a policy of salutary neglect by not enforcing them.

### Effects of new laws on British-Colonial relations

While earlier revenue-generating acts such as the Navigation Acts brought money to the colonists, the new laws after 1763 required colonists to pay money back to Britain. The British felt this was fair since the colonists were British subjects and since they had incurred debt protecting the Colonies. The colonists felt it was not only unfair, but illegal.

The development of local government in America had given the colonists a different view of the structure and role of government. This made it difficult for the British to understand the colonists' protests against what the British felt was a fair and reasonable solution to the mother country's financial problems.

## Increasing discontent in the American colonies

More and more colonists were born on American soil, decreasing any sense of kinship with the far away British rulers. Their new environment had led to new ideas of government and a strong view of the colonies as a separate entity from Britain. Colonists were allowed to self-govern in domestic issues, but Britain controlled international issues. In fact, the American colonies were largely left to form their own local government bodies, giving them more freedom than any other colonial territory. This gave the colonists a sense of independence, which led them to resent control from Britain. Threats during the French and Indian War led the colonists to call for unification in order to protect themselves.

## Difference between colonial government and British government

As new towns and other legislative districts developed in America, the colonists began to practice representative government. Colonial legislative bodies were made up of elected representatives chosen by male property owners in the districts. These individuals represented the interests of the districts from which they had been elected. By contrast, in Britain the Parliament represented the entire country. Parliament was not elected to represent individual districts. Instead, they represented specific classes. Because of this drastically different approach to government, the British did not understand the colonists' statement that they had no representation in the British Parliament.

## Acts of British Parliament

After the French and Indian Wars, the British Parliament passed four major acts:

- The Sugar Act, 1764—this act not only required taxes to be collected on molasses brought into the colonies, but gave British officials the right to search the homes of anyone suspected of violating it.
- The Stamp Act, 1765—this act taxed printed materials such as newspapers and legal documents. Protests led the Stamp Act to be repealed in 1766, but the repeal also included the Declaratory Act, which stated that Parliament had the right to govern the colonies.
- The Quartering Act, 1765—this act required colonists to provide accommodations and supplies for British troops. In addition, colonists were prohibited from settling west of the Appalachians until given permission by Britain.
- The Townshend Acts, 1767—these acts taxed paper, paint, lead and tea that came into the colonies. Colonists led boycotts in protest, and in Massachusetts leaders like Samuel and John Adams began to organize resistance against British rule.

## Boston Massacre

With the passage of the Stamp Act, nine colonies met in New York to demand its repeal. Elsewhere, protest arose in New York City, Philadelphia, Boston and other cities. These protests sometimes escalated into violence, often targeting ruling British officials. The passage of the Townshend Acts in 1767 led to additional tension in the colonies. The British sent troops to New York City and Boston. On March 5, 1770, protesters began to taunt the British troops, throwing snowballs. The soldiers responded by firing into the crowd. This clash between protesters and soldiers led to five deaths and eight injuries, and was christened the Boston Massacre. Shortly thereafter, Britain repealed the majority of the Townshend Acts.

### Tea Act and the Boston Tea Party

The majority of the Townshend Acts were repealed after the Boston Massacre in 1770, but Britain kept the tax on tea. In 1773, the Tea Act was passed. This allowed the East India Company to sell tea for much lower prices, and also allowed them to bypass American distributors, selling directly to shopkeepers instead. Colonial tea merchants saw this as a direct assault on their business. In December of 1773, the Sons of Liberty boarded ships in Boston Harbor and dumped 342 chests of tea into the sea in protest of the new laws. This act of protest came to be known as the Boston Tea Party.

### Coercive/Intolerable Acts

The Coercive Acts passed by Britain in 1774 were meant to punish Massachusetts for defying British authority. The four acts, also known as the Intolerable Acts:

- Shut down ports in Boston until the city paid back the value of the tea destroyed during the Boston Tea Party
- Required that local government officials in Massachusetts be appointed by the governor rather than being elected by the people
- Allowed trials of British soldiers to be transferred to Britain rather than being held in Massachusetts
- Required locals to provide lodging for British soldiers any time there was a disturbance, even if lodging required them to stay in private homes

These Acts led to the assembly of the First Continental Congress in Philadelphia on September 5, 1774. Fifty-five delegates met, representing 12 of the American colonies. They sought compromise with England over England's increasingly harsh efforts to control the colonies.

### First Continental Congress

The First Continental Congress met in Philadelphia on September 5, 1774. Their goal was to achieve a peaceful agreement with Britain. Made up of delegates from 12 of the 13 colonies, the Congress affirmed loyalty to Britain and the power of Parliament to dictate foreign affairs in the colonies. However, they demanded that the Intolerable Acts be repealed, and instituted a trade embargo with Britain until this came to pass.

In response, George III of England declared that the American colonies must submit or face military action. The British sought to end assemblies that opposed their policies. These assemblies gathered weapons and began to form militias. On April 19, 1775, the British military was ordered to disperse a meeting of the Massachusetts Assembly. A battle ensued on Lexington Common as the armed colonists resisted. The resulting battles became the Battle of Lexington and Concord—the first battles of the American Revolution.

## Second Continental Congress

The Second Continental Congress met in Philadelphia on May 10, 1775, a month after Lexington and Concord. Their discussions centered on defense of the American colonies and how to conduct the growing war, as well as local government. The delegates also discussed declaring independence from Britain, with many members in favor of this drastic move. They established an army, and on June 15, named George Washington as its commander-in-chief. By 1776, it was obvious that there was no turning back from full-scale war with Britain. The colonial delegates of the Continental Congress drafted the Declaration of Independence on July 4, 1776.

## Declaration of Independence

Penned by Thomas Jefferson and signed on July 4, 1776, the Declaration of Independence stated that King George III had violated the rights of the colonists and was establishing a tyrannical reign over them. Many of Jefferson's ideas of natural rights and property rights were shaped by seventeenth-century philosopher John Locke. Jefferson asserted all people's rights to "life, liberty and the pursuit of happiness." Locke's comparable idea asserted "life, liberty, and private property." Both felt that the purpose of government was to protect the rights of the people, and that individual rights were more important than individuals' obligations to the state.

## Battles of the Revolutionary War

The following are five major battles of the Revolutionary War and their significance:

- The Battle of Lexington and Concord (April 1775) is considered the first engagement of the Revolutionary War.
- The Battle of Bunker Hill (June 1775) was one of the bloodiest of the entire war. Although American troops withdrew, about half of the British army was lost. The colonists proved they could stand against professional British soldiers. In August, Britain declared that the American colonies were officially in a state of rebellion.
- The first colonial victory occurred in Trenton, New Jersey, when Washington and his troops crossed the Delaware River on Christmas Day, 1776 for a December 26 surprise attack on British and Hessian troops.
- The Battle of Saratoga effectively ended a plan to separate the New England colonies from their Southern counterparts. The surrender of British general John Burgoyne led to France joining the war as allies of the Americans, and is generally considered a turning point of the war.
- On October 19, 1781, General Cornwallis surrendered after a defeat in the Battle of Yorktown, ending the Revolutionary War.

## Treaty of Paris

The Treaty of Paris was signed on September 3, 1783, bringing an official end to the Revolutionary War. In this document, Britain officially recognized the United States of America as an independent nation. The treaty established the Mississippi River as the country's western border. The treaty also restored Florida to Spain, while France reclaimed African and Caribbean colonies seized by the British in 1763. On November 25, 1783, the last British troops departed from the newly born United States of America.

## Articles of Confederation

A precursor to the Constitution, the Articles of Confederation represented the first attempt of the newly independent colonies to establish the basics of government. The Continental Congress approved the Articles on November 15, 1777. They went into effect on March 1, 1781, following ratification by the thirteen states. The Articles prevented a central government from gaining too much power, instead giving power to a Congressional body made up of delegates from all thirteen states. However, the individual states retained final authority.

Without a strong central executive, though, this weak alliance among the new states proved ineffective in settling disputes or enforcing laws. The idea of a weak central government needed to be revised. Recognition of these weaknesses eventually led to the drafting of a new document, the Constitution.

## The Constitution

Delegates from twelve of the thirteen states (Rhode Island was not represented) met in Philadelphia in May of 1787, initially intending to revise the Articles of Confederation. However, it quickly became apparent that a simple revision would not provide the workable governmental structure the newly formed country needed. After vowing to keep all the proceedings secret until the final document was completed, the delegates set out to draft what would eventually become the Constitution of the United States of America. By keeping the negotiations secret, the delegates were able to present a completed document to the country for ratification, rather than having every small detail hammered out by the general public.

## Structure of proposed government

The delegates agreed that the new nation required a strong central government, but that its overall power should be limited. The various branches of the government should have balanced power, so that no one group could control the others. Final power belonged with the citizens who voted officials into office based on who would provide the best representation.

## Virginia Plan, New Jersey Plan, and the Great Compromise

Disagreement immediately occurred between delegates from large states and those from smaller states. James Madison and Edmund Randolph (the governor of Virginia) felt that representation in Congress should be based on state population. This was the Virginia Plan. The New Jersey Plan, presented by William Paterson, from New Jersey, proposed each state have equal representation. Finally, Roger Sherman from Connecticut formulated the Connecticut Compromise, also called the Great Compromise. The result was the familiar structure we have today. Each state has the equal representation of two Senators in the Senate, with the number of representatives in the House of Representatives based on population. This is called a bicameral Congress. Both houses may draft bills, but financial matters must originate in the House of Representatives.

## Three-fifths compromise

During debate on the US Constitution, a disagreement arose between the Northern and Southern states involving how slaves should be counted when determining a state's quota of representatives. In the South large numbers of slaves were commonly used to run plantations. Delegates wanted slaves to be counted to determine the number of representatives, but not counted to determine the amount of taxes the states would pay. The Northern states wanted exactly the opposite arrangement. The final decision was to count three-fifths of the slave population both for tax purposes and to determine representation. This was called the three-fifths compromise.

## Commerce Compromise

The Commerce Compromise also resulted from a North/South disagreement. In the North the economy was centered on industry and trade. The Southern economy was largely agricultural. The Northern states wanted to give the new government the ability to regulate exports as well as trade between the states. The South opposed this plan. Another compromise was in order. In the end, Congress received regulatory power over all trade, including the ability to collect tariffs on exported goods. In the South, this raised another red flag regarding the slave trade, as they were concerned about the effect on their economy if tariffs were levied on slaves. The final agreement allowed importing slaves to continue for twenty years without government intervention. Import taxes on slaves were limited, and after the year 1808, Congress could decide whether to allow continued imports of slaves.

## Objections against the Constitution

Once the Constitution was drafted, it was presented for approval by the states. Nine states needed to approve the document for it to become official. However, debate and discussion continued. Major concerns included:

- The lack of a bill of rights to protect individual freedoms
- States felt too much power was being handed over to the central government
- Voters wanted more control over their elected representatives

Discussion about necessary changes to the Constitution was divided into two camps: Federalists and Anti-Federalists. Federalists wanted a strong central government. Anti-Federalists wanted to prevent a tyrannical government from developing if a central government held too much power.

## Federalist and Anti-Federalist camps

Major Federalist leaders included Alexander Hamilton, John Jay and James Madison. They wrote a series of letters, called the Federalist Papers, aimed at convincing the states to ratify the Constitution. These were published in New York papers. Anti-Federalists included Thomas Jefferson and Patrick Henry. They argued against the Constitution as it was originally drafted in a series of Anti-Federalist Papers. The final compromise produced a strong central government controlled by checks and balances. A Bill of Rights was also added, becoming the first ten amendments to the Constitution. These amendments protected rights such as freedom of speech, freedom of religion, and other basic rights. Aside from various amendments added throughout the years, the United States Constitution has remained unchanged.

## Administration of the new government

The individuals who formed the first administration of the new government were:

- George Washington—elected as the first President of the United States in 1789
- John Adams—finished second in the election and became the first Vice President
- Thomas Jefferson—appointed by Washington as Secretary of State
- Alexander Hamilton—appointed Secretary of the Treasury

## Alien and Sedition Acts

When John Adams became president, a war was raging between Britain and France. While Adams and the Federalists backed the British, Thomas Jefferson and the Republican Party supported the French. The United States nearly went to war with France during this time period, while France worked to spread its international standing and influence under the leadership of Napoleon Bonaparte. The Alien and Sedition Acts grew out of this conflict, and made it illegal to speak in a hostile fashion against the existing government. They also allowed the president to deport anyone in the US who was not a citizen and who was suspected of treason or treasonous activity. When Jefferson became the third president in 1800, he repealed these four laws and pardoned anyone who had been convicted under them.

> **Review Video:** The Alien and Sedition Acts
> *Visit **mometrix.com/academy** and enter **Code**:* **633780**

## Political parties

Many in the US were against political parties after seeing the way parties, or factions, functioned in Britain. The factions in Britain were more interested in personal profit than the overall good of the country, and they did not want this to happen in the US. However, the differences of opinion between Thomas Jefferson and Alexander Hamilton led to formation of political parties. Hamilton favored a stronger central government, while Jefferson felt that more power should remain with the states. Jefferson was in favor of strict Constitutional interpretation, while Hamilton believed in a more flexible approach. As others joined the two camps, Hamilton backers began to term themselves Federalists while those supporting Jefferson became identified as Democratic-Republicans.

## Whig Party, Democratic Party, and Republican Party

Thomas Jefferson was elected president in 1800 and again in 1804. The Federalist Party began to decline, and its major figure, Alexander Hamilton, died in a duel with Aaron Burr in 1804. By 1816, the Federalist Party had virtually disappeared. New parties sprang up to take its place. After 1824, the Democratic-Republican Party suffered a split. The Whigs rose, backing John Quincy Adams and industrial growth. The new Democratic Party formed, in opposition to the Whigs, and their candidate, Andrew Jackson, was elected as president in 1828.

By the 1850s, issues regarding slavery led to the formation of the Republican Party, which was anti-slavery, while the Democratic Party, with a larger interest in the South, favored slavery. This Republican/Democrat division formed the basis of today's two-party system.

**Marbury v. Madison**

The main duty of the Supreme Court today is judicial review. This power was largely established by Marbury v. Madison. When John Adams was voted out of office in 1800, he worked, during his final days in office, to appoint Federalist judges to Supreme Court positions, knowing Jefferson, his replacement, held opposing views. As late as March 3, the day before Jefferson was to take office, Adams made last-minute appointments referred to as "Midnight Judges." One of the late appointments was William Marbury. The next day, March 4, Jefferson ordered his Secretary of State, James Madison, not to deliver Marbury's commission. This decision was backed by Chief Justice Marshall, who determined that the Judiciary Act of 1789, which granted the power to deliver commissions, was illegal in that it gave the Judicial Branch powers not granted in the Constitution. This case set precedent for the Supreme Court to nullify laws it found to be unconstitutional.

➢ **Review Video:** Marbury v. Madison
*Visit* ***mometrix.com/academy*** *and enter* ***Code*: 270990**

**McCulloch v. Maryland**

Judicial review was further exercised by the Supreme Court in McCulloch v. Maryland. When Congress chartered a national bank, the Second Bank of the United States, Maryland voted to tax any bank business dealing with banks chartered outside the state, including the federally chartered bank. Andrew McCulloch, an employee of the Second Bank of the US in Baltimore, refused to pay this tax. The resulting lawsuit from the State of Maryland went to the Supreme Court for judgment.

John Marshall, Chief Justice of the Supreme Court, stated that Congress was within its rights to charter a national bank. In addition, the State of Maryland did not have the power to levy a tax on the federal bank or on the federal government in general. In cases where state and federal government collided, precedent was set for the federal government to prevail.

**Effects of the Treaty of Paris on Native Americans**

After the Revolutionary War, the Treaty of Paris, which outlined the terms of surrender of the British to the Americans, granted large parcels of land to the US that were occupied by Native Americans. The new government attempted to claim the land, treating the natives as a conquered people. This approach proved unenforceable.

Next, the government tried purchasing the land from the Indians via a series of treaties as the country expanded westward. In practice, however, these treaties were not honored, and Native Americans were simply dislocated and forced to move farther and farther west, often with military action, as American expansion continued.

## Indian Removal Act of 1830 and the Treaty of New Echota

The Indian Removal Act of 1830 gave the new American government power to form treaties with Native Americans. In theory, America would claim land east of the Mississippi in exchange for land west of the Mississippi, to which the natives would relocate voluntarily. In practice, many tribal leaders were forced into signing the treaties, and relocation at times occurred by force. The Treaty of New Echota in 1835 was supposedly a treaty between the US government and Cherokee tribes in Georgia. However, the treaty was not signed by tribal leaders, but rather by a small portion of the represented people. The leaders protested and refused to leave, but President Martin Van Buren enforced the treaty by sending soldiers. During their forced relocation, more than 4,000 Cherokee Indians died on what became known as the Trail of Tears.

## Early economic trends by region

In the Northeast, the economy mostly depended on manufacturing, industry, and industrial development. This led to a dichotomy between rich business owners and industrial leaders and the much poorer workers who supported their businesses. The South continued to depend on agriculture, especially on large-scale farms or plantations worked mostly by slaves and indentured servants. In the West, where new settlements had begun to develop, the land was largely wild. Growing communities were essentially agricultural, raising crops and livestock. The differences between regions led each to support different interests both politically and economically.

## Louisiana Purchase

With tension still high between France and Britain, Napoleon was in need of money to support his continuing war efforts. To secure necessary funds, he decided to sell the Louisiana Territory to the US President Thomas Jefferson wanted to buy New Orleans, feeling US trade was made vulnerable to both Spain and France at that port. Instead, Napoleon sold him the entire territory for the bargain price of fifteen million dollars. The Louisiana Territory was larger than all the rest of the United States put together, and it eventually became fifteen additional states. Federalists in Congress were opposed to the purchase. They feared that the Louisiana Purchase would extend slavery, and that further western growth would weaken the power of the northern states.

## Early foreign policy

The three major ideas driving American foreign policy during its early years were:

- Isolationism—the early US government did not intend to establish colonies, though they did plan to grow larger within the bounds of North America.
- No entangling alliances—both George Washington and Thomas Jefferson were opposed to forming any permanent alliances with other countries or becoming involved in other countries' internal issues.
- Nationalism—a positive patriotic feeling about the United States blossomed quickly among its citizens, particularly after the War of 1812, when the US once again defeated Britain. The Industrial Revolution also sparked increased nationalism by allowing even the most far-flung areas of the US to communicate with each other via telegraph and the expanding railroad.

## War of 1812

The War of 1812 grew out of the continuing tension between France and Great Britain. Napoleon continued striving to conquer Britain, while the US continued trade with both countries, but favored France and the French colonies. Because of what Britain saw as an alliance between America and France, they determined to bring an end to trade between the two nations.

With the British preventing US trade with the French and the French preventing trade with the British, James Madison's presidency introduced acts to regulate international trade. If either Britain or France removed their restrictions, America would not trade with the other country. Napoleon acted first, and Madison prohibited trade with England. England saw this as the US formally siding with the French, and war ensued in 1812.

The War of 1812 has been called the Second American Revolution. It established the superiority of the US naval forces and reestablished US independence from Britain and Europe.

The British had two major objections to America's continued trade with France. First, they saw the US as helping France's war effort by providing supplies and goods. Second, the United States had grown into a competitor, taking trade and money away from British ships and tradesmen. In its attempts to end American trade with France, the British put into effect the Orders in Council, which made any and all French-owned ports off-limits to American ships. They also began to seize American ships and conscript their crews.

> ➢ **Review Video:** Opinions About the War of 1812
> *Visit **mometrix.com/academy** and enter **Code**:* **274558**

> ➢ **Review Video:** Results of the War of 1812
> *Visit **mometrix.com/academy** and enter **Code**:* **993725**

Military events

Two major naval battles, at Lake Erie and Lake Champlain, kept the British from invading the US via Canada. American attempts to conquer Canadian lands were not successful.

In another memorable British attack, the British invaded Washington DC and burned the White House on August 24, 1814. Legend has it that Dolley Madison, the First Lady, salvaged the portrait of George Washington from the fire. On Christmas Eve, 1814, the Treaty of Ghent officially ended the war. However, Andrew Jackson, unaware that the war was over, managed another victory at New Orleans on January 8, 1815. This victory improved American morale and led to a new wave of national pride and support known as the "Era of Good Feelings."

## Monroe Doctrine

On December 2, 1823, President Monroe delivered a message to Congress in which he introduced the Monroe Doctrine. In this address, he stated that any attempts by European powers to establish new colonies on the North American continent would be considered interference in American politics. The US would stay out of European matters, and expected

Europe to offer America the same courtesy. This approach to foreign policy stated in no uncertain terms that America would not tolerate any new European colonies in the New World, and that events occurring in Europe would no longer influence the policies and doctrines of the US.

**Lewis and Clark Expedition**

The purchase of the Louisiana Territory from France in 1803 more than doubled the size of the United States. President Thomas Jefferson wanted to have the area mapped and explored, since much of the territory was wilderness. He chose Meriwether Lewis and William Clark to head an expedition into the Louisiana Territory. After two years, Lewis and Clark returned, having traveled all the way to the Pacific Ocean. They brought maps, detailed journals, and a multitude of information about the wide expanse of land they had traversed. The Lewis and Clark Expedition opened up the west in the Louisiana Territory and beyond for further exploration and settlement.

➢ **Review Video:** The Lewis and Clark Expedition
*Visit* ***mometrix.com/academy*** *and enter* ***Code*****: 241256**

**Manifest Destiny**

In the 1800s, many believed America was destined by God to expand west, bringing as much of the North American continent as possible under the umbrella of US government. With the Northwest Ordinance and the Louisiana Purchase, over half of the continent became American. However, the rapid and relentless expansion brought conflict with the Native Americans, Great Britain, Mexico and Spain. One result of "Manifest Destiny" was the Mexican-American War from 1846 to 1848. By the end of the war, Texas, California, and a large portion of what is now the American Southwest joined the growing nation. Conflict also arose over the Oregon territory, shared by the US and Britain. In 1846, President James Polk resolved this problem by compromising with Britain, establishing a US boundary south of the 49th parallel.

➢ **Review Video:** Manifest Destiny
*Visit* ***mometrix.com/academy*** *and enter* ***Code*****: 962946**

**Mexican-American War**

Spain had held colonial interests in America since the 1540s—earlier even than Great Britain. In 1810, Mexico revolted against Spain and became a free nation in 1821. Texas followed suit, declaring its independence after an 1836 revolution. In 1844, the Democrats pressed President Tyler to annex Texas. Unlike his predecessor, Andrew Jackson, Tyler agreed to admit Texas into the Union and in 1845 Texas became a state.

During Mexico's war for independence, the nation incurred $4.5 million in war debts to the US Polk offered to forgive the debts in return for New Mexico and Upper California, but Mexico refused. In 1846, war was declared in response to a Mexican attack on American troops along the southern border of Texas. Additional conflict arose in Congress over the Wilmot Proviso, which proposed banning of slavery from any territory the US acquired from Mexico. The war ended in 1848.

## Gadsden Purchase and the 1853 post-war treaty with Mexico

After the Mexican-American war, a second treaty in 1853 determined hundreds of miles of America's southwest borders. In 1854, the Gadsden Purchase was finalized, providing even more territory to aid in the building of the transcontinental railroad. This purchase added what would eventually become the southernmost regions of Arizona and New Mexico to the growing nation. The modern outline of the United States was by this time nearly complete.

## American System

Spurred by the trade conflicts of the War of 1812, and supported by Henry Clay among others, the American System set up tariffs to help protect American interests from competition with overseas products. Reducing competition led to growth in employment and an overall increase in American industry. The higher tariffs also provided funds for the government to pay for various improvements. Congress passed high tariffs in 1816 and also chartered a federal bank. The Second Bank of the United States was given the job of regulating America's money supply.

## Jacksonian Democracy

Jacksonian Democracy is largely seen as a shift from politics favoring the wealthy to politics favoring the common man. All free white males were given the right to vote, not just property owners, as had been the case previously. Jackson's approach favored the patronage system, Laissez-faire economics, and relocation of the Indian tribes from the Southeast portion of the country. Jackson opposed the formation of a federal bank and allowed the Second Band of the United States to collapse by vetoing a bill to renew the charter. Jackson also faced the challenge of the Nullification Crisis when South Carolina claimed that it could ignore or nullify any federal law it considered unconstitutional. Jackson sent troops to the state to enforce the protested tariff laws, and a compromise engineered by Henry Clay in 1833 settled the matter for the time being.

- **Review Video:** Andrew Jackson as President
*Visit **mometrix.com/academy** and enter **Code**:* **667792**

- **Review Video:** Major Issues Under Andrew Jackson
*Visit **mometrix.com/academy** and enter **Code**:* **739251**

## Conflict between North and South

The conflict between North and South coalesced around the issue of slavery, but other elements contributed to the growing disagreement. Though most farmers in the South worked small farms with little or no slave labor, the huge plantations run by the South's rich depended on slaves or indentured servants to remain profitable. They had also become more dependent on cotton, with slave populations growing in concert with the rapid increase in cotton production.

In the North, a more diverse agricultural economy and the growth of industry made slaves rarer. The abolitionist movement grew steadily, with Harriet Beecher Stowe's *Uncle Tom's Cabin* giving many an idea to rally around. A collection of anti-slavery organizations formed, with many actively working to free slaves in the South, often bringing them to the northern states or Canada.

> ➢ **Review Video:** Conflict between the North and South
> *Visit* ***mometrix.com/academy*** *and enter* ***Code*****: 219819**

## Anti-slavery organizations

Five anti-slavery organizations and their significance are:

- American Colonization Society—Protestant churches formed this group, aimed at returning black slaves to Africa. Former slaves subsequently formed Liberia, but the colony did not do well, as the region was not well-suited for agriculture.
- American Anti-Slavery Society—William Lloyd Garrison, a Quaker, was the major force behind this group and its newspaper, *The Liberator.*
- Philadelphia Female Anti-Slavery Society—a women-only group formed by Margaretta Forten because women were not allowed to join the Anti-Slavery Society formed by her father.
- Anti-Slavery Convention of American Women—this group continued meeting even after pro-slavery factions burned down their original meeting place.
- Female Vigilant Society—an organization that raised funds to help the Underground Railroad, as well as slave refugees.

## Attitudes toward education

Horace Mann, among others, felt that schools could help children become better citizens, keep them away from crime, prevent poverty, and help American society become more unified. His *Common School Journal* brought his ideas of the importance of education into the public consciousness and proposed his suggestions for an improved American education system. Increased literacy led to increased awareness of current events, Western expansion, and other major developments of the time period. Public interest and participation in the arts and literature also increased. By the end of the 19th century, all children had access to a free public elementary education.

## Transportation

As America expanded its borders, it also developed new technology to travel the rapidly growing country. Roads and railroads traversed the nation, with the Transcontinental Railroad eventually allowing travel from one coast to the other. Canals and steamboats simplified water travel and made shipping easier and less expensive. The Erie Canal (1825) connected the Great Lakes with the Hudson River. Other canals connected other major waterways, further facilitating transportation and the shipment of goods.

With growing numbers of settlers moving into the West, wagon trails developed, including the Oregon Trail, California Trail and the Santa Fe Trail. The most common vehicles seen along these westbound trails were covered wagons, also known as prairie schooners.

## Industrial activity and major inventions

During the eighteenth century, goods were often manufactured in houses or small shops. With increased technology allowing for the use of machines, factories began to develop. In factories a large volume of salable goods could be produced in a much shorter amount of time. Many Americans, including increasing numbers of immigrants, found jobs in these factories, which were in constant need of labor. Another major invention was the cotton gin, which significantly decreased the processing time of cotton and was a major factor in the rapid expansion of cotton production in the South.

## Labor movements

In 1751, a group of bakers held a protest in which they stopped baking bread. This was technically the first American labor strike. In the 1830s and 1840s, labor movements began in earnest. Boston's masons, carpenters and stoneworkers protested the length of the workday, fighting to reduce it to ten hours. In 1844, a group of women in the textile industry also fought to reduce their workday to ten hours, forming the Lowell Female Labor Reform Association. Many other protests occurred and organizations developed through this time period with the same goal in mind.

## Second Great Awakening

Led by Protestant evangelical leaders, the Second Great Awakening occurred between 1800 and 1830. Several missionary groups grew out of the movement, including the American Home Missionary Society, which formed in 1826. The ideas behind the Second Great Awakening focused on personal responsibility, both as an individual and in response to injustice and suffering. The American Bible Society and the American Tract Society provided literature, while various traveling preachers spread the word. New denominations arose, including the Latter-day Saints and Seventh-day Adventists.

Another movement associated with the Second Great Awakening was the temperance movement, focused on ending the production and use of alcohol. One major organization behind the temperance movement was the Society for the Promotion of Temperance, formed in 1826 in Boston.

## Women's rights movement

The women's rights movement began in the 1840s with leaders including Elizabeth Cady Stanton, Sojourner Truth, Ernestine Rose, and Lucretia Mott. In 1869, Elizabeth Cady Stanton and Susan B. Anthony formed the National Woman Suffrage Association, fighting for women's right to vote.

In 1848 in Seneca Falls, the first women's rights convention was held, with about three hundred attendees. The two-day Seneca Falls Convention discussed the rights of women to vote (suffrage) as well as equal treatment in careers, legal proceedings, etc. The convention produced a "Declaration of Sentiments" which outlined a plan for women to attain the rights they deserved. Frederick Douglass supported the women's rights movement, as well as the abolition movement. In fact, women's rights and abolition movements often went hand-in-hand during this time period.

## Missouri Compromise

By 1819, the United States had developed a tenuous balance between slave and free states, with exactly twenty-two senators in Congress from each faction. However, Missouri was ready to join the union. As a slave state, it would tip the balance in Congress. To prevent this imbalance, the Missouri Compromise brought the northern part of Massachusetts into the union as Maine, establishing it as a free state to balance the admission of Missouri as a slave state. In addition, the remaining portion of the Louisiana Purchase was to remain free north of latitude 36°30'. Since cotton did not grow well this far north, this limitation was acceptable to congressmen representing the slave states.

However, the proposed Missouri constitution presented a problem, as it outlawed immigration of free blacks into the state. Another compromise was in order, this time proposed by Henry Clay. According to this new compromise, Missouri's would never pass a law that prevented anyone from entering the state. Through this and other work, Clay earned his title of the "Great Compromiser."

> **Review Video:** Missouri Compromise
> *Visit **mometrix.com/academy** and enter **Code**:* **848091**

## Popular sovereignty and the Compromise of 1850

In addition to the pro-slavery and anti-slavery factions, a third group rose who felt that each individual state should decide whether to allow or permit slavery within its borders. The idea that a state could make its own choices was referred to as popular sovereignty.

When California applied to join the union in 1849, the balance of congressional power was again threatened. The Compromise of 1850 introduced a group of laws meant to bring an end to the conflict:

- California's admittance as a free state
- The outlaw of the slave trade in Washington, D.C
- An increase in efforts to capture escaped slaves
- The right of New Mexico and Utah territories to decide individually whether to allow slavery

In spite of these measures, debate raged each time a new state prepared to enter the union.

## Kansas-Nebraska Act

With the creation of the Kansas and Nebraska territories in 1854, another debate began. Congress allowed popular sovereignty in these territories, but slavery opponents argued that the Missouri Compromise had already made slavery illegal in this region. In Kansas, two separate governments arose, one pro-slavery and one anti-slavery. Conflict between the two factions rose to violence, leading Kansas to gain the nickname of "Bleeding Kansas."

> **Review Video:** Sectional Crisis: The Kansas-Nebraska Act
> *Visit **mometrix.com/academy** and enter **Code**:* **982119**

## Dred Scott decision

Abolitionist factions coalesced around the case of Dred Scott, using his case to test the country's laws regarding slavery. Scott, a slave, had been taken by his owner from Missouri, which was a slave state. He then traveled to Illinois, a free state, then on to the Minnesota Territory, also free based on the Missouri Compromise. After several years, he returned to Missouri and his owner subsequently died. Abolitionists took Scott's case to court, stating that Scott was no longer a slave but free, since he had lived in free territory. The case went to the Supreme Court.

The Supreme Court stated that, because Scott, as a slave, was not a US citizen, his time in free states did not change his status. He also did not have the right to sue. In addition, the Court determined that the Missouri Compromise was unconstitutional, stating that Congress had overstepped its bounds by outlawing slavery in the territories.

> ➢ **Review Video:** Dred Scott Act
> *Visit **mometrix.com/academy** and enter **Code**:* **448931**

## Harper's Ferry and John Brown

John Brown, an abolitionist, had participated in several anti-slavery activities, including killing five pro-slavery men in retaliation, after the sacking of Lawrence, Kansas, an anti-slavery town. He and other abolitionists also banded together to pool their funds and build a runaway slave colony.

In 1859, Brown seized a federal arsenal in Harper's Ferry, located in what is now West Virginia. Brown intended to seize guns and ammunition and lead a slave rebellion. Robert E. Lee captured Brown and 21 followers, who were subsequently tried and hanged. While Northerners took the executions as an indication that the government supported slavery, Southerners were of the opinion that most of the North supported Brown and were, in general, anti-slavery.

## 1860 election

The 1860 Presidential candidates represented four different parties, each with a different opinion on slavery:

- John Breckinridge, representing the Southern Democrats, was pro-slavery but urged compromise to preserve the Union.
- Abraham Lincoln, of the Republican Party, was anti-slavery.
- Stephen Douglas, of the Northern Democrats, felt that the issue should be determined locally, on a state-by-state basis.
- John Bell, of the Constitutional Union Party, focused primarily on keeping the Union intact.

In the end, Abraham Lincoln won both the popular and electoral election. Southern states, who had sworn to secede from the Union if Lincoln was elected did so, led by South Carolina. Shortly thereafter, the Civil War began when Confederate shots were fired on Fort Sumter in Charleston.

## Advantages of the North and South in the Civil War

The Northern states had significant advantages, including:

- Larger population—the North consisted of 24 states while the South had 11.
- Better transportation and finances—with railroads primarily in the North, supply chains were much more dependable, as was overseas trade.
- Raw materials—the North held the majority of America's gold, as well as iron, copper, and other minerals vital to wartime.

The South's advantages included:

- Better-trained military officers—many of the Southern officers were West Point trained and had commanded in the Mexican and Indian wars.
- Familiarity with weapons—the climate and lifestyle of the South meant most of the people were experienced with both guns and horses. The industrial North had less extensive experience.
- Defensive position—the South felt that victory was guaranteed, since they were protecting their own lands, while the North would be invading.
- Well-defined goals—the South fought an ideological war to be allowed to govern themselves and preserve their way of life. The North originally fought to preserve the Union and later to free the slaves.

## Emancipation Proclamation

The Emancipation Proclamation, issued by President Lincoln on January 1, 1863, freed all slaves in Confederate states that were still in rebellion against the Union. While the original proclamation did not free any slaves in the states actually under Union control, it did set a precedent for the emancipation of slaves as the war progressed.

The Emancipation Proclamation worked in the Union's favor as many freed slaves and other black troops joined the Union Army. Almost 200,000 blacks fought in the Union army, and over 10,000 served in the navy. By the end of the war, over 4 million slaves had been freed, and in 1865 slavery was abolished in the 13th amendment to the Constitution.

➢ **Review Video:** Emancipation Proclamation
*Visit* ***mometrix.com/academy*** *and enter* ***Code*:** **511675**

## Civil War events

Six major events of the Civil War and their outcomes or significance are:

- The First Battle of Bull Run (July 21, 1861)—this was the first major land battle of the war. Observers, expecting to enjoy an entertaining skirmish, set up picnics nearby. Instead, they found themselves witness to a bloodbath. Union forces were defeated, and the battle set the course of the Civil War as long, bloody and costly.
- The Capture of Fort Henry by Ulysses S. Grant—this battle in February of 1862 marked the Union's first major victory.
- The Battle of Gettysburg (July 1-3, 1863)—often seen as the turning point of the war, Gettysburg also saw the largest number of casualties of the war, with over 50,000 dead, wounded, or missing. Robert E. Lee was defeated, and the Confederate army, significantly crippled, withdrew.

- The Overland Campaign (May and June of 1864)—Grant, now in command of all the Union armies, led this high casualty campaign that eventually positioned the Union for victory.
- Sherman's March to the Sea—William Tecumseh Sherman, in May of 1864, conquered Atlanta. He then continued to Savannah, destroying vast amounts of property as he went.
- Following Lee's defeat at the Appomattox Courthouse, General Grant accepted Lee's surrender in the home of Wilmer McLean in Appomattox, Virginia on April 9, 1865.

**Lincoln's assassination**

The Civil War ended with the surrender of the South on April 9, 1865. Five days later, Lincoln and his wife, Mary, attended the play *Our American Cousin* at the Ford Theater. John Wilkes Booth performed his part in a conspiracy to aid the Confederacy by shooting Lincoln in the back of the head. Booth was tracked down and killed by Union soldiers 12 days later. Lincoln, carried from the theater to a nearby house, died the next morning.

**Reconstruction and the Freedmen's Bureau**

In the aftermath of the Civil War, the South was left in chaos. From 1865 to 1877, government on all levels worked to help restore order to the South, ensure civil rights to the freed slaves, and bring the Confederate states back into the Union. This became known as the Reconstruction period. In 1866, Congress passed the Reconstruction Acts, placing former Confederate states under military rule and stating the grounds for readmission into the Union.

The Freedmen's Bureau was formed to help freedmen both with basic necessities like food and clothing and also with employment and finding of family members who had been separated during the war. Many in the South felt the Freedmen's Bureau worked to set freed slaves against their former owners. The Bureau was intended to help former slaves become self-sufficient, and to keep them from falling prey to those who would take advantage of them. It eventually closed due to lack of funding and to violence from the Ku Klux Klan.

**Radical and Moderate Republicans**

The Radical Republicans wished to treat the South quite harshly after the war. Thaddeus Stevens, the House Leader, suggested that the Confederate states be treated as if they were territories again, with ten years of military rule and territorial government before they would be readmitted. He also wanted to give all black men the right to vote. Former Confederate soldiers would be required to swear they had never supported the Confederacy (knows as the "Ironclad Oath") in order to be granted full rights as American citizens. In contrast, the moderate Republicans wanted only black men who were literate or who had served as Union troops to be able to vote. All Confederate soldiers except troop leaders would also be able to vote. Before his death, Lincoln had favored a more moderate approach to Reconstruction, hoping this approach might bring some states back into the Union before the end of the war.

## Black Codes, the Civil Rights Act, and impeachment of Andrew Johnson

The Black Codes were proposed to control freed slaves. They would not be allowed to bear arms, assemble, serve on juries, or testify against whites. Schools would be segregated, and unemployed blacks could be arrested and forced to work. The Civil Rights Act countered these codes, providing much wider rights for the freed slaves. Andrew Johnson, who became president after Lincoln's death, supported the Black Codes and vetoed the Civil Rights Act in 1865 and again in 1866. The second time, Congress overrode his veto and it became law. Two years later, Congress voted to impeach Johnson, the culmination of tensions between Congress and the president. He was tried and came within a single vote of being convicted, but ultimately was acquitted and finished his term in office.

## Thirteenth, Fourteenth and Fifteenth Amendments

The Thirteenth, Fourteenth and Fifteenth Amendments were all passed shortly after the end of the Civil War:

- The Thirteenth Amendment was ratified by the states on December 6, 1865. This amendment prohibited slavery in the United States.
- The Fourteenth Amendment overturned the Dred Scott decision, and was ratified July 9, 1868. American citizenship was redefined: a citizen was any person born or naturalized in the US, with all citizens guaranteed equal protection by all states. It also guaranteed citizens of any race the right to file a lawsuit or serve on a jury.
- The Fifteenth Amendment was ratified February 3, 1870. It states that no citizen of the United States can be denied the right to vote based on race, color, or previous status as a slave.

➢ **Review Video:** The 13th Amendment
*Visit **mometrix.com/academy** and enter **Code**:* **867407**

➢ **Review Video:** The 14th Amendment
*Visit **mometrix.com/academy** and enter **Code**:* **928755**

➢ **Review Video:** The 15th Amendment
*Visit **mometrix.com/academy** and enter **Code**:* **102009**

## Reconstruction

The three phases of Reconstruction are:

- Presidential Reconstruction—largely driven by President Andrew Johnson's policies, the Presidential phase of Reconstruction was lenient on the South and allowed continued discrimination against and control over blacks.
- Congressional Reconstruction—Congress, controlled largely by Radical Republicans, took a different stance, providing a wider range of civil rights for blacks and greater control over Southern government. Congressional Reconstruction is marked by military control of the former Confederate States.
- Redemption—gradually, the Confederate states were readmitted into the union. During this time, white Democrats took over the government of most of the South. In 1877, President Rutherford Hayes withdrew the last federal troops from the South.

## Carpetbaggers and Scalawags

The chaos in the south attracted a number of people seeking to fill the power vacuums and take advantage of the economic disruption. Scalawags were southern Whites who aligned with Freedmen to take over local governments. Many in the South who could have filled political offices refused to take the necessary oath required to grant them the right to vote, leaving many opportunities for Scalawags and others. Carpetbaggers were northerners who traveled to the South for various reasons. Some provided assistance, while others sought to make money or to acquire political power during this chaotic period.

## Transcontinental railroad

In 1869, the Union Pacific Railroad completed the first section of a planned transcontinental railroad. This section went from Omaha, Nebraska to Sacramento, California. Ninety percent of the workers were Chinese, working in very dangerous conditions for very low pay. With the rise of the railroad, products were much more easily transported across the country. While this was positive overall for industry throughout the country, it was often damaging to family farmers, who found themselves paying high shipping costs for smaller supply orders while larger companies received major discounts.

## Immigration limits

In 1870, the Naturalization Act put limits on US citizenship, allowing full citizenship only to whites and those of African descent. The Chinese Exclusion Act of 1882 put limits on Chinese immigration. The Immigration Act of 1882 taxed immigrants, charging fifty cents per person. These funds helped pay administrative costs for regulating immigration. Ellis Island opened in 1892 as a processing center for those arriving in New York. 1921 saw the Emergency Quota Act passed, also known as the Johnson Quota Act, which severely limited the number of immigrants allowed into the country.

## Nineteenth century changes in agriculture

Technological advancements

During the mid 1800s, irrigation techniques improved significantly. Advances occurred in cultivation and breeding, as well as fertilizer use and crop rotation. In the Great Plains, also known as the Great American Desert, the dense soil was finally cultivated with steel plows. In 1892, gasoline-powered tractors arrived, and were widely used by 1900. Other advancements in agriculture's toolset included barbed wire fences, combines, silos, deep-water wells, and the cream separator.

Government actions

Four major government actions that helped improve US agriculture in the nineteenth century are:

- The Department of Agriculture came into being in 1862, working for the interests of farmers and ranchers across the country.
- The Morrill Land-Grant Acts were a series of acts passed between 1862 and 1890, allowing land-grant colleges.
- In conjunction with land-grant colleges, the Hatch Act of 1887 brought agriculture experiment stations into the picture, helping discover new farming techniques.

- In 1914, the Smith-Lever Act provided cooperative programs to help educate people about food, home economics, community development and agriculture. Related agriculture extension programs helped farmers increase crop production to feed the rapidly growing nation.

### Inventors and inventions

Major inventors from the 1800s and their inventions are:

- Alexander Graham Bell—the telephone
- Orville and Wilbur Wright—the airplane
- Richard Gatling—the machine gun
- Walter Hunt, Elias Howe and Isaac Singer—the sewing machine
- Nikola Tesla—alternating current
- George Eastman—the Kodak camera
- Thomas Edison—light bulbs, motion pictures, the phonograph
- Samuel Morse—the telegraph
- Charles Goodyear—vulcanized rubber
- Cyrus McCormick—the reaper
- George Westinghouse—the transformer, the air brake

This was an active period for invention, with about 700,000 patents registered between 1860 and 1900.

### Gilded Age

The time period from the end of the Civil War to the beginning of the First World War is often referred to as the Gilded Age, or the Second Industrial Revolution. The US was changing from an agricultural-based economy to an industrial economy, with rapid growth accompanying the shift. In addition, the country itself was expanding, spreading into the seemingly unlimited West.

This time period saw the beginning of banks, department stores, chain stores, and trusts—all familiar features of the modern-day landscape. Cities also grew rapidly, and large numbers of immigrants arrived in the country, swelling the urban ranks.

> ➢ **Review Video:** The Gilded Age: An Overview
> *Visit **mometrix.com/academy** and enter **Code**:* **684770**

### Populist Party

A major recession struck the United States during the 1890s, with crop prices falling dramatically. Drought compounded the problems, leaving many American farmers in crippling debt. The Farmers' Alliance formed in 1875, drawing the rural poor into a single political entity.

Recession also affected the more industrial parts of the country. The Knights of Labor, formed in 1869 by Uriah Stephens, was able to unite workers into a union to protect their rights. Dissatisfied by views espoused by industrialists, these two groups, the Farmers Alliance and the Knights of Labor, joined to form the Populist Party, also known as the People's Party, in 1892. Some of the elements of the party's platform included:

- National currency
- Graduated income tax
- Government ownership of railroads as well as telegraph and telephone systems
- Secret ballots for voting
- Immigration restriction
- Single-term limits for President and Vice-President

The Populist Party was in favor of decreasing elitism and making the voice of the common man more easily heard in the political process.

**Labor movement**

One of the first large, well-organized strikes occurred in 1892. Called the Homestead Strike, it occurred when the Amalgamated Association of Iron and Steel Workers struck against the Carnegie Steel Company. Gunfire ensued, and Carnegie was able to eliminate the plant's union. In 1894, workers in the American Railway Union, led by Eugene Debs, initiated the Pullman Strike after the Pullman Palace Car Co. cut their wages by 28 percent. President Grover Cleveland called in troops to break up the strike on the grounds that it interfered with mail delivery. Mary Harris "Mother" Jones organized the Children's Crusade to protest child labor. A protest march proceeded to the home of President Theodore Roosevelt in 1903. Jones also worked with the United Mine Workers of America, and helped found the Industrial Workers of the World.

➢ **Review Video:** The Gilded Age: Labor Strikes
*Visit **mometrix.com/academy** and enter **Code**:* **683116**

➢ **Review Video:** The Gilded Age: Labor Unions
*Visit **mometrix.com/academy** and enter **Code**:* **749692**

**Panic of 1893**

Far from a US-centric event, the Panic of 1893 was an economic crisis that affected most of the globe. As a response, President Grover Cleveland repealed the Sherman Silver Purchase Act, afraid it had caused the downturn rather than boosting the economy as intended. The Panic led to bankruptcies, with banks and railroads going under and factory unemployment rising as high as 25 percent. In the end, the Republican Party regained power due to the economic crisis.

**Progressive Era**

From the 1890s to the end of the First World War, Progressives set forth an ideology that drove many levels of society and politics. The Progressives were in favor of workers' rights and safety, and wanted measures taken against waste and corruption. They felt science could help improve society, and that the government could—and should—provide answers to a variety of social problems. Progressives came from a wide variety of backgrounds, but were united in their desire to improve society.

Muckrakers

"Muckrakers" was a term used to identify aggressive investigative journalists who exposed scandals, corruption, and many other wrongs in late nineteenth century society. Among these intrepid writers were:

- Ida Tarbell—she exposed John D. Rockefeller's Standard Oil Trust.
- Jacob Riis—a photographer, he brought the living conditions of the poor in New York to the public's attention.
- Lincoln Steffens—he worked to expose political corruption in municipal government.
- Upton Sinclair—his book *The Jungle* led to reforms in the meat-packing industry.

Through the work of these journalists, many new policies came into being, including workmen's compensation, child labor laws, and trust-busting.

Sixteenth, Seventeenth, Eighteenth and Nineteenth Amendments

The early twentieth century saw several amendments made to the US Constitution:

- The Sixteenth Amendment (1913) established a federal income tax.
- The Seventeenth Amendment (1913) allowed popular election of senators.
- The Eighteenth Amendment (1919) prohibited the sale, production and transportation of alcohol. This amendment was later repealed by the Twenty-first Amendment.
- The Nineteenth Amendment (1920) gave women the right to vote.

These amendments largely grew out of the Progressive Era, as many citizens worked to improve American society.

Federal Trade Commission and elimination of trusts

Muckrakers such as Ida Tarbell and Lincoln Steffens brought to light the damaging trend of trusts—huge corporations working to monopolize areas of commerce so they could control prices and distribution. The Sherman Antitrust Act and the Clayton Antitrust Act set out guidelines for competition among corporations and set out to eliminate these trusts. The Federal Trade Commission was formed in 1914 in order to enforce antitrust measures and ensure that companies were operated fairly and did not create controlling monopolies.

> **Review Video:** The Progressive Era
> *Visit **mometrix.com/academy** and enter **Code**:* **293582**

**Government dealings with Native Americans**

America's westward expansion led to conflict and violent confrontations with Native Americans such as the Battle of Little Bighorn. In 1876, the American government ordered all Indians to relocate to reservations. Lack of compliance led to the Dawes Act in 1887, which ordered assimilation rather than separation: Native Americans were offered American citizenship and a piece of their tribal land if they would accept the lot chosen by the government and live on it separately from the tribe. This act remained in effect until 1934. Reformers also forced Indian children to attend Indian Boarding Schools, where they were not allowed to speak their native language and were immersed into a Euro-American culture and religion. Children were often abused in these schools, and were indoctrinated to abandon their identity as Native Americans. In 1890, the massacre at Wounded Knee, accompanied by Geronimo's surrender, led the Native Americans to work to preserve their culture rather than fight for their lands.

Native Americans in wartime

The Spanish-American war (1898) saw a number of Native Americans serving with Teddy Roosevelt in the Rough Riders. Apache scouts accompanied General John J. Pershing to Mexico, hoping to find Pancho Villa. More than 17,000 Native Americans were drafted into service for World War I, though at the time they were not considered legal citizens. In 1924, Indians were finally granted official citizenship by the Indian Citizenship Act.

After decades of relocation, forced assimilation, and genocide, the number of Native Americans in the US has greatly declined. Though many Native Americans have chosen—or have been forced—to assimilate, about 300 reservations exist today, with most of their inhabitants living in abject poverty.

## Spanish-American War

Spain had controlled Cuba since the fifteenth century. Over the centuries, the Spanish had quashed a variety of revolts. In 1886, slavery ended in Cuba, and another revolt was rising. In the meantime, the US had expressed interest in Cuba, offering Spain $130 million for the island in 1853, during Franklin Pierce's presidency. In 1898, the Cuban revolt was underway. In spite of various factions supporting the Cubans, the US President, William McKinley, refused to recognize the rebellion, preferring negotiation over involvement in war. Then the *Maine*, a US battleship in Havana Harbor, was blown up, killing 266 crew members. The US declared war two months later, and the war ended with a Spanish surrender in less than four months.

## Panama Canal

Initial work began on the Panama Canal in 1881, though the idea had been discussed since the 1500s. The canal greatly reduces the length and time needed to sail from one ocean to the other by connecting the Atlantic to the Pacific through the Isthmus of Panama, which joins South America to North America. Before the canal was built, travelers had to sail around the entire perimeter of South America to reach the West Coast of the US. The French began the work after successfully completing the Suez Canal, which connected the Mediterranean Sea to the Red Sea. However, due to disease and high expense the work moved slowly and after eight years the company went bankrupt, suspending work. The US purchased the holdings, and the first ship sailed through the canal in 1914. The Panama Canal was constructed as a lock-and-lake canal, with ships lifted on locks to travel from one lake to another over the rugged, mountainous terrain. In order to maintain control of the Canal Zone, the US assisted Panama in its battle for independence from Columbia.

## Roosevelt's "Big Stick Diplomacy" and foreign policy in South America

Theodore Roosevelt's famous quote, "Speak softly and carry a big stick," is supposedly of African origins, at least according to Roosevelt. He used this proverb to justify expanded involvement in foreign affairs during his tenure as President. The US military was deployed to protect American interests in Latin America. Roosevelt also worked to maintain an equal or greater influence in Latin America than those held by European interests. As a result, the US Navy grew larger, and the US generally became more involved in foreign affairs. Roosevelt felt that if any country was left vulnerable to control by Europe, due to economic issues or political instability, the US had not only a right to intervene, but was obligated to do so. This led to US involvement in Cuba, Nicaragua, Haiti and the Dominican Republic over several decades leading into the First and Second World Wars.

### William Howard Taft's "Dollar Diplomacy"

During William Howard Taft's presidency, Taft instituted "Dollar Diplomacy." This approach was America's effort to influence Latin America and East Asia through economic rather than military means. Taft saw past efforts in these areas to be political and warlike, while his efforts focused on peaceful economic goals. His justification of the policy was to protect the Panama Canal, which was vital to US trade interests.

In spite of Taft's assurance that Dollar Diplomacy was a peaceful approach, many interventions proved violent. During Latin American revolts, such as those in Nicaragua, the US sent troops to settle the revolutions. Afterwards, bankers moved in to help support the new leaders through loans. Dollar Diplomacy continued until 1913, when Woodrow Wilson was elected President.

### Woodrow Wilson's "Moral Diplomacy"

Turning away from Taft's "Dollar Diplomacy," Wilson instituted a foreign policy he referred to as "moral diplomacy." This approach still influences American foreign policy today. Wilson felt that representative government and democracy in all countries would lead to worldwide stability. Democratic governments, he felt, would be less likely to threaten American interests. He also saw the US and Great Britain as the great role models in this area, as well as champions of world peace and self-government. Free trade and international commerce would allow the US to speak out regarding world events.

Main elements of Wilson's policies included:

- Maintaining a strong military
- Promoting democracy throughout the world
- Expanding international trade to boost the American economy

### First World War

World War I occurred from 1914 to 1918 and was fought largely in Europe. Triggered by the assassination of Austrian Archduke Franz Ferdinand, the war rapidly escalated. At the beginning of the conflict, Woodrow Wilson declared the US neutral. Major events influencing US involvement included:

- Sinking of the *Lusitania*—the British passenger liner RMS *Lusitania* was sunk by a German U-boat in 1915. Among the 1,000 civilian victims were over 100 American citizens. Outraged by this act, many Americans began to push for US involvement in the war, using the *Lusitania* as a rallying cry.
- German U-boat aggression—Wilson continued to keep the US out of the war, using as his 1916 reelection slogan, "He kept us out of war." While he continued to work toward an end of the war, German U-boats began to indiscriminately attack

American and Canadian merchant ships carrying supplies to Germany's enemies in Europe.

- Zimmerman Telegram —the final event that brought the US into World War I was the interception of the Zimmerman Telegram (also known as the Zimmerman Note). In this telegram, Germany proposed forming an alliance with the Mexico if the US entered the war.

> **Review Video:** World War I: An Overview
> *Visit* ***mometrix.com/academy*** *and enter* ***Code*****: 994468**

**US efforts during World War I**

American railroads came under government control in December 1917. The widespread system was consolidated into a single system, with each region assigned a director. This greatly increased the efficiency of the railroad system, allowing the railroads to supply both domestic and military needs. Control returned to private ownership in 1920. In 1918, telegraph, telephone and cable services also came under Federal control, to be returned to private management the next year. The American Red Cross supported the war effort by knitting clothes for Army and Navy troops. They also helped supply hospital and refugee clothing and surgical dressings. Over eight million people participated in this effort. To generate wartime funds, the US government sold Liberty Bonds. In four issues, they sold nearly $25 billion—more than one fifth of Americans purchased them. After the war, a fifth bond drive was held, but sold "Victory Liberty Bonds."

**Wilson's Fourteen Points**

President Woodrow Wilson proposed Fourteen Points as the basis for a peace settlement to end the war. Presented to the US Congress in January 1918, the Fourteen Points included:

- Five points outlining general ideals
- Eight points to resolve immediate problems of political and territorial nature
- One point proposing an organization of nations (the League of Nations) with the intent of maintaining world peace

In November of that same year, Germany agreed to an armistice, assuming the final treaty would be based on the Fourteen Points. However, during the peace conference in Paris 1919, there was much disagreement, leading to a final agreement that punished Germany and the other Central Powers much more than originally intended. Henry Cabot Lodge, who had become the Foreign Relations Committee chairman in 1918, wanted an unconditional surrender from Germany and was concerned about the article in the Treaty of Versailles that gave the League of Nations power to declare war without a vote from the US Congress. A League of Nations was included in the Treaty of Versailles at Wilson's insistence. The Senate rejected the Treaty of Versailles, and in the end Wilson refused to concede to Lodge's demands. As a result, the US did not join the League of Nations.

> **Review Video:** Woodrow Wilson's Fourteen Points
> *Visit* ***mometrix.com/academy*** *and enter* ***Code*****: 335789**

## America during the 1920s

The post-war 1920s saw many Americans moving from the farm to the city, with growing prosperity in the US. The Roaring Twenties, or the Jazz Age, was driven largely by growth in the automobile and entertainment industries. Individuals like Charles Lindbergh, the first aviator to make a solo flight cross the Atlantic Ocean, added to the American admiration of individual accomplishment. Telephone lines, distribution of electricity, highways, the radio, and other inventions brought great changes to everyday life.

African-American cultural movements

The Harlem Renaissance saw a number of African-American artists settling in Harlem in New York. This community produced a number of well-known artists and writers, including Langston Hughes, Nella Larsen, Zora Neale Hurston, Claude McKay, Countee Cullen and Jean Toomer. The growth of jazz, also largely driven by African Americans, defined the Jazz Age. Its unconventional, improvisational style matched the growing sense of optimism and exploration of the decade. Originating as an offshoot of the blues, jazz began in New Orleans. Some significant jazz musicians were Duke Ellington, Louis Armstrong and Jelly Roll Morton. Big Band and Swing Jazz also developed in the 1920s. Well-known musicians of this movement included Bing Crosby, Frank Sinatra, Count Basie, Benny Goodman, Billie Holiday, Ella Fitzgerald and The Dorsey Brothers.

## National Origins Act of 1924

The National Origins Act (Johnson-Reed Act) placed limitations on immigration. The number of immigrants allowed into the US was based on the population of each nationality of immigrants who were living in the country in 1890. Only two percent of each nationality's 1890 population numbers were allowed to immigrate. This led to great disparities between immigrants from various nations, and Asian immigration was not allowed at all. Some of the impetus behind the Johnson-Reed Act came as a result of paranoia following the Russian Revolution. Fear of communist influences in the US led to a general fear of immigrants.

## Red Scare

World War I created many jobs, but after the war ended these jobs disappeared, leaving many unemployed. In the wake of these employment changes the International Workers of the World and the Socialist Party, headed by Eugene Debs, became more and more visible. Workers initiated strikes in an attempt to regain the favorable working conditions that had been put into place before the war. Unfortunately, many of these strikes became violent, and the actions were blamed on "Reds," or Communists, for trying to spread their views into America. With the recent Bolshevik Revolution in Russia, many Americans feared a similar revolution might occur in the US. The Red Scare ensued, with many individuals jailed for supposedly holding communist, anarchist or socialist beliefs.

## Growth of civil rights for African-Americans

Marcus Garvey founded the Universal Negro Improvement Association and African Communities League (UNIA-ACL), which became a large and active organization focused on building black nationalism. In 1909, the National Association for the Advancement of Colored People (NAACP) came into being, working to defeat Jim Crow laws. The NAACP also helped prevent racial segregation from becoming federal law, fought against lynchings, helped black soldiers in WWI become officers, and helped defend the Scottsboro Boys, who were unjustly accused of rape.

### Ku Klux Klan

In 1866, Confederate Army veterans came together to fight against Reconstruction in the South, forming a group called the Ku Klux Klan (KKK). With white supremacist beliefs, including anti-Semitism, nativism, anti-Catholicism, and overt racism, this organization relied heavily on violence to get its message across. In 1915, they grew again in power, using a film called *The Birth of a Nation*, by D.W. Griffith, to spread their ideas. In the 1920s, the reach of the KKK spread far into the North and Midwest, and members controlled a number of state governments. Its membership and power began to decline during the Great Depression, but experienced a resurgence later.

### American Civil Liberties Union

The American Civil Liberties Union (ACLU), founded in 1920, grew from the American Union Against Militarism. The ACLU helped conscientious objectors avoid going to war during WWI, and also helped those being prosecuted under the Espionage Act (1917) and the Sedition Act (1918), many of whom were immigrants. Their major goals were to protect immigrants and other citizens who were threatened with prosecution for their political beliefs, and to support labor unions, which were also under threat by the government during the Red Scare.

### Anti-Defamation League

In 1913, the Anti-Defamation League was formed to prevent anti-Semitic behavior and practices. Its actions also worked to prevent all forms of racism, and to prevent individuals from being discriminated against for any reason involving their race. They spoke against the Ku Klux Klan, as well as other racist or anti-Semitic organizations. This organization still works to fight discrimination against all minorities.

### Great Depression

The Great Depression, which began in 1929 with the stock market crash, grew out of several factors that had developed over the previous years including:

- Growing economic disparity between the rich and middle classes, with the rich amassing wealth much more quickly than the lower classes
- Disparity in economic distribution in industries
- Growing use of credit, leading to an inflated demand for some goods
- Government support of new industries rather than agriculture
- Risky stock market investments, leading to the stock market crash

Additional factors contributing to the Depression also included the Labor Day Hurricane in the Florida Keys (1935) and the Great Hurricane of 1938 in New England, along with the Dust Bowl in the Great Plains, which destroyed crops and resulted in the displacement of as many as 2.5 million people.

➢ **Review Video:** The Great Depression
*Visit **mometrix.com/academy** and enter **Code**:* **331401**

**Roosevelt administration**

Roosevelt's "New Deal"
Franklin D. Roosevelt was elected president in 1932 with his promise of a "New Deal" for Americans. His goals were to provide government work programs to provide jobs, wages and relief to numerous workers throughout the beleaguered US. Congress gave Roosevelt almost free rein to produce relief legislation. The goals of this legislation were:

- Relief—creating jobs for the high numbers of unemployed
- Recovery—stimulating the economy through the National Recovery Administration
- Reform—passing legislation to prevent future, similar economic crashes

The Roosevelt Administration also passed legislation regarding ecological issues, including the Soil Conservation Service, aimed at preventing another Dust Bowl.

Roosevelt's "alphabet organizations"
So-called "alphabet organizations" set up during Roosevelt's administration included:

- Civilian Conservation Corps (CCC)—provided jobs in the forestry service
- Agricultural Adjustment Administration (AAA)—increased agricultural income by adjusting both production and prices
- Tennessee Valley Authority (TVA)—organized projects to build dams in the Tennessee River for flood control and production of electricity, resulting in increased productivity for industries in the area, and easier navigation of the Tennessee River
- Public Works Administration (PWA) and Civil Works Administration (CWA)—provided a multitude of jobs, initiating over 34,000 projects
- Works Progress Administration (WPA)—helped unemployed persons to secure employment on government work projects or elsewhere

Actions taken to prevent future crashes and stabilize the economy
The Roosevelt administration passed several laws and established several institutions to initiate the "reform" portion of the New Deal, including:

- Glass-Steagall Act—separated investment from commercial banking
- Securities Exchange Commission (SEC)—helped regulate Wall Street investment practices, making them less dangerous to the overall economy
- Wagner Act—provided worker and union rights to improve relations between employees and employers
- Social Security Act of 1935—provided pensions as well as unemployment insurance

Other actions focused on insuring bank deposits and adjusting the value of American currency. Most of these regulatory agencies and government policies and programs still exist today.

**Labor regulations**

Three major regulations regarding labor that were passed after the Great Depression are:

- The Wagner Act (1935)—also known as the National Labor Relations Act, it established that unions were legal, protected members of unions, and required collective bargaining. This act was later amended by the Taft-Hartley Act of 1947 and the Landrum-Griffin Act of 1959, which further clarified certain elements.
- Davis-Bacon Act (1931)—provided fair compensation for contractors and subcontractors
- Walsh-Healey Act (1936)—established a minimum wage, child labor laws, safety standards, and overtime pay

**World War II**

Interventionist and Isolationist approaches to involvement

When war broke out in Europe in 1939, President Roosevelt stated that the US would remain neutral. However, his overall approach was considered "interventionist," as he was willing to provide aid to the Allies without actually entering the conflict. Thus the US supplied a wide variety of war materials to the Allied nations in the early years of the war.

Isolationists believed the US should not provide any aid to the Allies, including supplies. They felt Roosevelt, by assisting the Allies, was leading the US into a war for which it was not prepared. Led by Charles Lindbergh, the Isolationists believed that any involvement in the European conflict endangered the US by weakening its national defense.

➢ **Review Video:** World War II: An Overview
*Visit **mometrix.com/academy** and enter **Code**:* **254317**

US entry into the war

In 1937, Japan invaded China, prompting the US to eventually halt exports to Japan. Roosevelt also did not allow Japanese interests to withdraw money held in US banks. In 1941, General Tojo rose to power as the Japanese prime minister. Recognizing America's ability to bring a halt to Japan's expansion, he authorized the bombing of Pearl Harbor on December 7. The US responded by declaring war on Japan. Partially because of the Tripartite Pact among the Axis Powers, Germany and Italy then declared war on the US, later followed by Bulgaria, Hungary, and other Axis nations.

Surrender of Germany

In 1941, Hitler violated the non-aggression pact he had signed with Stalin two years earlier by invading the USSR. Stalin then joined the Allies. Stalin, Roosevelt and Winston Churchill planned to defeat Germany first, then Japan, bringing the war to an end.

In 1942-1943, the Allies drove Axis forces out of Africa. In addition, the Germans were soundly defeated at Stalingrad.

The Italian Campaign involved Allied operations in Italy between July 1943 and May 1945, including Italy's liberation. On June 6, 1944, known as D-Day, the Allies invaded France at Normandy. Soviet troops moved on the eastern front at the same time, driving German forces back. By April 25, 1945, Berlin was surrounded by Soviet troops. On May 7, Germany surrendered.

➢ **Review Video:** World War II: Germany
*Visit **mometrix.com/academy** and enter **Code**:* **951452**

Surrender of Japan
War continued with Japan after Germany's surrender. Japanese forces had taken a large portion of Southeast Asia and the Western Pacific, all the way to the Aleutian Islands in Alaska. General Doolittle bombed several Japanese cities while American troops scored a victory at Midway. Additional fighting in the Battle of the Coral Sea further weakened Japan's position. As a final blow, the US dropped two atomic bombs on Japan, one on Hiroshima and the other on Nagasaki. This was the first time atomic bombs had been used in warfare, and the devastation was horrific and demoralizing. Japan surrendered on September 2, 1945, which became V-J Day in the US.

➢ **Review Video:** World War II: Japan
*Visit **mometrix.com/academy** and enter **Code**:* **313104**

442nd Regimental Combat Team, the Tuskegee Airmen, and the Navajo Code Talkers
The 442nd Regimental Combat Team consisted of Japanese-Americans fighting in Europe for the US. The most highly decorated unit per member in US history, they suffered a 93% casualty rate during the war. The Tuskegee Airmen were African-American aviators, the first black Americans allowed to fly for the military. In spite of being ineligible to become official navy pilots, they flew over 15,000 missions and were highly decorated. The Navajo Code Talkers were native Navajo who used their traditional language to transmit information among Allied forces. Because Navajo is a language and not simply a code, the Axis powers were never able to translate it. Use of Navajo Code Talkers to transmit information was instrumental in the taking of Iwo Jima and other major victories of the war.

Women during World War II
Women served widely in the military during WWII, working in numerous positions, including the Flight Nurses Corps. Women also moved into the workforce while men were overseas, leading to over 19 million women in the US workforce by 1944. Rosie the Riveter stood as a symbol of these women and a means of recruiting others to take needed positions. Women, as well as their families left behind during wartime, also grew Victory Gardens to help provide food.

Atomic bomb
The atomic bomb, developed during WWII, was the most powerful bomb ever invented. A single bomb, carried by a single plane, held enough power to destroy an entire city. This devastating effect was demonstrated with the bombing of Hiroshima and Nagasaki in 1945 in what later became a controversial move, but ended the war. The bombings resulted in as many as 150,000 immediate deaths and many more as time passed after the bombings, mostly due to radiation poisoning.

Whatever the arguments against the use of "The Bomb," the post WWII era saw many countries develop similar weapons to match the newly expanded military power of the US. The impact of those developments and use of nuclear weapons continues to haunt international relations today.

**Yalta Conference and the Potsdam Conference**

In February 1945, Joseph Stalin, Franklin D. Roosevelt and Winston Churchill met in Yalta to discuss the post-war treatment of the Axis nations, particularly Germany. Though Germany had not yet surrendered, its defeat was imminent. After Germany's official surrender, Joseph Stalin, Harry Truman (Roosevelt's successor), and Clement Attlee (replacing Churchill partway through the conference) met to formalize those plans.

This meeting was called the Potsdam Conference. Basic provisions of these agreements included:

- Dividing Germany and Berlin into four zones of occupation
- Demilitarization of Germany
- Poland remaining under Soviet control
- Outlawing the Nazi Party
- Trials for Nazi leaders
- Relocation of numerous German citizens
- The USSR joining the United Nations, established in 1945
- Establishment of the United Nations Security Council, consisting of the US, the UK, the USSR, China and France

**Agreements made with post-war Japan**

General Douglas MacArthur led the American military occupation of Japan after the country surrendered. The goals of the US occupation included removing Japan's military and making the country a democracy. A 1947 constitution removed power from the emperor and gave it to the people, as well as granting voting rights to women. Japan was no longer allowed to declare war, and a group of 28 government officials were tried for war crimes. In 1951, the US finally signed a peace treaty with Japan. This treaty allowed Japan to rearm itself for purposes of self-defense, but stripped the country of the empire it had built overseas.

**Alien Registration Act and treatment of Japanese immigrants**

In 1940, the US passed the Alien Registration Act, which required all aliens older than fourteen to be fingerprinted and registered. They were also required to report changes of address within five days.

Tension between whites and Japanese immigrants in California, which had been building since the beginning of the century, came to a head with the bombing of Pearl Harbor in 1941. Believing that even those Japanese living in the US were likely to be loyal to their native country, the president ordered numerous Japanese to be arrested on suspicion of subversive action and isolated in exclusion zones known as War Relocation Camps. Approximately 120,000 Japanese-Americans, two-thirds of them US citizens, were sent to these camps during the war.

## General state of the US after World War II

Following WWII, the US became the strongest political power in the world, becoming a major player in world affairs and foreign policies. The US determined to stop the spread of communism, having named itself the "arsenal of democracy" during the war. In addition, America emerged with a greater sense of itself as a single, integrated nation, with many regional and economic differences diminished. The government worked for greater equality and the growth of communications increased contact among different areas of the country. Both the aftermath of the Great Depression and the necessities of WWII had given the government greater control over various institutions as well as the economy. This also meant that the American government took on greater responsibility for the well-being of its citizens, both in the domestic arena, such as providing basic needs, and in protecting them from foreign threats. This increased role of providing basic necessities for all Americans has been criticized by some as "the welfare state."

## Harry S. Truman

Harry S. Truman took over the presidency from Franklin D. Roosevelt near the end of WWII. He made the final decision to drop atomic bombs on Japan and played a major role in the final decisions regarding treatment of post-war Germany. On the domestic front, Truman initiated a 21-point plan known as the Fair Deal. This plan expanded Social Security, provided public housing, and made the Fair Employment Practice Committee permanent. Truman helped support Greece and Turkey (which were under threat from the USSR), supported South Korea against communist North Korea, and helped with recovery in Western Europe. He also participated in the formation of NATO, the North Atlantic Treaty Organization.

## Korean War

The Korean War began in 1950 and ended in 1953. For the first time in history, a world organization—the United Nations—played a military role in a war. North Korea sent communist troops into South Korea, seeking to bring the entire country under communist control. The UN sent out a call to member nations, asking them to support South Korea. Truman sent troops, as did many other UN member nations. The war ended three years later with a truce rather than a peace treaty, and Korea remains divided at the 38th parallel north, with communist rule remaining in the North and a democratic government ruling the South.

## Dwight D. Eisenhower

Eisenhower carried out a middle-of-the-road foreign policy and brought the US several steps forward in equal rights. He worked to minimize tensions during the Cold War, and negotiated a peace treaty with Russia after the death of Stalin. He enforced desegregation by sending troops to Little Rock Central High School in Arkansas, as well as ordering the desegregation of the military. Organizations formed during his administration included the Department of Health, Education and Welfare, and the National Aeronautics and Space Administration (NASA).

## John F. Kennedy

Although his term was cut short by his assassination, JFK instituted economic programs that led to a period of continuous expansion in the US unmatched since before WWII. He formed the Alliance for Progress and the Peace Corps, organizations intended to help developing nations. He also oversaw the passage of new civil rights legislation, and drafted plans to attack poverty and its causes, along with support of the arts. Kennedy's presidency ended when he was assassinated by Lee Harvey Oswald in 1963.

## Cuban Missile Crisis

The Cuban Missile Crisis occurred in 1962, during John F. Kennedy's presidency. Russian Premier Nikita Khrushchev decided to place nuclear missiles in Cuba to protect the island from invasion by the US. An American U-2 plane flying over the island photographed the missile bases as they were being built. Tensions rose, with the US concerned about nuclear missiles so close to its shores, and the USSR concerned about American missiles that had been placed in Turkey. Eventually, the missile sites were removed, and a US naval blockade turned back Soviet ships carrying missiles to Cuba. During negotiations, the US agreed to remove their missiles from Turkey and agreed to sell surplus wheat to the USSR. A telephone hotline between Moscow and Washington was set up to allow instant communication between the two heads of state to prevent similar incidents in the future.

## Lyndon B. Johnson

Kennedy's Vice President, Lyndon Johnson, assumed the presidency after Kennedy's assassination. He supported civil rights bills, tax cuts, and other wide-reaching legislation that Kennedy had also supported. Johnson saw America as a "Great Society," and enacted legislation to fight disease and poverty, renew urban areas, support education and environmental conservation. Medicare and Medicaid were instituted under his administration. He continued Kennedy's support of space exploration and he is also known, although less positively, for his handling of the Vietnam War.

## Civil Rights Movement

In the 1950s, post-war America was experiencing a rapid growth in prosperity. However, African-Americans found themselves left behind. Following the lead of Mahatma Gandhi, who led similar class struggles in India, African-Americans began to demand equal rights. Major figures in this struggle included:

- Rosa Parks—often called the "mother of the Civil Rights Movement," her refusal to give up her seat on the bus to a white man served as a seed from which the movement grew.
- Martin Luther King, Jr.—the best-known leader of the movement, King drew on Gandhi's beliefs and encouraged non-violent opposition. He led a march on Washington in 1963, received the Nobel Peace Prize in 1964, and was assassinated in 1968.
- Malcolm X—espousing less peaceful means of change, Malcolm X became a Black Muslim, and supported black nationalism.
- Stokely Carmichael—Carmichael originated the term "Black Power" and served as head of the Student Nonviolent Coordinating Committee. He believed in black pride

and black culture, and felt separate political and social institutions should be developed for blacks.

- Adam Clayton Powell—chairman of the Coordinating Committee for Employment, he led rent strikes and other actions, as well as a bus boycott, to increase the hiring of blacks.
- Jesse Jackson—Jackson was selected to head the Chicago Operation Breadbasket in 1966, and went on to organize boycotts and other actions. He also had an unsuccessful run for President.

Three major events of the Civil Rights Movement are:

- Montgomery Bus Boycott—in 1955, Rosa Parks refused to give her seat on the bus to a white man. As a result, she was tried and convicted of disorderly conduct and of violating local ordinances. A 381-day bus boycott ensued, protesting segregation on public buses.
- Desegregation of Little Rock—in 1957, after the Supreme Court decision on Brown v. Board of Education, which declared "separate but equal" unconstitutional, the Arkansas school board voted to desegregate their schools. Even though Arkansas was considered progressive, its governor brought in the Arkansas National Guard to prevent nine black students from entering Central High School in Little Rock. President Eisenhower responded by federalizing the National Guard and ordering them to stand down.
- Birmingham Campaign—protestors organized a variety of actions such as sit-ins and an organized march to launch a voting campaign. When the City of Birmingham declared the protests illegal, the protestors, including Martin Luther King, Jr., persisted and were arrested and jailed.

Three major pieces of legislation passed as a result of the Civil Rights movement are:

- Brown v. Board of Education (1954)—the Supreme Court declared that "separate but equal" accommodations and services were unconstitutional.
- Civil Rights Act of 1964—this declared discrimination illegal in employment, education, or public accommodation.
- Voting Rights Act of 1965—this act ended various activities practiced, mostly in the South, to bar blacks from exercising their voting rights. These included poll taxes and literacy tests.

### Vietnam War

After World War II, the US pledged, as part of its foreign policy, to come to the assistance of any country threatened by communism. When Vietnam was divided into a communist North and democratic South, much like Korea before it, the eventual attempts by the North to unify the country under Communist rule led to intervention by the US. On the home front, the Vietnam War became more and more unpopular politically, with Americans growing increasingly discontent with the inability of the US to achieve the goals it had set for the Asian country. When President Richard Nixon took office in 1969, his escalation of the war led to protests at Kent State in Ohio, during which several students were killed by National Guard troops. Protests continued, eventually resulting in the end of the compulsory draft in 1973. In that same year, the US departed Vietnam. In 1975, the south surrendered, and Vietnam became a unified country under communist rule.

## US Cold War foreign policy acts

The following are US Cold War foreign policy acts and how they affected international relationships, especially between the US and the Soviet Union:

- Marshall Plan—this sent aid to war-torn Europe after WWII, largely focusing on preventing the spread of communism.
- Containment Policy—proposed by George F. Kennan, the containment policy focused on containing the spread of Soviet communism.
- Truman Doctrine—Harry S. Truman stated that the US would provide both economic and military support to any country threatened by Soviet takeover.
- National Security Act—passed in 1947, this act reorganized the government's military departments into the Department of Defense, as well as creating the Central Intelligence Agency and the National Security Council.

The combination of these acts led to the Cold War, with Soviet communists attempting to spread their influence and the US and other countries trying to contain or stop this spread.

> ➢ **Review Video:** The Cold War: The United States and Russia
> *Visit **mometrix.com/academy** and enter **Code**:* **981433**

## NATO, the Warsaw Pact, and the Berlin Wall

NATO, the North Atlantic Treaty Organization, came into being in 1949. It essentially amounted to an agreement among the US and Western European countries that an attack on any one of these countries was to be considered an attack against the entire group.

Under the influence of the Soviet Union, the Eastern European countries of the USSR, Bulgaria, East Germany, Poland, Romania, Albania, Hungary, and Czechoslovakia responded with the Warsaw Pact, which created a similar agreement among those nations. In 1961, a wall was built to separate communist East Berlin from democratic West Berlin. This was a literal representation of the "Iron Curtain" that separated the democratic and communist countries through the world.

## Arms race

After World War II, major nations, particularly the US and USSR, rushed to develop highly advanced weapons systems such as the atomic bomb and later the hydrogen bomb. These countries seemed determined to outpace each other with the development of numerous, deadly weapons. These weapons were expensive and extremely dangerous, and it is possible that the war between US and Soviet interests remained "cold" due to the fear that one side or the other would use these powerful weapons.

## End of the Cold War

In the late 1980s, Mikhail Gorbachev led the Soviet Union. He introduced a series of reform programs. Ronald Reagan famously urged Gorbachev to tear down the Berlin Wall as a gesture of growing freedom in the Eastern Bloc, and in 1989 it was demolished, ending the separation of East and West Germany. The Soviet Union relinquished its power over the various republics in Eastern Europe, and they became independent nations with their own individual governments. In 1991, the USSR was dissolved and the Cold War also came to an end.

> ➢ **Review Video:** The Cold War: Resolution
> *Visit **mometrix.com/academy** and enter **Code**:* **843092**

## Technological advances after WWII

Numerous technological advances after the Second World War led to more effective treatment of diseases, more efficient communication and transportation, and new means of generating power. Advances in medicine increased the human lifespan in developed countries, and near-instantaneous communication opened up a myriad of possibilities. Some of these advances include:

- Discovery of penicillin (1928)
- Supersonic air travel (1947)
- Nuclear power plants (1951)
- Orbital satellite leading to manned space flight (Sputnik, 1957)
- First man on the moon (1969)

## US policy toward immigrants after World War II

Prior to WWII, the US had been limiting immigration for several decades. After WWII, policy shifted slightly to accommodate political refugees from Europe and elsewhere. So many people were displaced by the war that in 1946, the UN formed the International Refugee Organization to deal with the problem. In 1948, the US Congress passed the Displaced Persons Act, which allowed over 400,000 European refugees to enter the US, most of them concentration camp survivors and refugees from Eastern Europe.

In 1952, the United States Escapee Program (USEP) increased the quotas, allowing refugees from communist Europe to enter the US, as did the Refugee Relief Act, passed in 1953. At the same time, however, the Internal Security Act of 1950 allowed deportation of declared communists, and Asians were subjected to a quota based on race, rather than country of origin. Later changes included:

- Migration and Refugee Assistance Act (1962)—provided aid for refugees in need
- Immigration and Nationality Act (1965)—ended quotas based on nation of origin
- Immigration Reform and Control Act (1986)—prohibited the hiring of illegal immigrants, but also granted amnesty to about three million illegals already in the country

**Expansion of minority rights**

Several major acts have been passed, particularly since WWII, to protect the rights of minorities in America. These include:

- Civil Rights Act (1964)
- Voting Rights Act (1965)
- Age Discrimination Act (1967)
- Americans with Disabilities Act (1990)

Other important movements for civil rights included a prisoner's rights movement, movements for immigrant rights, and the women's rights movement. The National Organization for Women (NOW) was established in 1966 and worked to pass the Equal Rights Amendment. The amendment was passed, but not enough states ratified it for it to become part of the US Constitution.

**Richard Nixon (R, 1969-1974)**

Richard Nixon is best known for the Watergate scandal during his presidency, but other important events marked his tenure as president, including:

- End of the Vietnam War
- Improved diplomatic relations between the US and China, and the US and the USSR
- National Environmental Policy Act passed, providing for environmental protection
- Compulsory draft ended
- Supreme Court legalized abortion in Roe v. Wade
- Watergate

The Watergate scandal of 1972 ended Nixon's presidency. Rather than face impeachment and removal from office, he resigned in 1974.

**Gerald Ford (R, 1974-1977)**

Gerald Ford was appointed to the vice presidency after Nixon's vice president Spiro Agnew resigned in 1973 under charges of tax evasion. With Nixon's resignation, Ford became president.

Ford's presidency saw negotiations with Russia to limit nuclear arms, as well as struggles to deal with inflation, economic downturn, and energy shortages. Ford's policies sought to reduce governmental control of various businesses and reduce the role of government overall. He also worked to prevent escalation of conflicts in the Middle East.

**Jimmy Carter (D, 1977-1981)**

Jimmy Carter was elected as president in 1976. Faced with a budget deficit, high unemployment, and continued inflation, Carter also dealt with numerous matters of international diplomacy including:

- Torrijos-Carter Treaties—the US gave control of the Panama Canal to Panama.
- Camp David Accords—negotiations between Anwar el-Sadat, the president of Egypt, and Menachem Begin, the Israeli Prime Minister, led to a peace treaty between Egypt and Israel.

- Strategic Arms Limitation Talks (SALT)—these led to agreements and treaties between the US and the Soviet Union.
- Iran Hostage Crisis—after the Shah of Iran was deposed, an Islamic cleric, Ayatollah Khomeini, came to power. The shah came to the US for medical treatment and Iran demanded his return so he could stand trial. In retaliation, a group of Iranian students stormed the US Embassy in Iran. Fifty-two American hostages were held for 444 days.

Jimmy Carter was awarded the Nobel Peace Prize in 2002.

**Ronald Reagan (R, 1981-1989)**

Ronald Reagan, at 69, became the oldest American president. The two terms of his administration included notable events such as:

- Reaganomics, also known as supply-side, trickle-down, or free-market economics, involving major tax cuts
- Economic Recovery Tax Act of 1981
- First female justice appointed to the Supreme Court—Sandra Day O'Connor
- Massive increase in the national debt - from $1 trillion to $3 trillion
- Reduction of nuclear weapons via negotiations with Mikhail Gorbachev
- Iran-Contra scandal—cover-up of US involvement in revolutions in El Salvador and Nicaragua
- Deregulation of savings and loan industry
- Loss of the space shuttle *Challenger*

**George H. W. Bush (R, 1989-1993)**

Reagan's presidency was followed by a term under his former Vice President, George H. W. Bush. Bush's run for president included the famous "thousand points of light" speech, which was instrumental in increasing his standing in the election polls. During Bush's presidency, numerous international events took place, including:

- Fall of the Berlin wall and Germany's unification
- Panamanian dictator Manuel Noriega captured and tried on drug and racketeering charges
- Dissolution of the Soviet Union
- Gulf War, or Operation Desert Storm, triggered by Iraq's invasion of Kuwait
- Tiananmen Square Massacre in Beijing, China
- Ruby Ridge
- The arrival of the World Wide Web

**Bill Clinton (D, 1993-2001)**

William Jefferson "Bill" Clinton was the second president in US history to be impeached, but he was not convicted, and maintained high approval ratings in spite of the impeachment. Major events during his presidency included:

- Family and Medical Leave Act
- Don't Ask, Don't Tell, a compromise position regarding homosexuals serving in the military
- North American Free Trade Agreement, or NAFTA
- Defense of Marriage Act

- Oslo Accords
- Siege at Waco, Texas, involving the Branch Davidians led by David Koresh
- Bombing of the Murrah Federal Building in Oklahoma City, Oklahoma
- Troops sent to Haiti, Bosnia and Somalia to assist with domestic problems in those areas

### George W. Bush (R, 2001-2009)

George W. Bush, son of George Herbert Walker Bush, became president after Clinton. Major events during his presidency included:

- September 11, 2001, al-Qaeda terrorists hijack commercial airliners and fly into the World Trade Center towers and the Pentagon, killing nearly 3000 Americans
- US troops sent to Afghanistan to hunt down al-Qaeda leaders, including the head of the organization, Osama Bin Laden; beginning of the War on Terror
- US troops sent to Iraq, along with a multinational coalition, to depose Saddam Hussein and prevent his deployment of suspected weapons of mass destruction
- Subprime mortgage crisis and near collapse of the financial industry, leading to the Great Recession; first of multiple government bailouts of the financial industry

### Barack Obama (D, 2009-2017)

Barack Obama, a first-term senator from Illinois, became the first African-American president. Major events included:

- Multiple bailout packages and spending efforts, in an attempt to inject more money into a stagnant economy
- Massive increase in the national debt – from $10 trillion to $18 trillion
- Reinforcement of the War on Terror in Afghanistan and Iraq; additional deployment of troops in Libya and Syria
- Capture and execution of Osama Bin Laden
- Passage of the Affordable Care Act, legislation that greatly increased government involvement in the healthcare industry, and required every person living in the US to maintain health insurance coverage
- Moves to broaden gay rights, including the repeal of Clinton's Don't Ask, Don't Tell policy for homosexuals serving in the military

### Donald Trump (R, 2017- )

Donald Trump, a billionaire real estate tycoon with no prior political experience, was elected to the presidency in a surprise victory over former First Lady and Secretary of State (under Obama) Hillary Clinton. His platform focused on increasing immigration enforcement to curb illegal immigration, restricting foreign trade to improve the dwindling American manufacturing industry, and repealing the Affordable Care Act passed during the prior administration.

# World History

## Prehistory

Prehistory is the period of human history before writing was developed. The three major periods of prehistory are:

- Lower Paleolithic—Humans used crude tools.
- Upper Paleolithic—Humans began to develop a wider variety of tools. These tools were better made and more specialized. They also began to wear clothes, organize in groups with definite social structures, and to practice art. Most lived in caves during this time period.
- Neolithic—Social structures became even more complex, including growth of a sense of family and the ideas of religion and government. Humans learned to domesticate animals and produce crops, build houses, start fires with friction tools, and to knit, spin and weave.

## Anthropology

Anthropology is the study of human culture. Anthropologists study groups of humans, how they relate to each other, and the similarities and differences between these different groups and cultures. Anthropological research takes two approaches: cross-cultural research and comparative research. Most anthropologists work by living among different cultures and participating in those cultures in order to learn about them.

There are four major divisions within anthropology:

- Biological anthropology
- Cultural anthropology
- Linguistic anthropology
- Archaeology

## Archeology

Archeology studies past human cultures by evaluating what they leave behind. This can include bones, buildings, art, tools, pottery, graves, and even trash. Archeologists maintain detailed notes and records of their findings and use special tools to evaluate what they find. Photographs, notes, maps, artifacts, and surveys of the area can all contribute to evaluation of an archeological site. By studying all these elements of numerous archeological sites, scientists have been able to theorize that humans or near-humans have existed for about 600,000 years. Before that, more primitive humans are believed to have appeared about one million years ago. These humans eventually developed into Cro-Magnon man, and then Homo sapiens, or modern man.

## Human development from the Lower Paleolithic to the Iron Age

Human development has been divided into several phases:

- Lower Paleolithic or Early Stone Age, beginning two to three million years ago—early humans used tools like needles, hatchets, awls, and cutting tools.
- Middle Paleolithic or Middle Stone Age, beginning approximately 300,000 B.C.E.—sophisticated stone tools were developed, along with hunting, gathering, and ritual practices.

- Upper Paleolithic or Late Stone Age, beginning approximately 40,000 B.C.E.—including the Mesolithic and Neolithic eras, textiles and pottery are developed. Humans of this era discovered the wheel, began to practice agriculture, made polished tools, and had some domesticated animals.
- Bronze Age, beginning in approximately 3,000 B.C.E.—metals are discovered and the first civilizations emerge as humans become more technologically advanced.
- Iron Age, beginning in 1,200 to 1,000 B.C.E.—metal tools replace stone tools as humans develop knowledge of smelting.

## Civilizations

Civilizations are defined as having the following characteristics:
- Use of metal to make weapons and tools
- Written language
- A defined territorial state
- A calendar

The earliest civilizations developed in river valleys where reliable, fertile land was easily found, including:
- The Nile River Valley in Egypt
- Mesopotamia
- The Indus Valley
- Hwang Ho in China

The very earliest civilizations developed in the Tigris-Euphrates valley in Mesopotamia, which is now part of Iraq, and in Egypt's Nile valley. These civilizations arose between 5,000 and 3,000 B.C.E. The area where these civilizations grew is known as the Fertile Crescent. Geography and the availability of water made large-scale human habitation possible.

Importance of rivers and water

The earliest civilizations are also referred to as fluvial civilizations because they were founded near rivers. Rivers and the water they provide were vital to these early groupings, offering:
- Water for drinking, cultivating crops, and caring for domesticated animals
- A gathering place for wild animals that could be hunted
- Rich soil deposits as a result of regular flooding

Irrigation techniques helped direct water where it was most needed, to sustain herds of domestic animals and to nourish crops of increasing size and quality.

## Fertile Crescent

James Breasted, an archeologist from the University of Chicago, popularized the term "Fertile Crescent" to describe the area in the Near East where the earliest civilizations arose. The region includes modern day Iraq, Syria, Lebanon, Israel, Palestine, and Jordan. It is bordered on the south by the Syrian and Arabian Deserts, the west by the Mediterranean Sea, and to the north and east by the Taurus and Zagros Mountains respectively. This area not only provided the raw materials for the development of increasingly advanced civilizations, but also saw waves of migration and invasion, leading to the earliest wars and genocides as groups conquered and absorbed each other's cultures and inhabitants.

**Egyptian, Sumerian, Babylonian, and Assyrian cultures**

The Egyptians were one of the most advanced ancient cultures, having developed construction methods to build the great pyramids, as well as a form of writing known as hieroglyphics. Their religion was highly developed and complex, and included advanced techniques for the preservation of bodies after death. They also made paper by processing papyrus, a plant commonly found along the Nile, invented the decimal system, devised a solar calendar, and advanced overall knowledge of mathematics.

> ➢ **Review Video:** Egyptians
> *Visit **mometrix.com/academy** and enter **Code**:* **152695**

The Sumerians were the first to invent the wheel, and also brought irrigation systems into use. Their cuneiform writing was simpler than Egyptian hieroglyphs, and they developed the timekeeping system we still use today.

> ➢ **Review Video:** Early Mesopotamia: The Sumerians
> *Visit **mometrix.com/academy** and enter **Code**:* **987440**

The Babylonians are best known for the Code of Hammurabi, an advanced law code.

> ➢ **Review Video:** Early Mesopotamia: The Babylonians
> *Visit **mometrix.com/academy** and enter **Code**:* **340325**

The Assyrians developed horse-drawn chariots and an organized military.

**Hebrew, Persian, Minoan, and Mycenaean cultures**

The Hebrew or ancient Israelite culture developed the monotheistic religion that eventually developed into modern Judaism and Christianity.

The Persians were conquerors, but those they conquered were allowed to keep their own laws, customs, and religious traditions rather than being forced to accept those of their conquerors. They also developed an alphabet and practiced Zoroastrianism and Mithraism, religions that have influenced modern religious practice.

The Minoans used a syllabic writing system and built large, colorful palaces. These ornate buildings included sewage systems, running water, bathtubs, and even flushing toilets. Their script, known as Linear A, has yet to be deciphered.

The Mycenaeans practiced a religion that grew into the Greek pantheon, worshipping Zeus and other Olympian gods. They developed Linear B, a writing system used to write the earliest known form of Greek.

**Phoenicians and early culture in India and ancient China**

Skilled seafarers and navigators, the Phoenicians used the stars to navigate their ships at night. They developed a purple dye that was in great demand in the ancient world, and worked with glass and metals. They also devised a phonetic alphabet, using symbols to represent individual sounds rather than whole words or syllables.

In the Indus Valley, an urban civilization arose in what is now India. These ancient humans developed the concept of zero in mathematics, practiced an early form of the Hindu religion, and developed the caste system which is still prevalent in India today. Archeologists are still uncovering information about this highly developed ancient civilization.

In ancient China, human civilization developed along the Yangtze River. These people produced silk, grew millet, and made pottery, including Longshan black pottery.

**Civilizations of Mesopotamia**

The major civilizations of Mesopotamia, in what is now called the Middle East, were:

- Sumerians
- Amorites
- Hittites
- Assyrians
- Chaldeans
- Persians

These cultures controlled different areas of Mesopotamia during various time periods, but were similar in that they were autocratic: a single ruler served as the head of the government and often was the main religious ruler as well. These rulers were often tyrannical, militaristic leaders who controlled all aspects of life, including law, trade, and religious activity. Portions of the legacies of these civilizations remain in cultures today. These include mythologies, religious systems, mathematical innovations and even elements of various languages.

**Sumer**

Sumer, located in the southern part of Mesopotamia, consisted of a dozen city-states. Each city-state had its own gods, and the leader of each city-state also served as the high priest. Cultural legacies of Sumer include:

- The invention of writing
- Invention of the wheel
- The first library—established in Assyria by Ashurbanipal
- The Hanging Gardens of Babylon—one of the Seven Wonders of the Ancient World
- First written laws—Ur-Nammu's Codes and the Codes of Hammurabi
- The *Epic of Gilgamesh*—the first recorded epic story

**Kushite culture**

Kush, or Cush, was located in Nubia, south of ancient Egypt, and the earliest existing records of this civilization were found in Egyptian texts. At one time, Kush was the largest empire on the Nile River, ruling not only Nubia but Upper and Lower Egypt as well.

In Neolithic times, Kushites lived in villages, with buildings made of mud bricks. They were settled rather than nomadic, and practiced hunting and fishing, cultivated grain, and also herded cattle. Kerma, the capital, was a major center of trade.

Kush determined leadership through matrilineal descent of their kings, as did Egypt. Their heads of state, the Kandake or Kentake, were female. Their polytheistic religion included the primary Egyptian gods as well as regional gods, including a lion-headed god, which is commonly found in African cultures.

Archeological evidence indicates the Kushites were a mix of Mediterranean and Negroid peoples. Kush was conquered by the Aksumite Empire in the $4^{th}$ century CE.

### Minoan civilization

The Minoans lived on the island of Crete, just off the coast of Greece. This civilization reigned from approximately 4000 to 1400 B.C.E. and is considered to be the first advanced civilization in Europe. The Minoans developed writing systems known to linguists as Linear A and Linear B. Linear A has not yet been translated; Linear B evolved into classical Greek script. "Minoans" is not the name they used for themselves, but is instead a variation on the name of King Minos, a king in Greek mythology believed by some to have been a denizen of Crete. The Minoan civilization subsisted on trade, and their way of life was often disrupted by earthquakes and volcanoes. Much is still unknown about the Minoans, and archeologists continue to study their architecture and archeological remains. The Minoan culture eventually fell to Greek invaders and was supplanted by the Mycenaean civilization.

### Influences of ancient Indian civilization

The civilizations of ancient India gave rise to both Hinduism and Buddhism, major world religions that have influenced countries far from their place of origin. Practices such as yoga, increasingly popular in the West, can trace their roots to these earliest Indian civilizations, and the poses are still formally referred to by Sanskrit names. Literature from ancient India includes the *Mahabharata* containing the *Bhagavad Gita*, the *Ramayana*, *Arthashastra*, and the *Vedas*, a collection of sacred texts. Indo-European languages, including English, find their beginnings in these ancient cultures. Ancient Indo-Aryan languages such as Sanskrit are still used in some formal Hindu practices.

### Earliest civilizations in China

Many historians believe Chinese civilization is the oldest uninterrupted civilization in the world. The Neolithic age in China goes back to 10,000 B.C.E., with agriculture in China beginning as early as 5,000 B.C.E. Their system of writing dates to 1,500 B.C.E. The Yellow River served as the center for the earliest Chinese settlements. In Ningxia, in northwest China, there are carvings on cliffs that date back to the Paleolithic Period, indicating the extreme antiquity of Chinese culture. Literature from ancient China includes Confucius' *Analects*, the *Tao Te Ching*, and a variety of poetry.

### Ancient American cultures

Less is known of ancient American civilizations since less was left behind. Some of the more well-known cultures include:

- The Norte Chico civilization in Peru, an agricultural society of up to 30 individual communities, existed over 5,000 years ago. This culture is also known as the Caral-Supe civilization, and is the oldest known civilization in the Americas.

- The Anasazi, or Ancestral Pueblo People, lived in what is now the southwestern United States. Emerging about 1200 B.C.E., the Anasazi built complex adobe dwellings and were the forerunners of later Pueblo Indian cultures.
- The Maya emerged in southern Mexico and northern Central America as early as 2,600 B.C.E. They developed a written language and a complex calendar.

> ➢ **Review Video:** American Civilizations: Early Cultures
> *Visit **mometrix.com/academy** and enter **Code**:* **575452**

> ➢ **Review Video:** American Civilizations: The Mayas
> *Visit **mometrix.com/academy** and enter **Code**:* **556527**

**Mycenaean civilization**

In contrast to the Minoans, whom they displaced, the Mycenaeans relied more on conquest than on trade. Mycenaean states included Sparta, Athens, and Corinth. The history of this civilization, including the Trojan War, was recorded by the Greek poet, Homer. His work was largely considered mythical until archeologists discovered evidence of the city of Troy in Hisarlik, Turkey. Archeologists continue to add to the body of information about this ancient culture, translating documents written in Linear B, a script derived from the Minoan Linear A. It is theorized that the Mycenaean civilization was eventually destroyed in either a Dorian invasion or an attack by Greek invaders from the north.

**Dorian invasion**

A Dorian invasion does not refer to an invasion by a particular group of people, but rather is a hypothetical theory to explain the end of the Mycenaean civilization and the growth of classical Greece. Ancient tradition refers to these events as "the return of the Heracleidae," or the sons (descendents) of Hercules. Archeologists and historians still do not know exactly who conquered the Mycenaeans, but it is believed to have occurred around 1200 B.C.E., contemporaneous with the destruction of the Hittite civilization in what is now modern Turkey. The Hittites speak of an attack by people of the Aegean Sea, or the "Sea People." Only Athens was left intact.

**Spartans and Athenians**

Both powerful city-states, Sparta and Athens fought each other in the Peloponnesian War (431-404 B.C.E.). Despite their proximity, the Spartans and the Athenians nurtured contrasting cultures:

- The Spartans, located in Peloponnesus, were ruled by an oligarchic military state. They practiced farming, disallowed trade for Spartan citizens, and valued military arts and strict discipline. They emerged as the strongest military force in the area, and maintained this status for many years. In one memorable encounter, a small group of Spartans held off a huge army of Persians at Thermopylae.
- The Athenians were centered in Attica, where the land was rocky and unsuitable for farming. Like the Spartans, they descended from invaders who spoke Greek. Their government was very different from Sparta's; it was in Athens that democracy was created by Cleisthenes of Athens in 508 B.C.E. Athenians excelled in art, theater, architecture, and philosophy.

## Contributions of ancient Greece

Ancient Greece made numerous major contributions to cultural development, including:

- Theater—Aristophanes and other Greek playwrights laid the groundwork for modern theatrical performance.
- Alphabet—the Greek alphabet, derived from the Phoenician alphabet, developed into the Roman alphabet, and then into our modern-day alphabet.
- Geometry—Pythagoras and Euclid pioneered much of the system of geometry still taught today. Archimedes made various mathematical discoveries, including calculating a very accurate value of pi.
- Historical writing—much of ancient history doubles as mythology or religious texts. Herodotus and Thucydides made use of research and interpretation to record historical events.
- Philosophy—Socrates, Plato, and Aristotle served as the fathers of Western philosophy. Their work is still required reading for philosophy students.

## Alexander the Great

Born to Philip II of Macedon and tutored by Aristotle, Alexander the Great is considered one of the greatest conquerors in history. He conquered Egypt, the Achaemenid/Persian Empire, a powerful empire founded by Cyrus the Great that spanned three continents, and he traveled as far as India and the Iberian Peninsula. Though Alexander died from malaria at age 32, his conquering efforts spread Greek culture into the east. This cultural diffusion left a greater mark on history than did his empire, which fell apart due to internal conflict not long after his death. Trade between the East and West increased, as did an exchange of ideas and beliefs that influenced both regions greatly. The Hellenistic traditions his conquest spread were prevalent in Byzantine culture until as late as the 15th century.

## Hittite Empire

The Hittites were centered in what is now Turkey, but their empire extended into Palestine and Syria. They conquered the Babylonian civilization, but adopted their religion, laws, and literature. Overall, the Hittites tended to tolerate other religions, unlike many other contemporary cultures, and absorbed foreign gods into their own belief systems rather than forcing their religion onto peoples they conquered. The Hittite Empire reached its peak in 1600-1200 B.C.E. After a war with Egypt, which weakened them severely, they were eventually conquered by the Assyrians.

## Persian Wars

The Persian Empire, ruled by Cyrus the Great, encompassed an area from the Black Sea to Afghanistan, and beyond into Central Asia. After the death of Cyrus, Darius I became king in 522 B.C.E. The empire reached its zenith during his reign and Darius attempted to conquer Greece as well. From 499-449 B.C.E., the Greeks and Persians fought in the Persian Wars. The Peace of Callias brought an end to the fighting, after the Greeks were able to repel the invasion.

Battles of the Persian Wars included:

- The Battle of Marathon—heavily outnumbered Greek forces managed to achieve victory.
- The Battle of Thermopylae—a small band of Spartans held off a throng of Persian troops for several days before Persia defeated the Greeks and captured an evacuated Athens.
- The Battle of Salamis—this was a naval battle that again saw outnumbered Greeks achieving victory.
- The Battle of Plataea—this was another Greek victory, but one in which they outnumbered the Persians. This ended the invasion of Greece.

**Maurya Empire**

The Maurya Empire was a large, powerful empire established in India. It was one of the largest ever to rule in the Indian subcontinent, and existed from 322 to 185 B.C.E., ruled by Chandragupta Maurya after the withdrawal from India of Alexander the Great. The Maurya Empire was highly developed, including a standardized economic system, waterways, and private corporations. Trade to the Greeks and others became common, with goods including silk, exotic foods, and spices. Religious development included the rise of Buddhism and Jainism. The laws of the Maurya Empire protected not only civil and social rights of the citizens, but also protected animals, establishing protected zones for economically important creatures such as elephants, lions and tigers. This period of time in Indian history was largely peaceful, perhaps due to the strong Buddhist beliefs of many of its leaders. The empire finally fell after a succession of weak leaders, and was taken over by Demetrius, a Greco-Bactrian king who took advantage of this lapse in leadership to conquer southern Afghanistan and Pakistan around 180 B.C.E., forming the Indo-Greek Kingdom.

**Chinese dynasties**

In China, history was divided into a series of dynasties. The most famous of these, the Han dynasty, existed from 206 B.C.E. to 220 CE. Accomplishments of the Chinese Empires included:

- Building the Great Wall of China
- Numerous inventions, including paper, paper money, printing, and gunpowder
- High level of artistic development
- Silk production

The Chinese dynasties were comparable to Rome as far as their artistic and intellectual accomplishments, as well as the size and scope of their influence.

**Roman Republic and Empire**

Rome began humbly, in a single town that grew out of Etruscan settlements and traditions, founded, according to legend, by twin brothers Romulus and Remus, who were raised by wolves. Romulus killed Remus, and from his legacy grew Rome. A thousand years later, the Roman Empire covered a significant portion of the known world, from what is now Scotland, across Europe, and into the Middle East. Hellenization, or the spread of Greek culture throughout the world, served as an inspiration and a model for the spread of Roman culture. Rome brought in belief systems of conquered peoples as well as their technological and scientific accomplishments, melding the disparate parts into a Roman core. Rome began as a republic ruled by consuls, but after the assassination of Julius Caesar, it became an empire led by emperors. Rome's overall government was autocratic, but local officials came from the provinces where they lived. This limited administrative system was probably a major factor in the long life of the empire.

### Byzantine Empire

In the early fourth century, the Roman Empire split, with the eastern portion becoming the Eastern Empire, or the Byzantine Empire. In 330 CE, Constantine founded the city of Constantinople, which became the center of the Byzantine Empire. Its major influences came from Mesopotamia and Persia, in contrast to the Western Empire, which maintained traditions more closely linked to Greece and Carthage. Byzantium's position gave it an advantage over invaders from the west and the east, as well as control over trade from both regions. It protected the Western empire from invasion from the Persians and the Ottomans, and practiced a more centralized rule than in the West. The Byzantines were famous for lavish art and architecture, as well as the Code of Justinian, which collected Roman law into a clear system. The Byzantine Empire finally fell to the Ottomans in 1453.

### Nicene Creed

The Byzantine Empire was Christian-based but incorporated Greek language, philosophy and literature and drew its law and government policies from Rome. However, there was as yet no unified doctrine of Christianity, as it was a relatively new religion that had spread rapidly and without a great deal of organization. In 325, the First Council of Nicaea addressed this issue. From this conference came the Nicene Creed, addressing the Trinity and other basic Christian beliefs. The Council of Chalcedon in 451 further defined the view of the Trinity.

### Fall of the Western Roman Empire

Germanic tribes, including the Visigoths, Ostrogoths, Vandals, Saxons and Franks, controlled most of Europe. The Roman Empire faced major opposition on that front. The increasing size of the empire also made it harder to manage, leading to dissatisfaction throughout the empire as Roman government became less efficient. Germanic tribes refused to adhere to the Nicene Creed, instead following Arianism, which led the Roman Catholic Church to declare them heretics. The Franks proved a powerful military force in their defeat of the Muslims in 732. In 768, Charlemagne became king of the Franks. These tribes waged several wars against Rome, including the invasion of Britannia by the Angles and Saxons. Far-flung Rome lost control over this area of its Empire, and eventually Rome itself was invaded.

### Iconoclasm and conflict between Roman Catholic and Eastern Orthodox churches

Emperor Leo III ordered the destruction of all icons throughout the Byzantine Empire. Images of Jesus were replaced with crosses, and images of Jesus, Mary or other religious figures were considered blasphemy on grounds of idolatry. Pope Gregory II, called a synod to discuss the issue. The synod declared that the images were not heretical, and that strong disciplinary measures would result for anyone who destroyed them. Leo's response was an attempt to kill Pope Gregory, but this plan ended in failure.

## Viking invasions

Vikings invaded Northern France in the tenth century, eventually becoming the Normans. Originating in Scandinavia, the Vikings were accomplished seafarers with advanced knowledge of trade routes. With overpopulation plaguing their native lands, they began to travel. From the eighth to the eleventh centuries, they spread throughout Europe, conquering and colonizing. Vikings invaded and colonized England in several waves, including the Anglo-Saxon invasions that displaced Roman control. Their influence remained significant in England, affecting everything from the language of the country to place names and even the government and social structure. By 900, Vikings had settled in Iceland. They proceeded then to Greenland and eventually to North America, arriving in the New World even before the Spanish and British who claimed the lands several centuries later. They also traded with the Byzantine Empire until the eleventh century when their significant level of activity came to an end.

## Tenth century events in the West and the East

In Europe, the years 500-1000 CE are largely known as the Dark Ages. In the tenth century, numerous Viking invasions disrupted societies that had been more settled under Roman rule. Vikings settled in Northern France, eventually becoming the Normans. By the eleventh century, Europe would rise again into the High Middle Ages with the beginning of the Crusades.

In China, wars also raged. This led the Chinese to make use of gunpowder for the first time in warfare.

In the Americas, the Mayan Empire was winding down while the Toltec became more prominent. Pueblo Indian culture was also at its zenith.

In the East, the Muslims and the Byzantine Empire were experiencing a significant period of growth and development.

## European feudalism in the Middle Ages

A major element of the social and economic life of Europe, feudalism developed as a way to ensure European rulers would have the wherewithal to quickly raise an army when necessary. Vassals swore loyalty and promised to provide military service for lords, who in return offered a fief, or a parcel of land, for them to use to generate their livelihood. Vassals could work the land themselves, have it worked by peasants or serfs—workers who had few rights and were little more than slaves—or grant the fief to someone else. The king legally owned all the land, but in return promised to protect the vassals from invasion and war. Vassals returned a certain percentage of their income to the lords, who in turn passed a portion of their income on to the king. A similar practice was manorialism, in which the feudal system was applied to a self-contained manor. These manors were often owned by the lords who ran them, but were usually included in the same system of loyalty and promises of protection that drove feudalism.

## Influence of the Roman Catholic Church

The Roman Catholic Church extended significant influence both politically and economically throughout medieval society. The church supplied education, as there were no established schools or universities. To a large extent, the church had filled a power void left by various invasions throughout the former Roman Empire, leading it to exercise a role that was far more political than religious. Kings were heavily influenced by the Pope and other church officials, and churches controlled large amounts of land throughout Europe.

## Black Death

The Black Death, believed to be bubonic plague, most likely came to Europe on fleas carried by rats on sailing vessels. The plague killed more than a third of the entire population of Europe and effectively ended feudalism as a political system. Many who had formerly served as peasants or serfs found different work, as a demand for skilled labor grew. Nation-states grew in power, and in the face of the pandemic, many began to turn away from faith in God and toward the ideals of ancient Greece and Rome for government and other beliefs.

## Crusades

The Crusades began in the eleventh century and continued into the fifteenth. The major goal of these various military ventures was to slow the progression of Muslim forces into Europe and to expel them from the Holy Land, where they had taken control of Jerusalem and Palestine. Alexius I, the Byzantine emperor, called for helped from Pope Urban II when Palestine was taken. In 1095, the Pope, hoping to reunite Eastern and Western Christianity, encouraged all Christians to help the cause. Amidst great bloodshed, this Crusade recaptured Jerusalem, but over the next centuries, Jerusalem and other areas of the Holy Land changed hands numerous times. The Second Crusade (1147-1149) consisted of an unsuccessful attempt to retake Damascus. The Third Crusade, under Pope Gregory VIII, attempted to recapture Jerusalem, but failed. The Fourth Crusade, under Pope Innocent III, attempted to come into the Holy Land via Egypt. The Crusades led to greater power for the Pope and the Catholic Church in general and also opened numerous trading and cultural routes between Europe and the East.

## Developments through the eleventh century

Politics in India

After the Mauryan dynasty, the Guptas ruled India, maintaining a long period of peace and prosperity in the area. During this time, the Indian people invented the decimal system as well as the concept of zero. They produced cotton and calico, as well as other products in high demand in Europe and Asia, and developed a complex system of medicine. The Gupta Dynasty ended in the sixth century. First the Huns invaded, and then the Hephthalites (an Asian nomadic tribe) destroyed the weakened empire.

In the fourteenth century, Tamerlane, a Muslim who envisioned restoring Genghis Khan's empire, expanded India's borders and founded the Mogul Empire. His grandson Akbar promoted freedom of religion and built a wide-spread number of mosques, forts, and other buildings throughout the country.

Chinese and Japanese governments

After the Mongols, led by Genghis Khan and his grandson Kublai Khan, unified the Mongol Empire, China was led by the Ming Dynasty (1368-1644) and the Manchu (also known as Qing) Dynasty (1644-1912). Both dynasties were isolationist, ending China's interaction with other countries until the eighteenth century. The Ming Dynasty was known for its porcelain, while the Manchus focused on farming and road construction as the population grew.

Japan developed independently of China, but borrowed the Buddhist religion, the Chinese writing system, and other elements of Chinese society. Ruled by the divine emperor, Japan basically functioned on a feudal system led by daimyo, or warlords, and soldiers known as samurai. Japan remained isolationist, not interacting significantly with the rest of the world until the 1800s.

Africa

Much of Africa was difficult to traverse early on, due to the large amount of desert and other inhospitable terrain. Egypt remained important, though most of the northern coast became Muslim as their armies spread through the area. Ghana rose as a trade center in the ninth century, lasting into the twelfth century, primarily trading in gold, which it exchanges for Saharan salt. Mali rose somewhat later, with the trade center Timbuktu becoming an important exporter of goods such as iron, leather and tin. Mali also dealt in agricultural trade, becoming one of the most significant trading centers in West Africa. The Muslim religion dominated, and technological advancement was sparse.

African culture was largely defined through migration, as Arab merchants and others settled on the continent, particularly along the east coast. Scholars from the Muslim nations gravitated to Timbuktu, which in addition to its importance in trade, had also become a magnet for those seeking Islamic knowledge and education.

## Islam

Born in 570 CE, Muhammad began preaching around 613, leading his followers in a new religion called Islam, which means "submission to God's will." Before this time, the Arabian Peninsula was inhabited largely by Bedouins, nomads who battled amongst each other and lived in tribal organizations. But by the time Muhammad died in 632, most of Arabia had become Muslim to some extent. Muhammad conquered Mecca, where a temple called the Kaaba had long served as a center of the nomadic religions. He declared this temple the most sacred of Islam, and Mecca as the holy city. His writings became the Koran, or Qur'an, divine revelations he said had been delivered to him by the angel Gabriel.

Muhammad's teachings gave the formerly tribal Arabian people a sense of unity that had not existed in the area before. After his death, the converted Muslims of Arabia conquered a vast territory, creating an empire and bringing advances in literature, technology, science and art as Europe was declining under the scourge of the Black Death. Literature from this period includes the *Arabian Nights* and the *Rubaiyat* of Omar Khayyam. Later in its development, Islam split into two factions, the Shiite and the Sunni Muslims. Conflict continues today between these groups.

> ➢ **Review Video:** Islam
> *Visit* ***mometrix.com/academy*** *and enter* ***Code*:** **228482**

> ➢ **Review Video:** The Islamic Empire
> *Visit* ***mometrix.com/academy*** *and enter* ***Code*:** **511181**

### Ottoman Empire

By 1400, the Ottomans had grown in power in Anatolia and had begun attempts to take Constantinople. In 1453 they finally conquered the Byzantine capital and renamed it Istanbul. The Ottoman Empire's major strength, much like Rome before it, lay in its ability to unite widely disparate people through religious tolerance. This tolerance, which stemmed from the idea that Muslims, Christians, and Jews were fundamentally related and could coexist, enabled the Ottomans to develop a widely varied culture. They also believed in just laws and just government, with government centered in a monarch, known as the sultan.

### Renaissance

Renaissance literally means "rebirth." After the darkness of the Dark Ages and the Black Plague, interest rose again in the beliefs and politics of ancient Greece and Rome. Art, literature, music, science, and philosophy all burgeoned during the Renaissance. Many of the ideas of the Renaissance began in Florence, Italy, in the fourteenth century, spurred by the Medici family. Education for the upper classes expanded to include law, math, reading, writing, and classical Greek and Roman works. As the Renaissance progressed, the world was presented through art and literature in a realistic way that had never been explored before. This realism drove culture to new heights.

Artists, authors and scientists

Artists of the Renaissance included Leonardo da Vinci, also an inventor, Michelangelo, also an architect, and others who focused on realism in their work. In literature, major contributions came from humanist authors like Petrarch, Erasmus, Sir Thomas More, and Boccaccio, who believed man should focus on reality rather than on the ethereal. Shakespeare, Cervantes and Dante followed in their footsteps, and their works found a wide audience thanks to Gutenberg's development of the printing press. Scientific developments of the Renaissance included the work of Copernicus, Galileo and Kepler, who challenged the geocentric philosophies of the day by proving that the earth was not the center of the solar system.

> ➢ **Review Video:** Renaissance
> *Visit* ***mometrix.com/academy*** *and enter* ***Code*:** **145504**

## Reformation

The Reformation consisted of both the Protestant and the Catholic Reformation. The Protestant Reformation rose in Germany when Martin Luther protested abuses of the Catholic Church. John Calvin led the movement in Switzerland, while in England King Henry VIII made use of the Reformation's ideas to further his own political goals. The Catholic Reformation, or Counter-Reformation, occurred in response to the Protestant movement, leading to various changes in the Catholic Church. Some provided wider tolerance of different religious viewpoints, but others actually increased the persecution of those deemed to be heretics. From a religious standpoint, the Reformation occurred due to abuses by the Catholic Church such as indulgences and dispensations, religious offices being offered up for sale, and an increasingly dissolute clergy. Politically, the Reformation was driven by increased power of various ruling monarchs, who wished to take all power to themselves rather than allowing power to remain with the church. They also had begun to chafe at papal taxes and the church's increasing wealth. The ideas of the Protestant Revolution removed power from the Catholic Church and the Pope himself, playing nicely into the hands of those monarchs, such as Henry VIII, who wanted out from under the church's control.

> **Review Video:** The Reformation: The Protestants
> *Visit **mometrix.com/academy** and enter **Code**:* **604651**

## Scientific Revolution

In addition to holding power in the political realm, church doctrine also governed scientific belief. During the Scientific Revolution, astronomers and other scientists began to amass evidence that challenged the church's scientific doctrines. Major figures of the Scientific Revolution included:

- Nicolaus Copernicus—wrote *On the Revolutions of the Celestial Spheres*, arguing that the earth revolved around the sun
- Tycho Brahe—catalogued astronomical observations
- Johannes Kepler—developed laws of planetary motion
- Galileo Galilei—defended the heliocentric theories of Copernicus and Kepler, discovered four moons of Jupiter, and died under house arrest by the church, charged with heresy
- Isaac Newton—discovered gravity, studied optics, calculus and physics, and believed the workings of nature could be studied and proven through observation

> **Review Video:** The Scientific Revolution
> *Visit **mometrix.com/academy** and enter **Code**:* **972197**

## Enlightenment

During the Enlightenment, philosophers and scientists began to rely more and more on observation to support their ideas, rather than building on past beliefs, particularly those held by the church. A focus on ethics and logic drove their work. Major philosophers of the Enlightenment included:

- Rene Descartes—he famously wrote, "I think, therefore I am." He believed strongly in logic and rules of observation.
- David Hume—he pioneered empiricism and skepticism, believing that truth could only be found through direct experience, and that what others said to be true was always suspect.
- Immanuel Kant—he believed in self-examination and observation, and that the root of morality lay within human beings.
- Jean-Jacques Rousseau—he developed the idea of the social contract, that government existed by the agreement of the people, and that the government was obligated to protect the people and their basic rights. His ideas influenced John Locke and Thomas Jefferson.

➢ **Review Video:** The Enlightenment
*Visit **mometrix.com/academy** and enter **Code**:* **540039**

## American Revolution and French Revolution

Both the American and French Revolution came about as a protest against the excesses and overly controlling nature of their respective monarchs. In America, the British colonies had been left mostly to self-govern until the British monarchs began to increase control, spurring the colonies to revolt. In France, the nobility's excesses had led to increasingly difficult economic conditions, with inflation, heavy taxation and food shortages creating great burdens on the lower classes. Both revolutions led to the development of republics to replace the monarchies that were displaced. However, the French Revolution eventually led to the rise of the dictator Napoleon Bonaparte, while the American Revolution produced a working republic from the beginning.

In 1789, King Louis XVI, faced with a huge national debt, convened parliament. The Third Estate, or Commons, a division of the French parliament, then claimed power, and the king's resistance led to the storming of the Bastille, the royal prison. The people established a constitutional monarchy. When King Louis XVI and Marie Antoinette attempted to leave the country, they were executed on the guillotine.

From 1793 to 1794, Robespierre and extreme radicals, the Jacobins, instituted a Reign of Terror, executing tens of thousands of nobles as well as anyone considered an enemy of the Revolution. Robespierre was then executed, as well, and the Directory came into power, leading to a temporary return to bourgeois values. This governing body proved incompetent and corrupt, allowing Napoleon Bonaparte to come to power in 1799, first as a dictator, then as emperor. While the French Revolution threw off the power of a corrupt monarchy, its immediate results were likely not what the original perpetrators of the revolt had intended.

> **Review Video:** The Revolutionary War
> *Visit* ***mometrix.com/academy*** *and enter* ***Code*: 739570**

> **Review Video:** The French Revolution: Napoleon Bonaparte
> *Visit* ***mometrix.com/academy*** *and enter* ***Code*: 876330**

## Russian Revolution of 1905

In Russia, rule lay in the hands of the Czars, and the overall structure was feudalistic. Beneath the Czars was a group of rich nobles, landowners whose lands were worked by peasants and serfs. The Russo-Japanese War (1904-1905) made conditions much worse for the lower classes. When peasants demonstrated outside the Czar's Winter Palace, the palace guard fired upon the crowd. The demonstration had been organized by a trade union leader, and after the violent response, many unions as well as political parties blossomed and began to lead numerous strikes. When the economy ground to a halt, Czar Nicholas II signed a document known as the October Manifesto, which established a constitutional monarchy and gave legislative power to parliament. However, he violated the Manifesto shortly thereafter, disbanding parliament and ignoring the civil liberties granted by the Manifesto. This eventually led to the Bolshevik Revolution.

## Bolshevik Revolution of 1917

Throughout its modern history, Russia had lagged behind other countries in development. The continued existence of a feudal system, combined with harsh conditions and the overall size of the country, led to massive food shortages and increasingly harsh conditions for the majority of the population. The tyrannical rule of the Czars only made this worse, as did repeated losses in various military conflicts. Increasing poverty, decreasing supplies, and the Czar's violation of the October Manifesto which had given some political power and civil rights to the people finally came to a head with the Bolshevik Revolution.

Major events
A workers' strike in Petrograd in 1917 set the revolutionary wheels in motion when the army sided with the workers. While parliament set up a provisional government made up of nobles, the workers and military joined to form their own governmental system known as soviets, which consisted of local councils elected by the people. The ensuing chaos opened the doors for formerly exiled leaders Vladimir Lenin, Joseph Stalin and Leon Trotsky to move in and gain popular support as well as the support of the Red Guard. Overthrowing parliament, they took power, creating a communist state in Russia. This development led to the spread of communism throughout Eastern Europe and elsewhere, greatly affecting diplomatic policies throughout the world for several decades.

## Industrial Revolution

The Industrial Revolution began in Great Britain, bringing coal- and steam-powered machinery into widespread use. Industry began a period of rapid growth with these developments. Goods that had previously been produced in small workshops or even in homes were produced more efficiently and in much larger quantities in factories. Where society had been largely agrarian-based, the focus swiftly shifted to an industrial outlook. As electricity and internal combustion engines replaced coal and steam as energy sources, even more drastic and rapid changes occurred. Western European countries in particular turned to colonialism, taking control of portions of Africa and Asia to ensure access to the raw materials needed to produce factory goods. Specialized labor became very much in demand, and businesses grew rapidly, creating monopolies, increasing world trade, and developing large urban centers. Even agriculture changed fundamentally as the Industrial Revolution led to a second Agricultural Revolution with the addition of new technology to advance agricultural production.

➢ **Review Video:** The Industrial Revolution
*Visit **mometrix.com/academy** and enter **Code**:* **258668**

First and second phases
The first phase of the Industrial Revolution took place from roughly 1750 to 1830. The textile industry experienced major changes as more and more elements of the process became mechanized. Mining benefited from the steam engine. Transportation became easier and more widely available as waterways were improved and the railroad came into prominence. In the second phase, from 1830 to 1910, industries further improved in efficiency and new industries were introduced as photography, various chemical processes, and electricity became more widely available to produce new goods or new, improved versions of old goods. Petroleum and hydroelectricity became major sources of power. During this time, the Industrial Revolution spread out of Western Europe and into the US and Japan.

Political, social and economic side effects
The Industrial Revolution led to widespread education, a wider franchise, and the development of mass communication in the political arena. Economically, conflicts arose between companies and their employees, as struggles for fair treatment and fair wages increased. Unions gained power and became more active. Government regulation over industries increased, but at the same time, growing businesses fought for the right to free enterprise. In the social sphere, populations increased and began to concentrate around centers of industry. Cities became larger and more densely populated. Scientific advancements led to more efficient agriculture, greater supply of goods, and increased knowledge of medicine and sanitation, leading to better overall health.

## Nationalism in the eighteenth and nineteenth centuries

Nationalism, put simply, is a strong belief in, identification with, and allegiance to a particular nation and people. Nationalistic belief unified various areas that had previously seen themselves as fragmented, which led to patriotism and, in some cases, imperialism. As nationalism grew, individual nations sought to grow, bringing in other, smaller states that shared similar characteristics such as language and cultural beliefs. Unfortunately, a major side effect of these growing nationalistic beliefs was often conflict and outright war.

In Europe, imperialism led countries to spread their influence into Africa and Asia. Africa was eventually divided among several European countries that wanted the raw materials. Asia also came under European control, with the exception of China, Japan and Siam (now Thailand). In the US, Manifest Destiny became the rallying cry as the country expanded west. Italy and Germany formed larger nations from a variety of smaller states.

> **Review Video:** Nationalism
> *Visit* ***mometrix.com/academy*** *and enter* ***Code*****: 276165**

**World War I**

Europe

WWI began in 1914 with the assassination of Archduke Franz Ferdinand, heir to the throne of Austria-Hungary, by a Serbian national. This led to a conflict between Austria-Hungary and Serbia that quickly escalated into the First World War. Europe split into the Allies—Britain, France, and Russia, and later Italy, Japan, and the US, against the Central Powers—Austria-Hungary, Germany, the Ottoman Empire, and Bulgaria. As the war spread, countries beyond Europe became involved. The war left Europe deeply in debt, and particularly devastated the German economy. The ensuing Great Depression made matters worse, and economic devastation opened the door for communist, fascist, and socialist governments to gain power.

Trench warfare

Fighting during WWI largely took place in a series of trenches built along the Eastern and Western Fronts. These trenches added up to more than 24,000 miles. This produced fronts that stretched over 400 miles, from the coast of Belgium to the border of Switzerland. The Allies made use of straightforward open-air trenches with a front line, supporting lines, and communications lines. By contrast, the German trenches sometimes included well-equipped underground living quarters.

> **Review Video:** World War I
> *Visit* ***mometrix.com/academy*** *and enter* ***Code*****: 365382**

**Communism and Socialism**

At their roots, socialism and communism both focus on public ownership and distribution of goods and services. However, communism works toward revolution by drawing on what it sees to be inevitable class antagonism, eventually overthrowing the upper classes and the systems of capitalism.

Socialism makes use of democratic procedures, building on the existing order. This was particularly true of the utopian socialists, who saw industrial capitalism as oppressive, not allowing workers to prosper. While socialism struggled between the World Wars, communism took hold, especially in Eastern Europe. After WWII, democratic socialism became more common. Later, capitalism took a stronger hold again, and today most industrialized countries in the western world function under an economy that mixes elements of capitalism and socialism.

> **Review Video:** Socialism
> *Visit* ***mometrix.com/academy*** *and enter* ***Code*: 814221**

**Rise of the Nazi party**

The Great Depression had a particularly devastating effect on Germany's economy, especially after the US was no longer able to supply reconstruction loans to help the country regain its footing. With unemployment rising rapidly, dissatisfaction with the government grew. Fascist and Communist parties rose, promising change and improvement.

Led by Adolf Hitler, the fascist Nazi Party eventually gained power in Parliament based on these promises and the votes of desperate German workers. When Hitler became Chancellor, he launched numerous expansionist policies, violating the peace treaties that had ended WWI. His military buildup and conquering of neighboring countries sparked the aggression that soon led to WWII.

**Blitzkrieg**

The blitzkrieg, or "lightning war," consisted of fast, powerful surprise attacks that disrupted communications, made it difficult if not impossible for the victims to retaliate, and demoralized Germany's foes. The "blitz," or the aerial bombing of England in 1940, was one example, with bombings occurring in London and other cities 57 nights in a row. The Battle of Britain in 1940 also brought intense raids by Germany's air force, the Luftwaffe, mostly targeting ports and British air force bases. Eventually, Britain's Royal Air Force blocked the Luftwaffe, ending Germany's hopes for conquering Britain.

**Battle of the Bulge**

Following the D-Day Invasion, Allied forces gained considerable ground and began a major campaign to push through Europe. In December of 1944, Hitler launched a counteroffensive, attempting to retake Antwerp, an important port. The ensuing battle became the largest land battle on the war's Western Front, and was known as the Battle of the Ardennes, or the Battle of the Bulge. The battle lasted from December 16, 1944 to January 25, 1945. The Germans pushed forward, making inroads into Allied lines, but in the end the Allies brought the advance to a halt. The Germans were pushed back, with massive losses on both sides. However, those losses proved crippling to the German army.

**Holocaust**

As Germany sank deeper and deeper into dire economic straits, the tendency was to look for a person or group of people to blame for the problems of the country. With distrust of the Jewish people already ingrained, it was easy for German authorities to set up the Jews as scapegoats for Germany's problems. Under the rule of Hitler and the Nazi party, the "Final Solution" for the supposed Jewish problem was devised. Millions of Jews, as well as Gypsies, homosexuals, communists, Catholics, the mentally ill and others, simply named as criminals, were transported to concentration camps during the course of the war. At least six million were slaughtered in death camps such as Auschwitz, where horrible conditions and torture of prisoners were commonplace. The Allies were aware of rumors of mass slaughter throughout the war, but many discounted the reports. Only when troops went in to liberate the prisoners was the true horror of the concentration camps brought to light. The Holocaust resulted in massive loss of human life, but also in the loss and destruction of cultures. Because the genocide focused on specific ethnic groups, many traditions, histories, knowledge, and other cultural elements were lost, particularly among the Jewish and Gypsy populations. After World War II, the United Nations recognized genocide as a "crime against humanity." The UN passed the Universal Declaration of Human Rights in 1948 in order to further specify what rights the organization protected. Nazi war criminals faced justice during the Nuremberg Trials. There individuals, rather than their governments, were held accountable for war crimes.

➢ **Review Video:** The Holocaust
*Visit* ***mometrix.com/academy*** *and enter* ***Code*****: 219441**

### Cold War

With millions of military and civilian deaths and over 12 million persons displaced, WWII left large regions of Europe and Asia in disarray. Communist governments moved in with promises of renewed prosperity and economic stability. The Soviet Union backed communist regimes in much of Eastern Europe. In China, Mao Zedong led communist forces in the overthrow of the Chinese Nationalist Party and instituted a communist government in 1949. While the new communist governments restored a measure of stability to much of Eastern Europe, it brought its own problems, with dictatorial governments and an oppressive police force. The spread of communism also led to several years of tension between communist countries and the democratic west, as the west fought to slow the spread of oppressive regimes throughout the world. With both sides in possession of nuclear weapons, tensions rose. Each side feared the other would resort to nuclear attack. This standoff lasted until 1989, when the Berlin Wall fell. The Soviet Union was dissolved two years later.

### United Nations

The United Nations (UN) came into being toward the end of World War II. A successor to the less-than-successful League of Nations formed after World War I, the UN built and improved on those ideas. Since its inception, the UN has worked to bring the countries of the world together for diplomatic solutions to international problems, including sanctions and other restrictions. It has also initiated military action, calling for peacekeeping troops from member countries to move against countries violating UN policies. The Korean War was the first example of UN involvement in an international conflict.

### Decolonization

A rise of nationalism among European colonies led to many of them declaring independence. India and Pakistan became independent of Britain in 1947, and numerous

African and Asian colonies declared independence as well. This period of decolonization lasted into the 1960s. Some colonies moved successfully into independence but many, especially in Africa and Asia, struggled to create stable governments and economies, and suffered from ethnic and religious conflicts, some of which continue today.

**Korean War**

In 1910, Japan annexed Korea and maintained this control until 1945. After WWII, Soviet and US troops occupied Korea, with the Soviet Union controlling North Korea and the US controlling South Korea. In 1947, the UN ordered elections in Korea to unify the country but the Soviet Union refused to allow them to take place in North Korea, instead setting up a communist government. In 1950, the US withdrew troops, and the North Korean troops moved to invade South Korea. The Korean War was the first war in which the UN—or any international organization—played a major role. The US, Australia, Canada, France, Netherlands, Great Britain, Turkey, China, USSR and other countries sent troops at various times, for both sides, throughout the war. In 1953, the war ended in a truce, but no peace agreement was ever achieved, and Korea remains divided.

**Vietnam War and involvement of France**

Vietnam had previously been part of a French colony called French Indochina. The Vietnam War began with the First Indochina War from 1946-1954, in which France battled with the Democratic Republic of Vietnam, ruled by Ho Chi Minh. In 1954, a siege at Dien Bien Phu ended in a Vietnamese victory. Vietnam was then divided into North and South, much like Korea. Communist forces controlled the North and the South was controlled by South Vietnamese forces, supported by the US. Conflict ensued, leading to another war. US troops eventually led the fight, in support of South Vietnam. The war became a major political issue in the US, with many citizens protesting American involvement. In 1975, South Vietnam surrendered, and Vietnam became the Socialist Republic of Vietnam.

**Globalism**

In the modern era, globalism has emerged as a popular political ideology. Globalism is based in the idea that all people and all nations are interdependent. Each nation is dependent on one or more other nations for production of and markets for goods, and for income generation. Today's ease of international travel and communication, including technological advances such as the airplane, has heightened this sense of interdependence. The global economy, and the general idea of globalism, has shaped many economic and political choices since the beginning of the twentieth century. Many of today's issues, including environmental awareness, economic struggles, and continued warfare, often require the cooperation of many countries if they are to be dealt with effectively.

**Effects of globalization**

Countries worldwide often seek the same resources, leading to high demand, particularly for nonrenewable resources. This can result in heavy fluctuations in price. One major example is the demand for petroleum products such as oil and natural gas. Increased travel and communication make it possible to deal with diseases in remote locations; however, this also allows diseases to be spread via travelers.

A major factor contributing to increased globalization over the past few decades has been the Internet. By allowing instantaneous communication with anyone nearly anywhere on the globe, the Internet has led to interaction between far-flung individuals and countries, and an ever increasing awareness of events all over the world.

## Middle East in international relations and economics

The location on the globe, with ease of access to Europe and Asia, and its preponderance of oil deposits, makes the Middle Eastern countries crucial in many international issues, both diplomatic and economic. Because of its central location, the Middle East has been a hotbed for violence since before the beginning of recorded history. Conflicts over land, resources, and religious and political power continue in the area today, spurred by conflict over control of the area's vast oil fields as well as over territories that have been disputed for thousands of years.

> **Review Video:** Globalization: The Middle East
> *Visit* ***mometrix.com/academy*** *and enter* ***Code*: 655231**

## Genocide

The three major occurrences of genocide in modern history other than the Holocaust are:

- Armenian genocide—from 1914 to 1918, the Young Turks, heirs to the Ottoman Empire, slaughtered between 800,000 and 1.5 million Armenians. This constituted approximately half of the Armenian population at the time.
- Russian purges under Stalin—scholars have attributed deaths between 3 and 60 million, both directly and indirectly, to the policies and edicts of Joseph Stalin's regime. The deaths took place from 1921 to 1953, when Stalin died. In recent years, many scholars have settled on a number of deaths near 20 million but this is still disputed today.
- Rwandan genocide—in 1994, hundreds of thousands of Tutsi, as well as Hutu who sympathized with them, were slaughtered during the Rwandan Civil War. The UN did not act or authorize intervention during these atrocities.

# Geography and Culture

## Geography

Geography literally means the study of the earth. Geographers study physical characteristics of the earth as well as man-made borders and boundaries. They also study the distribution of life on the planet, such as where certain species of animals can be found or how different forms of life interact. Major elements of the study of geography include:

- Locations
- Regional characteristics
- Spatial relations
- Natural and manmade forces that change elements of the earth

These elements are studied from regional, topical, physical and human perspectives. Geography also focuses on the origins of the earth as well as the history and backgrounds of different human populations.

Physical and cultural geography

Physical geography is the study of the physical characteristics of the earth: how they relate to each other, how they were formed, and how they develop. These characteristics include climate, land, and water, and also how they affect human population in various areas. Different landforms in combination with various climates and other conditions determine characteristics of various cultures.

Cultural geography is the study of how the various aspects of physical geography affect individual cultures. Cultural geography also compares various cultures: how their lifestyles and customs are affected by their geographical location, climate, and other factors, and how they interact with their environment.

## Divisions of geographical study

The four divisions of geographical study and tools used are:

- Topical—the study of a single feature of the earth or one specific human activity that occurs world-wide.
- Physical—the various physical features of the earth, how they are created, the forces that change them, and how they are related to each other and to various human activities.
- Regional—specific characteristics of individual places and regions.
- Human—how human activity affects the environment. This includes study of political, historical, social, and cultural activities.

Tools used in geographical study include special research methods like mapping, field studies, statistics, interviews, mathematics, and use of various scientific instruments.

## Ancient geographers

The following are three important ancient geographers and their contributions to the study of geography:

- Eratosthenes lived in ancient Greek times, and mathematically calculated the circumference of the earth and the tilt of the earth's axis. He also created the first map of the world.
- Strabo wrote a description of the ancient world called *Geographica* in seventeen volumes.
- Ptolemy, primarily an astronomer, was also an experienced mapmaker. He wrote a treatise entitled *Geography*, which was used by Christopher Columbus in his travels.

## Analysis of areas of human population

In cities, towns, or other areas where many people have settled, geographers focus on distribution of populations, neighborhoods, industrial areas, transportation, and other elements important to the society in question. For example, they would map out the locations of hospitals, airports, factories, police stations, schools, and housing groups. They would also make note of how these facilities are distributed in relation to the areas of habitation, such as the number of schools in a certain neighborhood, or how many grocery stores are located in a specific suburban area. Another area of study and discussion is the distribution of towns themselves, from widely spaced rural towns to large cities that merge into each other to form a megalopolis.

## Cartographers and maps

A cartographer is a mapmaker. Mapmakers produce detailed illustrations of geographic areas to record where various features are located within that area. These illustrations can be compiled into maps, charts, graphs, and even globes. When constructing maps, cartographers must take into account the problem of distortion. Because the earth is round, a flat map does not accurately represent the correct proportions, especially if a very large geographical area is being depicted. Maps must be designed in such a way as to minimize this distortion and maximize accuracy. Accurately representing the earth's features on a flat surface is achieved through projection.

## Map projections

The three major types of projection used in creating world maps are:

- Cylindrical projection—this is created by wrapping the globe of the Earth in a cylindrical piece of paper, then using a light to project the globe onto the paper. The largest distortion occurs at the outermost edges.
- Conical projection—the paper is shaped like a cone and contacts the globe only at the cone's base. This type of projection is most useful for middle latitudes.
- Flat-Plane projections—also known as a Gnomonic projection, this type of map is projected onto a flat piece of paper that only touches the globe at a single point. Flat-plane projections make it possible to map out Great-Circle Routes, or the shortest route between one point and another on the globe, as a straight line.

Four specific types of map projections that are commonly used today are:

- Winkel tripel projection—this is the most common projection used for world maps, since it was accepted in 1998 by the National Geographic Society as a standard. The Winkel tripel projection balances size and shape, greatly reducing distortion.
- Robinson projection—east and west sections of the map are less distorted, but continental shapes are somewhat inaccurate.
- Goode homolosine projection—sizes and shapes are accurate, but distances are not. This projection basically represents a globe that has been cut into connected sections so that it can lie flat.
- Mercator projection—though distortion is high, particularly in areas farther from the equator, this cylindrical projection is commonly used by seafarers.

## Map elements

The five major elements of any map are:

- Title—this tells basic information about the map, such as the area represented.
- Legend—also known as the key, the legend explains what symbols used on a particular map represent, such as symbols for major landmarks.
- Grid—this most commonly represents the Geographic Grid System, or latitude and longitude marks used to precisely locate specific locations.
- Directions—a compass rose or other symbol is used to indicate the cardinal directions.
- Scale—this shows the relation between a certain distance on the map and the actual distance. For example, one inch might represent one mile, or ten miles, or even more depending on the size of the map.

> ➢ **Review Video:** Elements of a Map
> *Visit **mometrix.com/academy** and enter **Code**:* **437727**

## Equal area map and conformal map

An equal area map is designed such that the proportional sizes of various areas are accurate. For example, if one land mass is one-fifth the size of another, the lines on the map will be shifted to accommodate for distortion so that the proportional size is accurate. In many maps, areas farther from the equator are greatly distorted; this type of map compensates for this phenomenon. A conformal map focuses on representing the correct shape of geographical areas, with less concern for comparative size.

## Consistent scale map and thematic map

With a consistent scale map, the same scale, such as one inch=ten miles, is used throughout the entire map. This is most often used for maps of smaller areas, as maps that cover larger areas, such as the full globe, must make allowances for distortion. Maps of very large areas often make use of more than one scale, with scales closer to the center representing a larger area than those at the edges.

A thematic map is constructed to show very specific information about a chosen theme. For example, a thematic map might represent political information, such as how votes were distributed in an election, or could show population distribution or climatic features.

## Relief map

A relief map is constructed to show details of various elevations across the area of the map. Higher elevations are represented by different colors than lower elevations. Relief maps often also show additional details, such as the overall ruggedness or smoothness of an area. Mountains would be represented as ridged and rugged, while deserts would be shown as smooth.

Elevation in relief maps can also be represented by contour lines, or lines that connect points of the same elevation. Some relief maps even feature textures, reconstructing details in a sort of miniature model.

## Mountains, hills, plains, and valleys

- Mountains are elevated areas that measure 2,000 feet or more above sea level. Often steep and rugged, they usually occur in groups called chains or ranges. Six of the seven continents on Earth contain at least one range.
- Hills are of lower elevation than mountains, at about 500-2,000 feet. Hills are usually more rounded, and are found throughout every continent.
- Plains are large, flat areas and are usually very fertile. The majority of the Earth's population is supported by crops grown on vast plains.
- Valleys lie between hills and mountains. Depending on their location, their specific features can vary greatly, from fertile and habitable to rugged and inhospitable.

## Plateaus, deserts, deltas, mesas, basins, foothills, marshes, and swamps

- Plateaus are elevated, but flat on top. Some plateaus are extremely dry, such as the Kenya Plateau, because surrounding mountains prevent them from receiving moisture.
- Deserts receive less than ten inches of rain per year. They are usually large areas, such as the Sahara Desert in Africa or the Australian Outback.
- Deltas occur at river mouths. Because the rivers carry sediment to the deltas, these areas are often very fertile.
- Mesas are flat, steep-sided mountains or hills. The term is sometimes used to refer to plateaus.
- Basins are areas of low elevation where rivers drain.
- Foothills are the transitional area between the plains and the mountains, usually consisting of hills that gradually increase in size as they approach the mountain range.
- Marshes and swamps are also lowlands, but they are very wet and largely covered in vegetation such as reeds and rushes.

## Bodies of water

- Oceans are the largest bodies of water on Earth. They are salt water, and cover about two-thirds of the earth's surface. The five major oceans are the Atlantic, Pacific, Indian, Arctic, and Southern.

- Seas are generally also salt water, but are smaller than oceans and surrounded by land. Examples include the Mediterranean Sea, the Caribbean Sea, and the Caspian Sea.
- Lakes are bodies of freshwater found inland. Sixty percent of all lakes are located in Canada.
- Rivers are moving bodies of water that flow from higher elevations to lower. They usually start as rivulets or streams, and grow until they finally empty into a sea or an ocean.
- Canals, such as the Panama Canal and the Suez Canal, are manmade waterways connecting two large bodies of water.

➢ **Review Video:** Bodies of Water
*Visit **mometrix.com/academy** and enter **Code**:* **463122**

**Communities**

Communities, or groups of people who settle together in a specific area, typically gather where certain conditions exists. These conditions include:

- Easy access to resources such as food, water, and raw materials
- Ability to easily transport raw materials and goods, such as access to a waterway
- Room to house a sufficient work force

People also tend to form groups with others who are similar to them. In a typical community, people can be found who share values, a common language, and common or similar cultural characteristics and religious beliefs. These factors will determine the overall composition of a community as it develops.

**Cities**

Cities develop and grow as an area develops. Modern statistics show that over half of the world's people live in cities. That percentage is even higher in developed areas of the globe. Cities are currently growing more quickly in developing regions, and even established cities continue to experience growth throughout the world. In developing or developed areas, cities often are surrounded by a metropolitan area made up of both urban and suburban sections. In some places, cities have merged into each other and become a megalopolis—a single, huge city.

Cities develop differently in different areas of the world. The area available for cities to grow, as well as cultural and economic forces, drives how cities develop. For example, North American cities tend to cover wider areas. European cities tend to have better developed transportation systems. In Latin America, the richest inhabitants can be found in the city centers, while in North America wealthier inhabitants tend to live in suburban areas.

In other parts of the world, transportation and communication between cities is less developed. Recent technological innovations such as the cell phone have increased communication even in these areas. Urban areas must also maintain communication with rural areas in order to procure food, resources, and raw materials that cannot be produced within the city limits.

**Weather and climate**

Weather and climate are physical systems that affect geography. Though they deal with similar information, the way this information is measured and compiled is different. Weather involves daily conditions in the atmosphere that affect temperature, precipitation (rain, snow, hail, or sleet), wind speed, air pressure, and other factors. Weather focuses on the short-term—what the conditions will be today, tomorrow, or over the next few days.

In contrast, climate aggregates information about daily and seasonal weather conditions in a region over a long period of time. The climate takes into account average monthly and yearly temperatures, average precipitation over long periods of time, and the growing season of an area. Climates are classified according to latitude, or how close they lie to the earth's equator. The three major divisions are:

- Low Latitudes, lying from 0 to approximately 23.5 degrees latitude
- Middle Latitudes, found from approximately 23.5 to 66.5 degrees
- High Latitudes, found from approximately 66.5 degrees to the poles

Rainforests, savannas, and deserts occur in low latitudes:

- Rainforest climates, near the equator, experience high average temperatures and humidity, as well as relatively high rainfall.
- Savannas are found on either side of the rainforest region. Mostly grasslands, they typically experience dry winters and wet summers.
- Beyond the savannas lie the desert regions, with hot, dry climates, sparse rainfall, and temperature fluctuations of up to fifty degrees from day to night.

The climate regions found in the middle latitudes are:

- Mediterranean—the Mediterranean climate occurs between 30 and 40 degrees latitude, both north and south, on the western coasts of continents. Characteristics include a year-long growing season, hot, dry summers followed by mild winters, and sparse rainfall that occurs mostly during the winter months.
- Humid-subtropical—humid-subtropical regions are located on southeastern coastal areas. Winds that blow in over warm ocean currents produce long summers, mild winters, and a long growing season. These areas are highly productive, and support a larger part of the earth's population than any other climate.
- Humid-continental—the humid continental climate produces the familiar four seasons typical of a good portion of the US. Some of the most productive farmlands in the world lie in these climates. Winters are cold, summers are hot and humid.
- Marine—marine climates are found near water or on islands. Ocean winds help make these areas mild and rainy. Summers are cooler than humid-subtropical summers, but winters also bring milder temperatures due to the warmth of the ocean winds.
- Steppe—steppe climates, or prairie climates, are found far inland on large continents. Summers are hot and winters are cold, but rainfall is sparser than in continental climates.
- Desert—desert climates occur where steppe climates receive even less rainfall. Examples include the Gobi desert in Asia as well as desert areas of Australia and the southwestern US.

The high latitudes consist of two major climate areas, the tundra and taiga:

- Tundra means "marshy plain." Ground is frozen throughout long, cold winters, but there is little snowfall. During the short summers, it becomes wet and marshy. Tundras are not amenable to crops, but many plants and animals have adapted to the conditions.
- Taigas lie south of tundra regions, and include the largest forest areas in the world, as well as swamps and marshes. Large mineral deposits exist here, as well as many animals valued for their fur. In the winter, taiga regions are colder than the tundra, and summers are hotter. The growing season is short.

A vertical climate exists in high mountain ranges. Increasing elevation leads to varying temperatures, growing conditions, types of vegetation and animals, and occurrence of human habitation, often encompassing elements of various other climate regions.

> **Review Video:** Weather and Climate
> *Visit **mometrix.com/academy** and enter **Code**:* **996776**

Factors that affect climate

Because the earth is tilted, its rotation brings about changes in seasons. Regions closer to the equator, and those nearest the poles, experience very little change in seasonal temperatures. Mid-range latitudes are most likely to experience distinct seasons. Large bodies of water also affect climate. Ocean currents and wind patterns can change the climate for an area that lies in typically cold latitude, such as England, to a much more temperate climate. Mountains can affect both short-term weather and long-term climates. Some deserts occur because precipitation is stopped by the wall of a mountain range.

Over time, established climate patterns can shift and change. While the issue is hotly debated, it has been theorized that human activity has also led to climate change.

### Human systems

Human systems affect geography in the way in which they settle, form groups that grow into large-scale habitations, and even create permanent changes in the landscape. Geographers study movements of people, how they distribute goods among each other and to other settlements or cultures, and how ideas grow and spread. Migrations, wars, forced relocations, and trade can all spread cultural ideas, language, goods and other practices to wide-spread areas. Some major migrations or the conquering of one people by another have significantly changed cultures throughout history. In addition, human systems can lead to various conflicts or alliances to control access to and the use of natural resources.

North America

North America consists of 23 countries, including (in decreasing population order) the United States of America, Mexico, Canada, Guatemala, Cuba, Haiti, and the Dominican Republic. The US and Canada support similarly diverse cultures, as both were formed from groups of native races as well as large numbers of immigrants. Many North American cultures come from a mixture of indigenous and colonial European influences. Agriculture is important to North American countries, while service industries and technology also play a large part in the economy. On average, North America supports a high standard of living and a high level of development and supports trade with countries throughout the world.

South America

Including Brazil (largest in area and population), Colombia, Argentina, Venezuela, Peru, and 10 more countries or territories, South America is largely defined by its prevailing languages. The majority of countries in South America speak Spanish or Portuguese. Most of South America has experienced a similar history, having been originally dominated by Native cultures, conquered by European nations. The countries of South America have since gained independence, but there is a wide disparity between various countries' economic and political factors. Most South American countries rely on only one or two exports, usually agricultural, with suitable lands often controlled by rich families. Most societies in South America feature major separations between classes, both economically and socially. Challenges faced by developing South American countries include geographical limitations, economic issues, and sustainable development, including the need to preserve the existing rainforests.

Europe

Europe contains a wide variety of cultures, ethnic groups, physical geographical features, climates, and resources, all of which have influenced the distribution of its varied population. Europe in general is industrialized and developed, with cultural differences giving each individual country its own unique characteristics. Greek and Roman influences played a major role in European culture, as did Christianity. European countries spread their beliefs and cultural elements throughout the world by means of migration and colonization. They have had a significant influence on nearly every other continent in the world. While Western Europe has been largely democratic, Eastern Europe functioned under communist rule for many years. The recent formation of the European Union (EU) has increased stability and positive diplomatic relations among European nations. Like other industrialized regions, Europe is now focusing on various environmental issues.

Russia

After numerous conflicts, Russia became a Communist state, known as the USSR. With the collapse of the USSR in 1991, the country has struggled in its transition to a market-driven economy. Attempts to build a workable system have led to the destruction of natural resources as well as problems with nuclear power, including accidents such as Chernobyl. To complete the transition to a market economy, Russia needs to improve its transportation and communication systems, and find a way to more efficiently use its natural resources.

The population of Russia is not distributed evenly, with three quarters of the population living west of the Ural Mountains. The people of Russia encompass over a hundred different ethnic groups. Over eighty percent of the population is ethnically Russian, and Russian is the official language of the country.

North Africa and Southwest and Central Asia

The largely desert climate of these areas has led most population centers to rise around sources of water, such as the Nile River. This area is the home of the earliest known civilizations and the origin of Christianity, Judaism, and Islam. After serving as the site of huge, independent civilizations in ancient times, North Africa and Southwest and Central Asia were largely parceled out as European colonies during the eighteenth and nineteenth centuries. The beginning of the twentieth century saw many of these countries gain their independence. Islam has served as a unifying force for large portions of these areas, and many of the inhabitants speak Arabic. In spite of the arid climate, agriculture is a large business, but the most valuable resource is oil. Centuries of conflict throughout this area have led to ongoing political problems. These political problems have also contributed to environmental issues.

Sub-Saharan Africa

South of the Sahara Desert, Africa is divided into a number of culturally diverse nations. The inhabitants are unevenly distributed due to geographical limitations that prevent settlement in vast areas. AIDS has become a major plague throughout this part of Africa, killing millions, largely due to restrictive beliefs that prevent education about the disease, as well as abject poverty and unsettled political situations that make it impossible to manage the pandemic. The population of this area of Africa is widely diverse due to extensive migration. Many of the people still rely on subsistence farming for their welfare. Starvation and poverty are rampant due to drought and political instability. Some areas are far more stable than others due to greater availability of resources. These have been able to begin the process of industrialization.

South Asia

South Asia is home to one of the first human civilizations, which grew up in the Indus River Valley. With a great deal of disparity between rural and urban life, South Asia has much to do to improve the quality of life for its lower classes. Two major religions, Hinduism and Buddhism, have their origins in this region. Parts of South Asia, most notably India, were subject to British rule for several decades, and are still working to improve independent governments and social systems. Overall, South Asia is very culturally diverse, with a wide mix of religions and languages throughout. Many individuals are farmers, but a growing number have found prosperity in the spread of high-tech industries. Industrialization is growing in South Asia, but continues to face environmental, social, religious and economic challenges.

East Asia

Governments in East Asia are varied, ranging from communist to democratic governments, with some governments that mix both approaches. Isolationism throughout the area limited the countries' contact with other nations until the early twentieth century. The unevenly distributed population of East Asia consists of over one and a half billion people with widely diverse ethnic backgrounds, religions and languages. More residents live in urban areas than in rural areas, creating shortages of farm workers at times. Japan, Taiwan and South Korea are overall more urban, while China and Mongolia are more rural. Japan stands as the most industrial country of East Asia. Some areas of East Asia are suffering from major environmental issues. Japan has dealt with many of these problems and now has some of the strictest environmental laws in the world.

Southeast Asia

Much of Southeast Asia was colonized by European countries during the eighteenth and nineteenth centuries, with the exception of Siam, now known as Thailand. All Southeast Asian countries are now independent, but the twentieth century saw numerous conflicts between communist and democratic forces.

Southeast Asia has been heavily influenced by both Buddhist and Muslim religions. Industrialization is growing, with the population moving in large numbers from rural to urban areas. Some have moved to avoid conflict, oppression, and poverty.

Natural disasters, including volcanoes, typhoons, and flash flooding, are fairly common in Southeast Asia, creating extensive economic damage and societal disruption.

The South Pacific

South Pacific cultures originally migrated from Southeast Asia, creating hunter-gatherer or sometimes settled agricultural communities. European countries moved in during later centuries, seeking the plentiful natural resources of the area. Today, some South Pacific islands remain under the control of foreign governments, and culture in these areas mixes modern, industrialized society with indigenous culture. Population is unevenly distributed, largely due to the inhabitability of many parts of the South Pacific, such as the extremely hot desert areas of Australia. Agriculture still drives much of the economy, with tourism growing. Antarctica remains the only continent not claimed by a single country. There are no permanent human habitations in Antarctica, but scientists and explorers visit the area on a temporary basis.

## Human-environment interaction

Geography also studies the ways people interact with, use, and change their environment. The effects, reasons, and consequences of these changes are studied, as are the ways the environment limits or influences human behavior. This kind of study can help determine the best course of action when a nation or group of people are considering making changes to the environment, such as building a dam or removing natural landscape to build or expand roads. Study of the consequences can help determine if these actions are manageable and how long-term, detrimental results can be mitigated.

## Physical geography and climate

North America

The largest amount of North America is the US and Canada, which have a similar distribution of geographical features, mountain ranges in both east and west, stretches of fertile plains through the center, and lakes and waterways. Both areas were shaped by glaciers, which also deposited highly fertile soil. Because they are so large, Canada and the US experience several varieties of climate, including continental climates with four seasons in median areas, tropical climates in the southern part of the US, and arctic climes in the far north. The remaining area of North America is comprised primarily of islands, including the Caribbean Isles and Greenland.

South America

South America contains a wide variety of geographical features including high mountains such as the Andes, wide plains, and high altitude plateaus. The region contains numerous natural resources, but many of them have remained unused due to various obstacles, including political issues, geographic barriers, and lack of sufficient economic power. Climate zones in South America are largely tropical, with rainforests and savannas, but vertical climate zones and grasslands also exist in places.

Europe

Europe spans a wide area with a variety of climate zones. In the east and south are mountain ranges, while the north is dominated by a plains region. The long coastline and the island nature of some countries, such as Britain, mean the climate is often warmer than other lands at similar latitudes, as the area is warmed by ocean currents. Many areas of western Europe have a moderate climate, while areas of the south are dominated by the classic Mediterranean climate. Europe carries a high level of natural resources. Numerous waterways help connect the inner regions with the coastal areas. Much of Europe is industrialized, and agriculture has been developed for thousands of years.

Russia

Russia's area encompasses part of Asia and Europe. From the standpoint of square footage alone, Russia is the largest country in the world. Due to its size, Russia encompasses a wide variety of climatic regions, including plains, plateaus, mountains, and tundra.

Russia's climate can be quite harsh, with rivers that are frozen most of the year, making transportation of the country's rich natural resources more difficult. Siberia, in northern Russia, is dominated by permafrost. Native peoples in this area still follow a hunting and gathering lifestyle, living in portable yurts and subsisting largely on herds of reindeer or caribou. Other areas include taiga with extensive, dense woods in north central Russia and more temperate steppes and grasslands in the southwest.

North Africa and Southwest and Central Asia

This area of the world is complex in its geographical structure and climate, incorporating seas, peninsulas, rivers, mountains, and numerous other features. Earthquakes are common, with tectonic plates in the area remaining active. Much of the world's oil lies in this area. The tendency of the large rivers of North Africa, especially the Nile, to follow a set pattern of drought and extreme fertility, led people to settle there from prehistoric times. As technology has advanced, people have tamed this river, making its activity more predictable and the land around it more productive. The extremely arid nature of many other parts of this area has also led to human intervention such as irrigation to increase agricultural production.

Sub-Saharan Africa

South of the Sahara Desert, the high elevations and other geographical characteristics have made it very difficult for human travel or settlement to occur. The geography of the area is dominated by a series of plateaus. There are also mountain ranges and a large rift valley in the eastern part of the continent. Contrasting the wide desert areas, Sub-Saharan Africa contains numerous lakes, rivers, and world-famous waterfalls. The area has tropical climates, including rainforests, savannas, steppes, and desert areas. The main natural resources are minerals, including gems and water.

South Asia

The longest alluvial plain, a plain caused by shifting floodplains of major rivers and river systems over time, exists in South Asia. South Asia boasts three major river systems in the Ganges, Indus, and Brahmaputra. It also has large deposits of minerals, including iron ore that is in great demand internationally. South Asia holds mountains, plains, plateaus, and numerous islands. The climates range from tropical to highlands and desert areas. South Asia also experiences monsoon winds that cause a long rainy season. Variations in climate, elevation and human activity influence agricultural production.

East Asia

East Asia includes North and South Korea, Mongolia, China, Japan, and Taiwan. Mineral resources are plentiful but not evenly distributed throughout. The coastlines are long, and while the population is large, farmlands are sparse. As a result, the surrounding oceans have become a major source of sustenance. East Asia is large enough to also encompass several climate regions. Ocean currents provide milder climates to coastal areas, while monsoons provide the majority of the rainfall for the region. Typhoons are somewhat common, as are earthquakes, volcanoes and tsunamis. The latter occur because of the tectonic plates that meet beneath the continent and remain somewhat active.

Southeast Asia

Southeast Asia lies largely on the equator, and roughly half of the countries of the region are island nations. These countries include Indonesia, the Philippines, Vietnam, Thailand, Myanmar, and Malaysia (which is partially on the mainland and partially an island country). The island nations of Southeast Asia feature mountains that are considered part of the Ring of Fire, an area where tectonic plates remain active, leading to extensive volcanic activity as well as earthquakes and tsunamis. Southeast Asia boasts many rivers as well as abundant natural resources, including gems, fossil fuels and minerals. There are basically two seasons—wet and dry. The wet season arrives with the monsoons. In general, Southeast Asia consists of tropical rainforest climates, but there are some mountain areas and tropical savannas.

Australia, Oceania and Antarctica

In the far southern hemisphere of the globe, Australia and Oceania present their own climatic combinations. Australia, the only island on earth that is also a continent, has extensive deserts as well as mountains and lowlands. The economy is driven by agriculture, including ranches and farms, and minerals. While the steppes bordering extremely arid inland areas are suitable for livestock, only the coastal areas receive sufficient rainfall for crops without using irrigation. Oceania refers to over 10,000 Pacific islands created by volcanic activity. Most of these have tropical climates with wet and dry seasons. New Zealand, Australia's nearest neighbor, boasts rich forests as well as mountain ranges and relatively moderate temperatures, including rainfall throughout the year. Antarctica is covered with ice. Its major resource consists of scientific information. It supports some wildlife, such as penguins, and little vegetation, mostly mosses or lichens.

## Plate tectonics

According to the geological theory of plate tectonics, the earth's crust is made up of ten major and several minor tectonic plates. These plates are the solid areas of the crust. They float on top of the earth's mantle, which is made up of molten rock. Because the plates float on this liquid component of the earth's crust, they move, creating major changes in the earth's surface. These changes can happen very slowly over a long time period, such as in continental drift, or rapidly, such as when earthquakes occur. Interaction between the different continental plates can create mountain ranges, volcanic activity, major earthquakes, and deep rifts.

Plate boundaries

Plate tectonics defines three types of plate boundaries, determined by the way in which the edges of the plates interact. These plate boundaries are:

- Convergent boundaries—the bordering plates move toward one another. When they collide directly, this is known as continental collision, which can create very large, high mountain ranges such as the Himalayas and the Andes. If one plate slides under the other, this is called subduction. Subduction can lead to intense volcanic activity. One example is the Ring of Fire that lies along the northern Pacific coastlines.

- Divergent boundaries—plates move away from each other. This movement leads to rifts such as the Mid-Atlantic Ridge and east Africa's Great Rift Valley.
- Transform boundaries—plate boundaries slide in opposite directions against each other. Intense pressure builds up along transform boundaries as the plates grind along each other's edges, leading to earthquakes. Many major fault lines, including the San Andreas Fault, lie along transform boundaries.

➤ **Review Video:** Plate Tectonics
*Visit* ***mometrix.com/academy*** *and enter* ***Code*****: 623693**

**Erosion, weathering, transportation and deposition**

Erosion involves movement of any loose material on the earth's surface. This can include soil, sand, or rock fragments. These loose fragments can be displaced by natural forces such as wind, water, ice, plant cover, and human factors. Mechanical erosion occurs due to natural forces. Chemical erosion occurs as a result of human intervention and activities. Weathering occurs when atmospheric elements affect the earth's surface. Water, heat, ice, and pressure all lead to weathering. Transportation refers to loose material being moved by wind, water or ice. Glacial movement, for example, carries everything from pebbles to boulders, sometimes over long distances. Deposition is the result of transportation. When material is transported, it is eventually deposited, and builds up to create formations like moraines and sand dunes.

**Effects of human interaction and conflict on geographical boundaries**

Human societies and their interaction have led to divisions of territories into countries and various other subdivisions. While these divisions are at their root artificial, they are important to geographers in the discussion of interactions of various populations. Geographical divisions often occur through conflict between different human populations. The reasons behind these divisions include:

- Control of resources
- Control of important trade routes
- Control of populations

Conflict often occurs due to religious, political, language, or race differences. Natural resources are finite and so often lead to conflict over how they are distributed among populations.

**State sovereignty**

State sovereignty recognizes the division of geographical areas into areas controlled by various governments or groups of people. These groups control not only the territory, but also all its natural resources and the inhabitants of the area. The entire planet Earth is divided into political or administratively sovereign areas recognized to be controlled by a particular government with the exception of the continent of Antarctica.

## Alliances

Alliances form between different countries based on similar interests, political goals, cultural values, or military issues. Six existing international alliances include:

- North Atlantic Treaty Organization (NATO)
- Common Market
- European Union (EU)
- United Nations (UN)
- Caribbean Community
- Council of Arab Economic Unity

In addition, very large companies and multi-national corporations can create alliances and various kinds of competition based on the need to control resources, production, and the overall marketplace.

## Agricultural revolution

The agricultural revolution began approximately six thousand years ago when the plow was invented in Mesopotamia. Using a plow drawn by animals, people were able to cultivate crops in large quantities rather than gathering available seeds and grains and planting them by hand. Because large-scale agriculture was labor intensive, this led to the development of stable communities where people gathered to make farming possible. As stable farming communities replaced groups of nomadic hunter-gatherers, human society underwent profound changes. Societies became dependent on limited numbers of crops as well as subject to the vagaries of weather. Trading livestock and surplus agricultural output led to the growth of large-scale commerce and trade routes.

## Modification of surrounding environments by human populations

The agricultural revolution led human societies to begin changing their surroundings in order to accommodate their needs for shelter and room to cultivate food and to provide for domestic animals. Clearing ground for crops, redirecting waterways for irrigation purposes, and building permanent settlements all create major changes in the environment. Large-scale agriculture can lead to loose topsoil and damaging erosion. Building large cities leads to degraded air quality, water pollution from energy consumption, and many other side effects that can severely damage the environment. Recently, many countries have taken action by passing laws to reduce human impact on the environment and reduce the potentially damaging side effects. This is called environmental policy.

## Ecology

Ecology is the study of the way living creatures interact with their environment. Biogeography explores the way physical features of the earth affect living creatures. Ecology bases its studies on three different levels of the environment:

- Ecosystem—this is a specific physical environment and all the organisms that live there.
- Biome—this is a group of ecosystems, usually consisting of a large area with similar flora and fauna as well as similar climate and soil. Examples of biomes include deserts, tropical rain forests, taigas, and tundra.

- Habitat—this is an area in which a specific species usually lives. The habitat includes the necessary soil, water, and resources for that particular species, as well as predators and other species that compete for the same resources.

**Interactions between species**

Different interactions occur among species and members of single species within a habitat. These interactions fall into three categories:

- Competition competition occurs when different animals, either of the same species or of different species, compete for the same resources. Robins can compete with other robins for available food, but other insectivores also compete for these same resources.
- Predation— predation occurs when one species depends on the other species for food, such as a fox who subsists on small mammals.
- Symbiosis — symbiosis occurs when two different species exist in the same environment without negatively affecting each other. Some symbiotic relationships are beneficial to one or both organisms without harm occurring to either.

**Ability to adapt**

If a species is relocated from one habitat to another, it must adapt in order to survive. Some species are more capable of adapting than others. Those that cannot adapt will not survive. There are different ways a creature can adapt, including behavior modification as well as structure or physiological changes. Adaptation is also vital if an organism's environment changes around it. Although the creature has not been relocated, it finds itself in a new environment that requires changes in order to survive. The more readily an organism can adapt, the more likely it is to survive. The almost infinite ability of humans to adapt is a major reason why they are able to survive in almost any habitat in any area of the world.

**Biodiversity**

Biodiversity refers to the variety of habitats that exist on the planet, as well as the variety of organisms that can exist within these habitats. A greater level of biodiversity makes it more likely that an individual habitat will flourish along with the species that depend upon it. Changes in habitat, including climate change, human intervention, or other factors, can reduce biodiversity by causing the extinction of certain species.

# Government

### Political science

Political science focuses on studying different governments and how they compare to each other, general political theory, ways political theory is put into action, how nations and governments interact with each other, and a general study of governmental structure and function. Other elements of political science include the study of elections, governmental administration at various levels, development and action of political parties, and how values such as freedom, power, justice and equality are expressed in different political cultures. Political science also encompasses elements of other disciplines, including:

- History—how historical events have shaped political thought and process
- Sociology—the effects of various stages of social development on the growth and development of government and politics
- Anthropology—the effects of governmental process on the culture of an individual group and its relationships with other groups
- Economics—how government policies regulate distribution of products and how they can control and/or influence the economy in general

### Government

Based on general political theory, the four major purposes of any given government are:

- Ensuring national security—the government protects against international, domestic and terrorist attacks and also ensures ongoing security through negotiating and establishing relationships with other governments.
- Providing public services—the government should "promote the general welfare," as stated in the Preamble to the US Constitution, by meeting the needs of its citizens.
- Ensuring social order—the government supplies means of settling conflicts among citizens as well as making laws to govern the nation, state, or city.
- Making decisions regarding the economy—laws help form the economic policy of the country, regarding both domestic and international trade and related issues. The government also has the ability to distribute goods and wealth to some extent among its citizens.

### Origin of the state

There are four main theories regarding the origin of the state:

- Evolutionary—the state evolved from the family, with the head of state the equivalent of the family's patriarch or matriarch.
- Force—one person or group of people brought everyone in an area under their control, forming the first government.
- Divine Right—certain people were chosen by the prevailing deity to be the rulers of the nation, which is itself created by the deity or deities.
- Social Contract—there is no natural order. The people allow themselves to be governed to maintain social order, while the state in turn promises to protect the people they govern. If the government fails to protect its people, the people have the right to seek new leaders.

**Influences of philosophers on political study**

Ancient Greek philosophers Aristotle and Plato believed political science would lead to order in political matters, and that this scientifically organized order would create stable, just societies.

Thomas Aquinas adapted the ideas of Aristotle to a Christian perspective. His ideas stated that individuals should have certain rights, but also certain duties, and that these rights and duties should determine the type and extent of government rule. In stating that laws should limit the role of government, he laid the groundwork for ideas that would eventually become modern constitutionalism.

Niccolò Machiavelli, author of *The Prince*, was a proponent of politics based on power. He is often considered the founder of modern political science.

Thomas Hobbes, author of *Leviathan* (1651), believed that individual's lives were focused solely on a quest for power, and that the state must work to control this urge. Hobbes felt that people were completely unable to live harmoniously without the intervention of a powerful, undivided government.

John Locke published *Two Treatises of Government* in 1689. This work argued against the ideas of Thomas Hobbes. He put forth the theory of *tabula rasa*—that people are born with minds like blank slates. Individual minds are molded by experience, not innate knowledge or intuition. He also believed that all men should be independent and equal. Many of Locke's ideas found their way into the Constitution of the United States.

The two French philosophers, Montesquieu and Rousseau, heavily influenced the French Revolution (1789-1799). They believed government policies and ideas should change to alleviate existing problems, an idea referred to as "liberalism." Rousseau in particular directly influenced the Revolution with writings such as *The Social Contract* (1762) and *Declaration of the Rights of Man and of the Citizen* (1789). Other ideas Rousseau and Montesquieu espoused included:

- Individual freedom and community welfare are of equal importance
- Man's innate goodness leads to natural harmony
- Reason develops with the rise of civilized society
- Individual citizens carry certain obligations to the existing government

David Hume and Jeremy Bentham believed politics should have as its main goal maintaining "the greatest happiness for the greatest number." Hume also believed in empiricism, or that ideas should not be believed until the proof has been observed. He was a natural skeptic and always sought out the truth of matters rather than believing what he was told.

John Stuart Mill, a British philosopher as well as an economist, believed in progressive policies such as women's suffrage, emancipation, and the development of labor unions and farming cooperatives.

Johann Fichte and Georg Hegel, German philosophers in the late eighteenth and early nineteenth centuries, supported a form of liberalism grounded largely in socialism and a sense of nationalism.

## Political orientations

The four main political orientations are:

- Liberal—liberals believe that government should work to increase equality, even at the expense of some freedoms. Government should assist those in need. Focus on enforced social justice and free basic services for everyone.
- Conservative—a conservative believes that government should be limited in most cases. The government should allow its citizens to help one another and solve their own problems rather than enforcing solutions. Business should not be overregulated, allowing a free market.
- Moderate—this ideology incorporates some liberal and some conservative values, generally falling somewhere between in overall belief.
- Libertarian—libertarians believe that the government's role should be limited to protecting the life and liberty of citizens. Government should not be involved in any citizen's life unless that citizen is encroaching upon the rights of another.

## Principles of government

The six major principles of government as outlined in the United States Constitution are:

- Federalism—the power of the government does not belong entirely to the national government, but is divided between federal and state governments.
- Popular sovereignty—the government is determined by the people, and gains its authority and power from the people.
- Separation of powers—the government is divided into three branches, executive, legislative, and judicial, with each branch having its own set of powers.
- Judicial review—courts at all levels of government can declare laws invalid if they contradict the constitutions of individual states, or the US Constitution, with the Supreme Court serving as the final judicial authority on decisions of this kind.
- Checks and balances—no single branch can act without input from another, and each branch has the power to "check" any other, as well as balance other branches' powers.
- Limited government—governmental powers are limited and certain individual rights are defined as inviolable by the government.

## Powers delegated to the national government

The structure of the US government divides power between national and state governments. Powers delegated to the federal government by the Constitution are:

- Expressed powers—powers directly defined in the Constitution, including power to declare war, regulate commerce, make money, and collect taxes
- Implied powers—powers the national government must have in order to carry out the expressed powers
- Inherent powers—powers inherent to any government, not expressly defined in the Constitution

Some of these powers, such as collection and levying of taxes, are also granted to the individual state governments.

## Federalism

The way federalism should be practiced has been the subject of debate since writing of the Constitution. There were—and still are—two main factions regarding this issue:

- States' rights—those favoring the states' rights position feel that the state governments should take the lead in performing local actions to manage various problems.
- Nationalist—those favoring a nationalist position feel the national government should take the lead to deal with those same matters.

The flexibility of the Constitution has allowed the US government to shift and adapt as the needs of the country have changed. Power has often shifted from the state governments to the national government and back again, and both levels of government have developed various ways to influence each other.

Federalism has three major effects on public policy in the US:

- Determining whether the local, state, or national government originates policy
- Affecting how policies are made
- Ensuring policy-making functions under a set of limitations

Federalism also influences the political balance of power in the US by:

- making it difficult, if not impossible, for a single political party to seize total power
- ensuring that individuals can participate in the political system at various levels
- making it possible for individuals working within the system to be able to affect policy at some level, whether local or more widespread

## Branches of the US government

The following are the three branches of the US Federal government and the individuals that belong to each branch:

- Legislative Branch—this consists of the two Houses of Congress: the House of Representatives and the Senate. All members of the Legislative Branch are elected officials.
- Executive Branch—this branch is made up of the President, Vice President, presidential advisors, and other various cabinet members. Advisors and cabinet are appointed by the President, but must be approved by Congress.
- Judicial Branch—the federal court system, headed by the Supreme Court.

The three branches of the Federal government each have specific roles and responsibilities:

- The Legislative Branch is largely concerned with law-making. All laws must be approved by Congress before they go into effect. They are also responsible for regulating money and trade, approving presidential appointments, and establishing organizations like the postal service and federal courts. Congress can also propose amendments to the Constitution, and can impeach, or bring charges against, the President. Only Congress can declare war.
- The Executive Branch carries out laws, treaties, and war declarations enacted by Congress. The President can also veto bills approved by Congress, and serves as commander-in-chief of the US military. The president appoints cabinet members, ambassadors to foreign countries, and federal judges.

- The Judicial Branch makes decisions on challenges as to whether laws passed by Congress meet the requirements of the US Constitution. The Supreme Court may also choose to review decisions made by lower courts to determine their constitutionality.

> **Review Video:** The Three Branches of the US Government
> *Visit **mometrix.com/academy** and enter **Code**:* **718704**

**US citizenship**

Anyone born in the US, born abroad to a US citizen, or who has gone through a process of naturalization is considered a citizen of the United States. It is possible to lose US citizenship as a result of conviction of certain crimes such as treason. Citizenship may also be lost if a citizen pledges an oath to another country or serves in the military of a country engaged in hostilities with the US. A US citizen can also choose to hold dual citizenship, work as an expatriate in another country without losing US citizenship, or even to renounce citizenship if he or she so chooses.

Citizens are granted certain rights under the US government. The most important of these are defined in the Bill of Rights, and include freedom of speech, religion, assembly, and a variety of other rights the government is not allowed to remove. A US citizen also has a number of duties:

- Paying taxes
- Loyalty to the government (though the US does not prosecute those who criticize or seek to change the government)
- Support and defense of the Constitution
- Serving in the Armed Forces when required by law
- Obeying laws as set forth by the various levels of government.

Responsibilities of a US citizen include:

- Voting in elections
- Respecting one another's rights and not infringing on them
- Staying informed about various political and national issues
- Respecting one another's beliefs

**Bill of Rights**

The first ten amendments of the US Constitution are known as the Bill of Rights. These amendments prevent the government from infringing upon certain freedoms that the founding fathers felt were natural rights that already belonged to all people. These rights included freedom of speech, freedom of religion, the right to bear arms, and freedom of assembly. Many of the rights were formulated in direct response to the way the colonists felt they had been mistreated by the British government.

The first ten amendments were passed by Congress in 1789. Three-fourths of the existing thirteen states had ratified them by December of 1791, making them official additions to the Constitution. The rights granted in the Bill of Rights are:

- First Amendment—freedom of religion, speech, freedom of the press, and the right to assemble and to petition the government
- Second Amendment—the right to bear arms
- Third Amendment—Congress cannot force individuals to house troops
- Fourth Amendment—protection from unreasonable search and seizure
- Fifth Amendment—no individual is required to testify against himself, and no individual may be tried twice for the same crime
- Sixth Amendment—right to criminal trial by jury, right to legal counsel
- Seventh Amendment—right to civil trial by jury
- Eighth Amendment—protection from excessive bail or cruel and unusual punishment
- Ninth Amendment—prevents rights not explicitly named in the Constitution from being taken away because they are not named
- Tenth Amendment—any rights not directly delegated to the national government, or not directly prohibited by the government from the states, belong to the states or to the people

In some cases, the government restricts certain elements of First Amendment rights. Some examples include:

- Freedom of religion—when a religion espouses illegal activities, the government often restricts these forms of religious expression. Examples include polygamy, animal sacrifice, and use of illicit drugs or illegal substances.
- Freedom of speech—this can be restricted if exercise of free speech endangers other people.
- Freedom of the press—laws prevent the press from publishing falsehoods.

In emergency situations such as wartime, stricter restrictions are sometimes placed on these rights, especially rights to free speech and assembly, and freedom of the press, in order to protect national security.

> **Review Video:** The Bill of Rights
> *Visit **mometrix.com/academy** and enter **Code**:* **585149**

### Constitutional rights of criminals

The US Constitution makes allowances for the rights of criminals, or anyone who has transgressed established laws. There must be laws to protect citizens from criminals, but those accused of crimes must also be protected and their basic rights as individuals preserved. In addition, the Constitution protects individuals from the power of authorities to prevent police forces and other enforcement organizations from becoming oppressive. The fourth, fifth, sixth and eighth amendments specifically address these rights.

### Equal protection under the law for all individuals

When the Founding Fathers wrote in the Declaration of Independence that "all men are created equal," they actually were referring to men, and in fact defined citizens as white men who owned land. However, as the country has developed and changed, the definition has expanded to more wholly include all people.

"Equality" does not mean all people are inherently the same, but it does mean they all should be granted the same rights and should be treated the same by the government. Amendments to the Constitution have granted citizenship and voting rights to all Americans regardless of race or gender. The Supreme Court evaluates various laws and court decisions to determine if they properly represent the idea of equal protection. One sample case was Brown v. Board of Education in 1954, which declared separate-but-equal treatment to be unconstitutional.

### Civil liberty challenges addressed in current political discussions

The civil rights movements of the 1960s and ongoing struggle for the rights of women and other minorities have sparked challenges to existing law. In addition, debate has raged over how much information the government should be required to divulge to the public. Major issues in today's political climate include:

- Continued debate over women's rights, especially regarding equal pay for equal work
- Debate over affirmative action to encourage hiring of minorities
- Debate over civil rights of homosexuals, including marriage and military service
- Decisions as to whether minorities should be compensated for past discriminatory practices
- Balance between the public's right to know and the government's need to maintain national security
- Balance between the public's right to privacy and national security

### Civil liberties and civil rights

While the terms "civil liberties" and "civil rights" are often used synonymously, in actuality their definitions are slightly different. The two concepts work together, however, to define the basics of a free state:

- "Civil liberties" defines the role of the state in providing equal rights and opportunities to individuals within that state. An example is non-discrimination policies with regards to granting citizenship.
- "Civil rights" defines the limitations of governmental rights, describing those rights that belong to individuals and which cannot be infringed upon by the government. Examples of these rights include freedom of religion, political freedom, and overall freedom to live as one chooses.

### Suffrage and franchise

Suffrage and franchise both refer to the right to vote. As the US developed as a nation, there was much debate over which individuals should hold this right. In the early years, only white male landowners were granted suffrage. By the nineteenth century, most states had franchised, or granted the right to vote to, all adult white males. The Fifteenth Amendment of 1870 granted suffrage to former slave men. The Nineteenth Amendment gave women the right to vote in 1920, and in 1971 the Twenty-sixth Amendment expanded voting rights to include any US citizen over the age of eighteen. However, those who have not been granted full citizenship and citizens who have committed certain crimes do not have voting rights.

## Changes in voting process

The first elections in the US were held by public ballot. However, election abuses soon became common, since public ballot made it easy to intimidate, threaten, or otherwise influence the votes of individuals or groups of individuals. New practices were put into play, including registering voters before elections took place, and using a secret or Australian ballot. In 1892, the introduction of the voting machine further privatized the voting process, since it allowed complete privacy for voting. Today debate continues about the accuracy of various voting methods, including high-tech voting machines and even low-tech punch cards.

## Political parties

Different types and numbers of political parties can have a significant effect on how a government is run. If there is a single party, or a one-party system, the government is defined by that one party, and all policy is based on that party's beliefs. In a two-party system, two parties with different viewpoints compete for power and influence. The US is basically a two-party system, with checks and balances to make it difficult for one party to gain complete power over the other. There are also multi-party systems, with three or more parties. In multiparty systems, various parties will often come to agreements in order to form a majority and shift the balance of power.

George Washington was adamantly against the establishment of political parties, based on the abuses perpetrated by such parties in Britain. However, political parties developed in US politics almost from the beginning. Major parties throughout US history have included:

- Federalists and Democratic-Republicans—these parties formed in the late 1700s and disagreed on the balance of power between national and state government.
- Democrats and Whigs—these developed before the Civil War, based on disagreements about various issues such as slavery.
- Democrats and Republicans—the Republican Party developed after the Civil War, and the two parties debated issues centering on the treatment of the post-war South.

While third parties sometimes enter the picture in US politics, the government is basically a two-party system, dominated by the Democrats and Republicans.

> ➢ **Review Video:** Political Parties
> *Visit* ***mometrix.com/academy*** *and enter* ***Code*****: 640197**

## Functions of political parties

Political parties form organizations at all levels of government. Activities of individual parties include:

- Recruiting and backing candidates for offices
- Discussing various issues with the public, increasing public awareness
- Working toward compromise on difficult issues
- Staffing government offices and providing administrative support

At the administrative level, parties work to ensure that viable candidates are available for elections and that offices and staff are in place to support candidates as they run for office and afterwards, when they are elected.

**Process for choosing political candidate**

Historically, in the quest for political office, a potential candidate has followed one of the following four processes:

- Nominating convention—an official meeting of the members of a party for the express purpose of nominating candidates for upcoming elections. The Democratic National Convention and the Republican National Convention, convened to announce candidates for presidency, are examples of this kind of gathering.
- Caucus—a meeting, usually attended by a party's leaders. Some states still use caucuses, but not all.
- Primary election—the most common method of choosing candidates today, the primary is a publicly held election to choose candidates.
- Petition—signatures are gathered to place a candidate on the ballot. Petitions can also be used to place legislation on a ballot.

**Citizen participation in political process**

In addition to voting for elected officials, American citizens are able to participate in the political process through several other avenues. These include:

- Participating in local government
- Participating in caucuses for large elections
- Volunteering to help political parties
- Running for election to local, state, or national offices

Individuals can also donate money to political causes, or support political groups that focus on specific causes such as abortion, wildlife conservation or women's rights. These groups often make use of representatives who lobby legislators to act in support of their efforts.

**Campaign funding**

Political campaigns are very expensive. In addition to the basic necessities of a campaign office, including office supplies, office space, etc., a large quantity of the money that funds a political campaign goes toward advertising. Money to fund a political campaign can come from several sources including:

- The candidate's personal funds
- Donations by individuals
- Special interest groups

The most significant source of campaign funding is special interest groups. Groups in favor of certain policies will donate money to candidates they believe will support those policies. Special interest groups also do their own advertising in support of candidates they endorse.

**Free press and the media**

The right to free speech guaranteed in the first amendment to the Constitution allows the media to report on government and political activities without fear of retribution. Because the media has access to information about the government, its policies and actions, as well as debates and discussions that occur in Congress, it can keep the public informed about the inner workings of the government. The media can also draw attention to injustices, imbalances of power, and other transgressions the government or government officials might commit. However, media outlets may, like special interest groups, align themselves with certain political viewpoints and skew their reports to fit that viewpoint. The rise of the Internet has made media reporting even more complex, as news can be found from an infinite variety of sources, both reliable and unreliable.

### Anarchism, communism and dictatorship

Anarchists believe that all government should be eliminated and that individuals should rule themselves. Historically, anarchists have used violence and assassination to further their beliefs.

Communism is based on class conflict, revolution and a one-party state. Ideally, a communist government would involve a single government for the entire world. Communist government controls the production and flow of goods and services rather than leaving this to companies or individuals.

Dictatorship involves rule by a single individual. If rule is enforced by a small group, this is referred to as an oligarchy. Dictators tend to rule with a violent hand, using a highly repressive police force to ensure control over the populace.

### Fascism and monarchy

Fascism centers on a single leader and is, ideologically, an oppositional belief to communism. Fascism includes a single party state and centralized control. The power of the fascist leader lies in the "cult of personality," and the fascist state often focuses on expansion and conquering of other nations. Monarchy was the major form of government for Europe through most of its history. A monarchy is led by a king or a queen. This position is hereditary, and the rulers are not elected. In modern times, constitutional monarchy has developed, where the king and queen still exist but most of the governmental decisions are made by democratic institutions such as a parliament.

### Presidential system and socialism

A presidential system, like a parliamentary system, has a legislature and political parties, but there is no difference between the head of state and the head of government. Instead of separating these functions, an elected president performs both. Election of the president can be direct or indirect, and the president may not necessarily belong to the largest political party. In socialism, the state controls production of goods, though it does not necessarily own all means of production. The state also provides a variety of social services to citizens and helps guide the economy. A democratic form of government often exists in socialist countries.

### Totalitarian and authoritarian systems of government

A totalitarian system believes everything should be under the control of the government, from resource production to the press to religion and other social institutions. All aspects of life under a totalitarian system must conform to the ideals of the government. Authoritarian governments practice widespread state authority, but do not necessarily dismantle all public institutions. If a church, for example, exists as an organization but poses no threat to the authority of the state, an authoritarian government might leave it as it is. While all totalitarian governments are by definition authoritarian, a government can be authoritarian without becoming totalitarian.

> **Review Video:** Authoritarian and Totalitarian Systems of Government
> *Visit **mometrix.com/academy** and enter **Code**:* **104046**

**Parliamentary and democratic systems of government**

In a parliamentary system, government involves a legislature and a variety of political parties. The head of government, usually a Prime Minister, is typically the head of the dominant party. A head of state can be elected, or this position can be taken by a monarch, as in Great Britain's constitutional monarchy system.

In a democratic system of government, the people elect their government representatives. The word "democracy" is a Greek term that means "rule of the people." There are two forms of democracy—direct and indirect. In a direct democracy, each issue or election is decided by a vote where each individual is counted separately. An indirect democracy employs a legislature that votes on issues that affect large numbers of people whom the legislative members represent. Democracy can exist as a parliamentary system or a presidential system. The US is a presidential, indirect democracy.

**Realism, liberalism, institutionalism, and constructivism**

The theory of realism states that nations are by nature aggressive, and work in their own self-interest. Relations between nations are determined by military and economic strength. The nation is seen as the highest authority. Liberalism believes states can cooperate, and that they act based on capability rather than power. This term was originally coined to describe Woodrow Wilson's theories on international cooperation. In institutionalism, institutions provide structure and incentive for cooperation among nations. Institutions are defined as a set of rules used to make international decisions. These institutions also help distribute power and determine how nations will interact. Constructivism, like liberalism, is based on international cooperation, but recognizes that perceptions countries have of each other can affect their relations.

> **Review Video:** Classical Liberalism
> *Visit **mometrix.com/academy** and enter **Code**:* **535938**

**Foreign policy**

Foreign policy is a set of goals, policies and strategies that determine how an individual nation will interact with other countries. These strategies shift, sometimes quickly and drastically, according to actions or changes occurring in the other countries. However, a nation's foreign policy is often based on a certain set of ideals and national needs.

Examples of US foreign policy include isolationism versus internationalism. In the 1800s, the US leaned more toward isolationism, exhibiting a reluctance to become involved in foreign affairs. The World Wars led to a period of internationalism, as the US entered these wars in support of other countries and joined the United Nations. Today's foreign policy tends more toward interdependence, or globalism, recognizing the widespread affects of issues like economic health.

US foreign policy is largely determined by Congress and the president, influenced by the secretary of state, secretary of defense, and the national security adviser. Executive officials carry out policies. The main departments in charge of these day-to-day issues are the US Department of State, also referred to as the State Department. The Department of State carries out policy, negotiates treaties, maintains diplomatic relations, assists citizens traveling in foreign countries, and ensures that the president is properly informed of any international issues. The Department of Defense, the largest executive department in the US, supervises the armed forces and provides assistance to the President in his role as Commander-in-chief.

## International organizations

Two types of international organizations are:

- Intergovernmental organizations (IGOs). These organizations are made up of members from various national governments. The UN is an example of an intergovernmental organization. Treaties among the member nations determine the functions and powers of these groups.
- Nongovernmental organizations (NGOs). An NGO lies outside the scope of any government and is usually supported through private donations. An example of an NGO is the International Red Cross, which works with governments all over the world when their countries are in crisis, but is formally affiliated with no particular country or government.

## Diplomats

Diplomats are individuals who reside in foreign countries in order to maintain communications between that country and their home country. They help negotiate trade agreements and environmental policies, as well as conveying official information to foreign governments. They also help to resolve conflicts between the countries, often working to sort out issues without making the conflicts official in any way. Diplomats, or ambassadors, are appointed in the US by the president. Appointments must be approved by Congress.

## UN

The United Nations (UN) helps form international policies by hosting representatives of various countries who then provide input into policy decisions. Countries who are members of the UN must agree to abide by all final UN resolutions, but this is not always the case in practice, as dissent is not uncommon. If countries do not follow UN resolutions, the UN can decide on sanctions against those countries, often economic sanctions, such as trade restriction. The UN can also send military forces to problem areas, with "peace keeping" troops brought in from member nations. An example of this function is the Korean War, the first war in which an international organization played a major role.

# Economics

## Economics

Economics is the study of the ways specific societies allocate resources to individuals and groups within that society. Also important are the choices society makes regarding what efforts or initiatives are funded and which are not. Since resources in any society are finite, allocation becomes a vivid reflection of that society's values. In general, the economic system that drives an individual society is based on:

- What goods are produced
- How those goods are produced
- Who acquires the goods or benefits from them

Economics consists of two main categories: macroeconomics, which studies larger systems, and microeconomics, which studies smaller systems.

## Market economy

A market economy is based on supply and demand. Demand has to do with what customers want and need, as well as what quantity those consumers are able to purchase based on other economic factors. Supply refers to how much can be produced to meet demand, or how much suppliers are willing and able to sell. Where the needs of consumers meet the needs of suppliers is referred to as a market equilibrium price. This price varies depending on many factors, including the overall health of a society's economy, overall beliefs and considerations of individuals in society. The following is a list of terms defined in the context of a market economy:

- Elasticity—this is based on how the quantity of a particular product responds to the price demanded for that product. If quantity responds quickly to changes in price, the supply/demand for that product is said to be elastic. If it does not respond quickly, then the supply/demand is inelastic.
- Market efficiency—this occurs when a market is capable of producing output high enough to meet consumer demand, that market is efficient.
- Comparative advantage—in the field of international trade, this refers to a country focusing on a specific product that it can produce it more efficiently and more cheaply, or at a lower opportunity cost, than another country, thus giving it a comparative advantage in production.

> **Review Video:** Market Economy
> *Visit **mometrix.com/academy** and enter **Code:*** **460547**

Comparison to planned economy

In a market economy, supply and demand are determined by consumers. In a planned economy, a public entity or planning authority makes the decisions about what resources will be produced, how they will be produced, and who will be able to benefit from them. The means of production, such as factories, are also owned by a public entity rather than by private interests. In market socialism, the economic structure falls somewhere between the market economy and the planned economy. Planning authorities determine allocation of resources at higher economic levels, while consumer goods are driven by a market economy.

### Microeconomics

While economics generally studies how resources are allocated, microeconomics focuses on economic factors such as the way consumers behave, how income is distributed, and output and input markets. Studies are limited to the industry or firm level, rather than an entire country or society. Among the elements studied in microeconomics are factors of production, costs of production, and factor income. These factors determine production decisions of individual firms, based on resources and costs.

> **Review Video:** Microeconomics
> *Visit **mometrix.com/academy** and enter **Code**:* **779207**

### Classification of markets

The conditions prevailing in a given market are used to classify markets. Conditions considered include:

- Existence of competition
- Number and size of suppliers
- Influence of suppliers over price
- Variety of available products
- Ease of entering the market

Once these questions are answered, an economist can classify a certain market according to its structure and the nature of competition within the market.

### Market failure

When any of the elements for a successfully competitive market are missing, this can lead to a market failure. Certain elements are necessary to create what economists call "perfect competition." If one of these factors is weak or lacking, the market is classified as having "imperfect competition." Worse than imperfect competition, though, is a market failure. There are five major types of market failure:

- Inadequate competition
- Inadequate information
- Immobile resources
- Negative externalities, or side effects
- Failure to provide public goods

Externalities are side effects of a market that affect third parties. These effects can be either negative or positive.

> **Review Video:** Market Failure
> *Visit **mometrix.com/academy** and enter **Code**:* **198450**

## Factors of production and costs of production

Every good and service requires certain resources, or inputs. These inputs are referred to as factors of production. Every good and service requires four factors of production:

- Labor
- Capital
- Land
- Entrepreneurship

These factors can be fixed or variable, and can produce fixed or variable costs. Examples of fixed costs include land and equipment. Variable costs include labor. The total of fixed and variable costs makes up the cost of production.

## Factor income

Factors of production each have an associated factor income. Factors that earn income include:

- Labor—earns wages
- Capital—earns interest
- Land—earns rent
- Entrepreneurship—earns profit

Each factor's income is determined by its contribution. In a market economy, this income is not guaranteed to be equal. How scarce the factor is and the weight of its contribution to the overall production process determines the final factor income.

## Output market

The four kinds of market structures in an output market are:

- Perfect competition—all existing firms sell an identical product. The firms are not able to control the final price. In addition, there is nothing that makes it difficult to become involved in or leave the industry. Anything that would prevent entering or leaving an industry is called a barrier to entry. An example of this market structure is agriculture.
- Monopoly—a single seller controls the product and its price. Barriers to entry, such as prohibitively high fixed cost structures, prevent other sellers from entering the market.
- Monopolistic competition—a number of firms sell similar products, but they are not identical, such as different brands of clothes or food. Barriers to entry are low.
- Oligopoly—only a few firms control the production and distribution of products, such as automobiles. Barriers to entry are high, preventing large numbers of firms from entering the market.

## Monopolies

Four types of monopolies are:

- Natural monopoly—a single supplier has a distinct advantage over the others.
- Geographic monopoly—only one business offers the product in a certain area.
- Technological monopoly—a single company controls the technology necessary to supply the product.

- Government monopoly—a government agency is the only provider of a specific good or service.

Control by the US government

The US government has passed several acts to regulate businesses, including:

- Sherman Antitrust Act (1890)—this prohibited trusts, monopolies, and any other situations that eliminated competition.
- Clayton Antitrust Act (1914)—this prohibited price discrimination.
- Robinson-Patman Act (1936)—this strengthened provisions of the Clayton Antitrust Act, requiring businesses to offer the same pricing on products to any customer.

The government has also taken other actions to ensure competition, including requirements for public disclosure. The Securities and Exchange Commission (SEC) requires companies that provide public stock to provide financial reports on a regular basis. Because of the nature of their business, banks are further regulated and required to provide various information to the government.

## Marketing and utility

Marketing consists of all of the activity necessary to convince consumers to acquire goods. One major way to move products into the hands of consumers is to convince them that any single product will satisfy a need. The ability of a product or service to satisfy the need of a consumer is called utility. There are four types of utility:

- Form utility—a product's desirability lies in its physical characteristics.
- Place utility—a product's desirability is connected to its location and convenience.
- Time utility—a product's desirability is determined by its availability at a certain time.
- Ownership utility—a product's desirability is increased because ownership of the product passes to the consumer.

Marketing behavior will stress any or all of these types of utility when marketing to the consumer.

## Determining a product's market

Successful marketing depends not only on convincing customers they need the product, but also on focusing the marketing towards those who already have a need or desire for the product. Before releasing a product into the general marketplace, many producers will test markets to determine which will be the most receptive to the product.

There are three steps usually taken to evaluate a product's market:

- Market research—this involves researching a market to determine if it will be receptive to the product.
- Market surveys—a part of market research, market surveys ask consumers specific questions to help determine the marketability of a product to a specific group.
- Test marketing—this includes releasing the product into a small geographical area to see how it sells. Often test marketing is followed by wider marketing if the product does well.

### Marketing plan

- Product—this includes any elements pertaining directly to the product, such as packaging, presentation, or services to include along with it.
- Price—this calculates cost of production, distribution, advertising, etc., as well as the desired profit to determine the final price.
- Place—this determines which outlets will be used to sell the product, whether traditional outlets or through direct mail or Internet marketing.
- Promotion—this involves ways to let consumers know the product is available, through advertising and other means.

Once these elements have all been determined, the producer can proceed with production and distribution of his product.

> **Review Video:** Marketing Plan
> *Visit **mometrix.com/academy** and enter **Code**:* **983409**

### Distribution channels

Distribution channels determine the route a product takes on its journey from producer to consumer, and can also influence the final price and availability of the product. There are two major forms of distributions: wholesale and retail. A wholesale distributor buys in large quantities and then resells smaller amounts to other businesses. Retailers sell directly to the consumers rather than to businesses. In the modern marketplace, additional distribution channels have grown up with the rise of markets such as club warehouse stores as well as purchasing through catalogs or over the Internet. Most of these newer distribution channels bring products more directly to the consumer, eliminating the need for middlemen.

### Distribution of income and poverty

Distribution of income in any society ranges from poorest to richest. In most societies, income is not distributed evenly. To determine income distribution, family incomes are ranked from lowest to highest. These rankings are divided into five sections called quintiles, which are compared to each other. The uneven distribution of income is often linked to higher levels of education and ability in the upper classes, but can also be due to other factors such as discrimination and existing monopolies. The income gap in America continues to grow, largely due to growth in the service industry, changes in the American family unit and reduced influence of labor unions. Poverty is defined by comparing incomes to poverty guidelines. Poverty guidelines determine the level of income necessary for a family to function. Those below the poverty line are often eligible for assistance from government agencies.

### Consumer behavior

The two major types of consumer behavior as defined in macroeconomics are:

- Marginal propensity to consume defines the tendency of consumers to increase spending in conjunction with increases in income. In general, individuals with greater income will buy more. As individuals increase their income through job changes or growth of experience, they will also increase spending.

- Utility is a term that describes the satisfaction experienced by a consumer in relation to acquiring and using a good or service. Providers of goods and services will stress utility to convince consumers they want the products being presented.

## Macroeconomics

Macroeconomics examines economies on a much larger level than microeconomics. While microeconomics studies economics on a firm or industry level, macroeconomics looks at economic trends and structures on a national level. Variables studied in macroeconomics include:

- Output
- Consumption
- Investment
- Government spending
- Net exports

The overall economic condition of a nation is defined as the Gross Domestic Product, or GDP. GDP measures a nation's economic output over a limited time period, such as a year.

> **Review Video:** Microeconomics and Macroeconomics
> *Visit **mometrix.com/academy** and enter **Code**:* **538837**

## GDP

The two major ways to measure the Gross Domestic Product of a country are:

- The expenditures approach calculates the GDP based on how much money is spent in each individual sector.
- The income approach calculates the GDP based on how much money is earned in each sector.

Both methods yield the same results and both of these calculation methods are based on four economic sectors that make up a country's macro-economy:

- Consumers
- Business
- Government
- Foreign sector

Several factors must be considered in order to accurately calculate the GDP using the incomes approach. Income factors are:

- Wages paid to laborers, or Compensation of Employees
- Rental income derived from land
- Interest income derived from invested capital
- Entrepreneurial income

Entrepreneurial income consists of two forms. Proprietor's income is income that comes back to the entrepreneur himself. Corporate profit is income that goes back into the corporation as a whole. Corporate profit is divided by the corporation into corporate profits taxes, dividends, and retained earnings. Two other figures must be subtracted in the incomes approach. These are indirect business taxes, including property and sales taxes, and depreciation.

Effects of the population
Changes in population can affect the calculation of a nation's GDP, particularly since GDP and GNP (Gross National Product) are generally measured per capita. If a country's economic production is low, but the population is high, the income per individual will be lower than if the income is high and the population is lower. Also, if the population grows quickly and the income grows slowly, individual income will remain low or even drop drastically. Population growth can also affect overall economic growth. Economic growth requires both that consumers purchase goods and workers produce them. A population that does not grow quickly enough will not supply enough workers to support rapid economic growth.

Ideal balance in an economy and phases in national economies
Ideally, an economy functions efficiently, with the aggregate supply, or the amount of national output, equal to the aggregate demand, or the amount of the output that is purchased. In these cases, the economy is stable and prosperous. However, economies more typically go through phases. These phases are:

- Boom—GDP is high and the economy prospers
- Recession—GDP falls, unemployment rises
- Trough—the recession reaches its lowest point
- Recovery—unemployment lessens, prices rise, and the economy begins to stabilize again

These phases tend to repeat in cycles that are not necessarily predictable or regular.

## Unemployment and inflation

When demand outstrips supply, prices are driven artificially high, or inflated. This occurs when too much spending causes an imbalance in the economy. In general, inflation occurs because an economy is growing too quickly. When there is too little spending and supply has moved far beyond demand, a surplus of product results. Companies cut back on production, reduce the number of employees, and unemployment rises as people lose their jobs. This imbalance occurs when an economy becomes sluggish. In general, both these economic instability situations are caused by an imbalance between supply and demand. Government intervention may be necessary to stabilize an economy when either inflation or unemployment becomes too serious.

Forms of unemployment

- Frictional—when workers change jobs and are unemployed while waiting for new jobs
- Structural—when economic shifts reduce the need for workers
- Cyclical—when natural business cycles bring about loss of jobs
- Seasonal—when seasonal cycles reduce the need for certain jobs
- Technological—when advances in technology result in elimination of certain jobs

Any of these factors can increase unemployment in certain sectors. Inflation is classified by the overall rate at which it occurs:

- Creeping inflation—this is an inflation rate of about 1-3% annually.
- Walking inflation—this is an inflation rate of 3-10% annually.

- Galloping inflation—this is a high inflation rate of more than 10% but less than 1000% annually.
- Hyperinflation—this is an inflation rate over 1000% per year. Hyperinflation usually leads to complete monetary collapse in a society, as individuals become unable to generate sufficient income to purchase necessary goods.

Government intervention policies

When an economy becomes too imbalanced, either due to excessive spending or not enough spending, government intervention often becomes necessary to put the economy back on track. Government Fiscal Policy can take several forms, including:

- Contractionary policy
- Expansionary policy
- Monetary policy

Contractionary policies help counteract inflation. These include increasing taxes and decreasing government spending to slow spending in the overall economy. Expansionary policies increase government spending and lower taxes in order to reduce unemployment and increase the level of spending in the economy overall. Monetary policy can take several forms, and affects the amount of funds available to banks for making loans.

## Populations and population growth

Populations are studied by size, rates of growth due to immigration, the overall fertility rate, and life expectancy. For example, though the population of the United States is considerably larger than it was two hundred years ago, the rate of population growth has decreased greatly, from about three percent per year to less than one percent per year. In the US, the fertility rate is fairly low, with most choosing not to have large families, and life expectancy is high, creating a projected imbalance between older and younger people in the near future. In addition, immigration and the mixing of racially diverse cultures are projected to increase the percentages of Asians, Hispanics and African-Americans.

## Money

Money is used in three major ways:

- As an accounting unit
- As a store of value
- As an exchange medium

In general, money must be acceptable throughout a society in exchange for debts or to purchase goods and services. Money should be relatively scarce, its value should remain stable, and it should be easily carried, durable, and easy to divide up. There are three basic types of money: commodity, representative and fiat. Commodity money includes gems or precious metals. Representative money can be exchanged for items such as gold or silver which have inherent value. Fiat money, or legal tender, has no inherent value but has been declared to function as money by the government. It is often backed by gold or silver, but not necessarily on a one-to-one ratio.

US money

Money in the US is not just currency. When economists calculate the amount of money available, they must take into account other factors such as deposits that have been placed in checking accounts, debit cards and "near moneys" such as savings accounts, that can be quickly converted into cash. Currency, checkable deposits and traveler's checks, referred to as M1, are added up, and then M2 is calculated by adding savings deposits, CDs and various other monetary deposits. The final result is the total quantity of available money.

### Monetary policy and the Federal Reserve System

The Federal Reserve System, also known as the Fed, implements all monetary policy in the US. Monetary policy regulates the amount of money available in the American banking system. The Fed can decrease or increase the amount of available money for loans, thus helping regulate the national economy. Monetary policies implemented by the Fed are part of expansionary or contractionary monetary policies that help counteract inflation or unemployment. The discount rate is an interest rate charged by the Fed when banks borrow money from them. A lower discount rate leads banks to borrow more money, leading to increased spending. A higher discount rate has the opposite effect.

➢ **Review Video:** Monetary Policy
*Visit **mometrix.com/academy** and enter **Code**:* **662298**

### Banks

Banks earn their income by loaning out money and charging interest on those loans. If less money is available, fewer loans can be made, which affects the amount of spending in the overall economy. While banks function by making loans, they are not allowed to loan out all the money they hold in deposit. The amount of money they must maintain in reserve is known as the reserve ratio. If the reserve ratio is raised, less money is available for loans and spending decreases. A lower reserve ratio increases available funds and increases spending. This ratio is determined by the Federal Reserve System.

### Open Market Operations

The Federal Reserve System can also expand or contract the overall money supply through open market operations. In this case, the Fed can buy or sell bonds it has purchased from banks or individuals. When the Fed buys bonds, more money is put into circulation, creating an expansionary situation to stimulate the economy. When the Fed sells bonds, money is withdrawn from the system, creating a contractionary situation to slow an economy suffering from inflation. Because of international financial markets, however, American banks often borrow and lend money in markets outside the US. By shifting their attention to international markets, domestic banks and other businesses can circumvent whatever contractionary policies the Fed may have put into place.

### International trade

International trade can take advantage of broader markets, bringing a wider variety of products within easy reach. By contrast, it can also allow individual countries to specialize in particular products that they can produce easily, such as those for which they have easy access to raw materials. Other products, more difficult to make domestically, can be acquired through trade with other nations. International trade requires efficient use of native resources as well as sufficient disposable income to purchase native and imported products. Many countries in the world engage extensively in international trade, but others still face major economic challenges.

**Developing nations**

The five major characteristics of a developing nation are:

- Low GDP
- Rapid growth of population
- Economy that depends on subsistence agriculture
- Poor conditions, including high infant mortality rates, high disease rates, poor sanitation, and insufficient housing
- Low literacy rate

Developing nations often function under oppressive governments that do not provide private property rights and withhold education and other rights from women. They also often feature an extreme disparity between upper and lower classes, with little opportunity for the lower classes to improve their position.

<u>Stages of economic development</u>
Economic development occurs in three stages that are defined by the activities that drive the economy:

- Agricultural stage
- Manufacturing stage
- Service sector stage

In developing countries, it is often difficult to acquire the necessary funding to provide equipment and training to move into the advanced stages of economic development. Some can receive help from developed countries via foreign aid and investment or international organizations such as the International Monetary Fund or the World Bank. Having developed countries provide monetary, technical, or military assistance can help developing countries move forward to the next stage in their development.

<u>Obstacles to economic growth</u>
Developing nations typically struggle to overcome obstacles that prevent or slow economic development. Major obstacles can include:

- Rapid, uncontrolled population growth
- Trade restrictions
- Misused resources, often perpetrated by the government
- Traditional beliefs that can slow or reject change

Corrupt, oppressive governments often hamper the economic growth of developing nations, creating huge economic disparities and making it impossible for individuals to advance, in turn preventing overall growth. Governments sometimes export currency, called capital flight, which is detrimental to a country's economic development. In general, countries are more likely to experience economic growth if their governments encourage entrepreneurship and provide private property rights.

**Problems with rapid industrialization**

Rapid growth throughout the world leaves some nations behind, and sometimes spurs their governments to move forward too quickly into industrialization and artificially rapid economic growth. While slow or nonexistent economic growth causes problems in a country, overly rapid industrialization carries its own issues. Four major problems encountered due to rapid industrialization are:

- Use of technology not suited to the products or services being supplied
- Poor investment of capital
- Lack of time for the population to adapt to new paradigms
- Lack of time to experience all stages of development and adjust to each stage

Economic failures in Indonesia were largely due to rapid growth that was poorly handled.

**E-commerce**

The growth of the Internet has brought many changes to our society, not the least of which is the modern way of business. Where supply channels used to move in certain necessary ways, many of these channels are now bypassed as e-commerce makes it possible for nearly any individual to set up a direct market to consumers, as well as direct interaction with suppliers. Competition is fierce. In many instances e-commerce can provide nearly instantaneous gratification, with a wide variety of products. Whoever provides the best product most quickly often rises to the top of a marketplace. How this added element to the marketplace will affect the economy in the future remains to be seen. Many industries are still struggling with the best ways to adapt to the rapid, continuous changes.

**Knowledge economy**

The knowledge economy is a growing sector in the economy of developed countries, and includes the trade and development of:

- Data
- Intellectual property
- Technology, especially in the area of communications

Knowledge as a resource is steadily becoming more and more important. What is now being called the Information Age may prove to bring about changes in life and culture as significant as those brought on by the Agricultural and Industrial Revolutions.

**Cybernomics**

Related to the knowledge economy is what has been dubbed "cybernomics," or economics driven by e-commerce and other computer-based markets and products. Marketing has changed drastically with the growth of cyber communication, allowing suppliers to connect one-on-one with their customers. Other issues coming to the fore regarding cybernomics include:

- Secure online trade
- Intellectual property rights
- Rights to privacy
- Bringing developing nations into the fold

As these issues are debated and new laws and policies developed, the face of many industries continues to undergo drastic change. Many of the old ways of doing business no longer work, leaving industries scrambling to function profitably within the new system.

# Practice Test

## Practice Questions

1. Some countries in the Americas still have large populations of indigenous or partly indigenous peoples. Of the following, which pair of countries does not have comparatively as large of an indigenous population as the other countries?
   a. Guatemala and Peru
   b. Ecuador and Bolivia
   c. Paraguay and Mexico
   d. Argentina and Uruguay

2. Which of the following statements is *not* true regarding English expansionism in the 16th century?
   a. England's defeat of the Spanish Armada in 1588 brought a decisive end to their war with Spain.
   b. King Henry VIII's desire to divorce Catherine of Aragon strengthened English expansionism.
   c. Queen Elizabeth's support for the Protestant Reformation strengthened English expansionism.
   d. Sir Francis Drake and other English sea captains plundered the Spaniards' plunders of Indians.

3. Which of the following is *not* correct regarding the Virginia Companies?
   a. One of these companies, the Virginia Company of Plymouth, made its base in North America.
   b. One of these companies, the Virginia Company of London, made its base in Massachusetts.
   c. One company had a charter to colonize America between the Hudson and Cape Fear rivers.
   d. One company had a charter to colonize America from the Potomac River to north Maine.

4. Which of the following conquistadores unwittingly gave smallpox to the Indians and destroyed the Aztec empire in Mexico?
   a. Balboa
   b. Ponce de Leon
   c. Cortes
   d. De Vaca

5. Which statement best describes the significance of the Peter Zenger trial in colonial America?
   a. It was the earliest American case on the right to bear arms.
   b. It established a precedent for freedom of the press.
   c. It was the earliest American case on right of peaceable assembly.
   d. It established a precedent for freedom of religion.

6. Which of these factors was *not* a direct contributor to the beginning of the American Revolution?

a. The attitudes of American colonists toward Great Britain following the French and Indian War
b. The attitudes of leaders in Great Britain toward the American colonies and imperialism
c. James Otis's court argument against Great Britain's Writs of Assistance as breaking natural law
d. Lord Grenville's Proclamation of 1763, Sugar Act, Currency Act, and especially Stamp Act

7. Which of the following statements is *not* true regarding the Tea Act of 1773?

a. The British East India Company was suffering financially because Americans were buying tea smuggled from Holland.
b. Parliament granted concessions to the British East India Company to ship tea straight to America, bypassing England.
c. Colonists found that even with added taxes, tea directly shipped by the British East India Company cost less, and they bought it.
d. American colonists refused to buy less expensive tea from the British East India Company on the principle of taxation.

8. Which of the following is true concerning the formation of new state governments in the new United States of America following freedom from British rule?

a. By the end of 1777, new constitutions had been created for twelve of the American states.
b. The states of Connecticut and Massachusetts retained their colonial charters, minus the British parts.
c. The state of Massachusetts required a special convention for its constitution, setting a good example.
d. The state of Massachusetts did not formally begin to use its new constitution until 1778.

9. Which of the following is *not* a true statement regarding the Louisiana Purchase?

a. Jefferson sent a delegation to Paris to endeavor to purchase only the city of New Orleans from Napoleon.
b. Napoleon, anticipating U.S. intrusions into Louisiana, offered to sell the U.S. the entire Louisiana territory.
c. The American delegation accepted Napoleon's offer, though they were only authorized to buy New Orleans.
d. The Louisiana Purchase, once it was completed, increased the territory of the U.S. by 50% overnight.

10. Which of these was *not* a factor that contributed to the duel in which Aaron Burr killed Alexander Hamilton?

a. Some Federalists who opposed U.S. Western expansion were attempting to organize a movement to secede from the Union.
b. Alexander Hamilton challenged Aaron Burr to a duel because he objected to U.S. expansion into the West, which Burr supported.
c. Secessionist Federalists tried to enlist Aaron Burr's support for their cause by backing him in his run for Governor of New York.
d. Alexander Hamilton was the leader of the group that opposed Aaron Burr's campaign to run for New York Governor.

11. Which of the following did *not* occur during the War of 1812?

a. Early in the war, the U.S. executed a three-pronged invasion of Canada and succeeded on two of three fronts.
b. Early in the war, Americans won naval battles against the British, but were soon beaten back by the British.
c. Admiral Oliver Hazard Perry's fleet defeated the British navy on Lake Erie in September, 1813.
d. William Henry Harrison invaded Canada and defeated the British and the Indians in the Battle of the Thames.

12. Which of the following was *not* an immediate effect of rapid urban growth in the 1800s?

a. Poor sanitation conditions in the cities
b. Epidemics of diseases in the cities
c. Inadequate police and fire protection
d. Widespread urban political corruption

13. Which of the following laws was instrumental in spurring westward migration to the Great Plains between 1860 and 1880?

a. The Homestead Act
b. The Timber Culture Act
c. The Desert Land Act
d. All of these laws were instrumental in spurring westward migration to the Great Plains during that period.

14. What did *not* contribute to ending America's neutrality in World War I?

a. Germany's declaration of a war zone surrounding the British Isles in February, 1913
b. Germany's declaration of a war on Russia after Archduke Ferdinand's assassination
c. Germany's sinking the British ship *Lusitania,* which killed 128 American passengers
d. Germany's declaration of unrestricted submarine warfare on all ships in the war zone

15. Of the following international diplomatic conferences, which one made US-Soviet differences apparent?

a. The Potsdam conference
b. The conference at Yalta
c. Dumbarton Oaks conference
d. The Tehran conference

16. Which statement about relations between the Middle East and the US and Europe in the 1950s is *not* correct?

a. President Nasser of Egypt refused to align with the US in the Cold War.
b. President Eisenhower removed US funding from the Aswan Dam in 1956.
c. President Nasser nationalized the Suez Canal, which was owned by England.
d. In 1956, Egypt attacked Israel, and England and France joined in the war.

17. Of the following, which person or group was *not* instrumental in postwar advancement of civil rights and desegregation during the 1940s and 1950s?

a. The President
b. The Supreme Court
c. The Congress
d. The NAACP

18. Of the programs enacted by President Lyndon B. Johnson's administration, which was most closely related to John F. Kennedy's legacy?

a. The Economic Opportunity Act
b. The Civil Rights Act
c. The Great Society program
d. All of these were equally related to JFK's legacy.

19. Which statement regarding US international trade policy in the 1990s is *not* correct?

a. In 1994, the General Agreement on Tariffs and Trade (GATT) was approved by Congress.
b. The GATT was between 57 countries who agreed they would remove or reduce many of their tariffs.
c. The GATT created the World Trade Organization (WTO) to settle international trade differences.
d. The NAFTA (North American Free Trade Agreement), ratified in 1994, had originally been set up by George H.W. Bush's administration.

20. Which statement about factors related to the growth of the US economy between 1945 and 1970 is *not* correct?

a. The Baby Boom's greatly increased birth rates contributed to economic growth during this time.
b. The reduction in military spending after World War II contributed to the stronger US economy.
c. Government programs and growing affluence nearly quadrupled college enrollments in 20 years.
d. Increased mobility and bigger families caused fast suburban expansion, especially in the Sunbelt.

21. Which of the following statements regarding immigration to America during the 1980s is *not* true?

a. Twice as many immigrants came to America during the 1980s than during the 1970s.
b. Latin Americans comprised the largest proportion of immigrants to America in the 1980s.
c. Most immigrants to the US in the 1980s were Latin American, Asian, and Caribbean.
d. The 1986 Immigration Reform and Control Act reduced illegal Mexican immigration.

22. Which is *not* correct regarding black activism during the 1960s?
    a. There was a riot in the Los Angeles ghetto of Watts in 1965.
    b. There was a riot involving black activists in Newark, New Jersey, after the Watts riot.
    c. The Mississippi Freedom Democrats unseated that state's delegation at the convention.
    d. There was a riot involving black activists in Detroit, Michigan, after the riot in Watts.

23. What was the earliest written language in Mesopotamia?
    a. Sumerian
    b. Elamite
    c. Akkadian
    d. Aramaic

24. During which of these periods were pyramids *not* built in Egypt?
    a. The Old Kingdom
    b. The Middle Kingdom
    c. The New Kingdom
    d. The Third Dynasty

25. Which of the following is *not* true about the Crusades?
    a. Their purpose was for European rulers to retake the Middle East from Muslims
    b. The Crusades succeeded at European kings' goal of reclaiming the "holy land"
    c. The Crusades accelerated the already incipient decline of the Byzantine Empire
    d. Egypt saw a return as a major Middle Eastern power as a result of the Crusades

26. Which of the following events did *not* contribute to the growth of the Italian Renaissance?
    a. The Black Death killed 1/3 of the population of Europe
    b. The lower classes benefited from the need for laborers
    c. The middle classes developed from a need for services
    d. All these events contributed to the Italian Renaissance

27. Which of the following is *not* correct regarding assumptions of mercantilism?
    a. The money and the wealth of a nation are identical properties
    b. In order to prosper, a nation should try to increase its imports
    c. In order to prosper, a nation should try to increase its exports
    d. Economic protectionism by national governments is advisable

28. Which of the following is *not* true about the English Civil Wars between 1641 and 1651?
    a. These wars all were waged between Royalists and Parliamentarians
    b. The outcome of this series of civil wars was victory for Parliament
    c. These wars legalized Parliament's consent as requisite to monarchy
    d. Two of the wars in this time involved supporters of King Charles I

29. Which of the following choices is/are *not* considered among causes of the French Revolution?
    a. Famines causing malnutrition and starvation
    b. War debt, Court spending, bad monetary system
    c. Resentment against the Catholic Church's rule
    d. Resentment against the Protestant Reformation

30. Which statement best describes the role played by the French economy in causing the 1789 French Revolution?
a. France's very large national debt led to heavy tax burdens on the French peasantry.
b. Nearly sixty percent of annual national expenditures financed luxuries for the French nobility.
c. Reforms in the guild system allowed many peasants to rise to the middle class.
d. The king's attempt to curtail free trade led skilled journeymen to rebel against the monarchy.

31. Which of the following statements is accurate regarding the end of the First World War?
a. The Treaty of Versailles brought peace among all countries involved in the war
b. The Treaty of Versailles contained a clause for establishing the United Nations
c. President Woodrow Wilson had proposed forming a coalition of world nations
d. President Wilson succeeded in getting the USA to ratify the League of Nations

32. How did Russia's participation in World War I influence the Russian Revolution?
a. Civilian suffering and military setbacks served as a catalyst for revolutionary forces.
b. Nicholas III capitalized on battlefield successes to temporarily silence critics.
c. The government eased laws banning collective action by factory workers to appease social discontent about the war.
d. Anti-government protesters temporarily ceased protesting to show patriotism in a difficult war.

33. During the decolonization of the Cold War years, which of the following events occurred chronologically latest?
a. The Eastern Bloc and Satellite states became independent from the Soviet Union
b. Canada became totally independent from British Parliament via the Canada Act
c. The Bahamas, in the Caribbean, became independent from the United Kingdom
d. The Algerian War ended, and Algeria became independent from France

34. Why was U.S. industrialization confined to the Northeast until after the Civil War?
a. Because the Civil War delayed the development of water-powered manufacturing
b. Because the Northeast had faster-running rivers than the rivers found in the South
c. Because Slater's first cotton mill with horse-drawn production lost so much money
d. Because the technical innovations for milling textiles had not as yet been invented

35. Which of the following statements is *not* an accurate statement about the Puritans in England?
a. The Puritans unconditionally gave all their support to the English Reformation
b. The Puritans saw the Church of England as too much like the Catholic Church
c. The Puritans became a chief political power because of the English Civil War
d. The Puritans' clergy mainly departed from the Church of England after 1662

36. Which of the following statements is *not* true about the Gilded Age in America?
a. The Gilded Age was the era of the "robber barons" in the business world
b. The Gilded Age got its name from the excesses of the wealthy upper class
c. The Gilded Age had philanthropy Carnegie called the "Gospel of Wealth"
d. The Gilded Age is a term whose origins have not been identified clearly

37. Which of the following is *not* true about Democracy and the formation of the United States?
  a. The founding fathers stated in the Constitution that the USA would be a democracy
  b. The Declaration of Independence did not dictate democracy but stated its principles
  c. The United States Constitution stipulated that government be elected by the people
  d. The United States Constitution had terms to protect some, but not all, of the people

38. Which of the following statements does *not* describe the average European diet BEFORE the expansion of trade routes?
  a. Europeans ate for survival, not enjoyment.
  b. They had an abundance of preservatives such as salt that could make food last longer.
  c. Grain-based foods such as porridge and bread were staple meals.
  d. Spices were unavailable.

39. Which of these is true concerning the French Revolution, America, and Europe?
  a. When France's revolution spread and they went to war with other European countries, George Washington allied with the French.
  b. During the time period around 1792, American merchants were conducting trading with countries on both sides of the war.
  c. American traders conducted business with various countries, profiting the most from the British West Indies.
  d. The Spanish navy retaliated against America for trading with the French by capturing American trading ships.

40. Which group overtook Rome in the mid-600s B.C. and established much of its infrastructure, including sewers, roads, and fortifications, only to be driven out of the city in 509 B.C.?
  a. Latins.
  b. Etruscans.
  c. Greeks.
  d. Persians.

41. The writers of The Federalist Papers published under the pen name "Publius." Who were the authors?
  a. James Madison, John Jay, and Alexander Hamilton
  b. George Washington, Thomas Jefferson, and James Madison
  c. Alexander Hamilton, Benjamin Franklin, and Thomas Jefferson
  d. Benjamin Franklin, John Jay, and Thomas Jefferson

42. Social studies education has many practical applications. Which of the following is the most direct application of teaching high school seniors the structure of the U.S. government?
  a. Knowledge of the fundamentals of federalism
  b. Informed participation in school elections
  c. Knowledge of a system of checks and balances
  d. Informed participation in U.S. political processes

43. The U.S. government is best understood as a federalist government because:
a. the legislative branch consists of two representative bodies.
b. it is a representative democracy rather than a direct democracy.
c. political power is divided between the federal government and the states.
d. a national Constitution shapes national legislation.

44. One reason the Articles of Confederation created a weak government was because it limited Congress's ability to do what?
a. Declare war
b. Conduct a census
c. Vote
d. Tax

45. The philosophy of the late 17th-18th centuries that influenced the Constitution was from the Age of:
a. Enlightenment
b. Empire
c. Discovery
d. Industry

46. The votes of how many states were needed to ratify the Constitution?
a. Five
b. Ten
c. Nine
d. Seven

47. Virginian ______________ advocated a stronger central government and was influential at the Constitutional Convention.
a. Benjamin Franklin
b. James Madison
c. George Mason
d. Robert Yates

48. Power divided between local and central branches of government is a definition of what term?
a. Bicameralism
b. Checks and balances
c. Legislative oversight
d. Federalism

49. The Senate and the House of Representatives are an example of:
a. Bicameralism
b. Checks and balances
c. Legislative oversight
d. Federalism

50. The Vice President succeeds the President in case of death, illness or impeachment. What is the order of succession for the next three successors, according to the Presidential Succession Act of 1947?

a. President Pro Tempore of the Senate, Secretary of State, and Secretary of Defense
b. Speaker of the House, President Pro Tempore of the Senate, and Secretary of State
c. President Pro Tempore of the Senate, Speaker of the House, and Secretary of State
d. Secretary of State, Secretary of Defense, and Speaker of the House

51. The President has the power to veto legislation. How is this power limited?

I. Congress can override the veto
II. The President cannot line veto
III. The President cannot propose legislation

a. I and III
b. II only
c. I and II
d. I only

52. The civil rights act that outlawed segregation in schools and public places also:

a. Gave minorities the right to vote
b. Established women's right to vote
c. Outlawed unequal voter registration
d. Provided protection for children

53. Which of the following is a power held only by the federal government?

a. The power to levy taxes, borrow money, and spend money
b. The power to award copyrights and patents to people or groups
c. The power to establish the criteria that qualify a person to vote
d. The power to ratify proposed amendments to the Constitution

54. Of the following actions, which one requires a three-fourths majority?

a. State approval of a proposed amendment to the Constitution
b. Submitting a proposal for an amendment to the Constitution
c. Ratification for appointments to the Presidency in the Senate
d. The introduction of charges for an impeachment in the House

55. Which of the following statements is *not* correct about U.S. westward expansion and Manifest Destiny?

a. The idea that U.S. freedom and values should be shared with, even forced upon, as many people as possible had existed for many years.
b. The term "Manifest Destiny" and the idea it represented had been used for many years prior to the 1830s.
c. Many Americans believed that America as a nation should ultimately be extended to include Canada and Mexico.
d. Increased nationalism after the resolution of the War of 1812 and rapid population growth added to Manifest Destiny.

56. Presidential candidates are eligible for public funding if they raise $5,000 per state in how many states?
   a. Twenty
   b. Ten
   c. Twenty-five
   d. Seventeen

57. What judicial system did America borrow from England?
   a. Due process
   b. Federal law
   c. Commerce law
   d. Common law

58. Which of the following is a possible absolute location for New Orleans?
   a. 30° S, 90° E
   b. 30° N, 90° E
   c. 30° S, 90° W
   d. 30° N, 90° W

59. On which type of map are different countries represented in different colors, with no two adjacent countries sharing a color?
   a. Physical map
   b. Political map
   c. Climate map
   d. Contour map

60. Which of the following statements about the equator is true?
   a. It intersects four continents.
   b. It is to the north of both horse latitudes.
   c. It is located at 0° longitude.
   d. It is not very windy.

61. The apparent distance between Greenland and Norway is greatest on a(n)
   a. Mercator Map.
   b. Conic Projection Map.
   c. Contour Map.
   d. Equal-Area Projection Map.

62. Which of the following is *not* a method of representing relief on a physical map?
   a. Symbols
   b. Color
   c. Shading
   d. Contour Lines

63. Which map describes the movement of people, trends, or materials across a physical area?
   a. Political Map
   b. Cartogram
   c. Qualitative Map
   d. Flow-line Map

64. What is the most common type of volcano on earth?
  a. Lava dome
  b. Composite volcano
  c. Shield volcano
  d. Cinder cone

65. Water is continuously recycled in the hydrosphere. By which process does water return to the atmosphere after precipitation?
  a. Percolation
  b. Cohesion
  c. Evaporation
  d. Condensation

66. Which type of rock is formed by extreme heat and pressure?
  a. Limestone
  b. Metamorphic
  c. Sedimentary
  d. Igneous

67. Which part of a hurricane features the strongest winds and greatest rainfall?
  a. Eye wall
  b. Front
  c. Eye
  d. Outward spiral

68. Which of the following are not included in a geographical definition of Southeast Asia?
  a. Myanmar, Laos, Cambodia, and Thailand
  b. Vietnam, the Malay Peninsula, and Brunei
  c. East Malaysia, Indonesia, and the Philippines
  d. These are all geographical parts of Southeast Asia

69. Which of the following exemplifies the multiplier effect of large cities?
  a. The presence of specialized equipment for an industry attracts even more business.
  b. The large population lowers the price of goods.
  c. Public transportation means more people can commute to work.
  d. A local newspaper can afford to give away the Sunday edition.

70. For thousands of years, Africans have cultivated the grasslands south of the Sahara Desert, an area known as the
  a. Qattara Depression.
  b. Great Rift Valley.
  c. Congo Basin.
  d. Sahel.

71. Tracy needs to determine the shortest route between Lima and Lisbon. Which of the following maps should she use?
  a. Azimuthal projection with the North Pole at the center
  b. Azimuthal projection with Lisbon at the center
  c. Robinson projection of the Eastern Hemisphere
  d. Robinson projection of the Western Hemisphere

72. Which of the following countries are separated by a geometric border?
   a. Turkish Cyprus and Greek Cyprus
   b. North Korea and South Korea
   c. France and Spain
   d. England and Ireland

73. During one year in Grassley County, there are 750 births, 350 deaths, 80 immigrations, and 50 emigrations. What is the natural increase rate for this year?
   a. 400
   b. 830
   c. 430
   d. More information is required.

74. Which of the following is *not* one of the world's four major population agglomerations?
   a. North Africa
   b. Eastern North America
   c. South Asia
   d. Europe

75. Which of the following statements concerning choice theory are correct?
   I. Scarcity forces people, including producers, to make choices
   II. Producers make choices and, as a result, face trade-offs
   III. Opportunity cost is one way to measure the cost of a choice
   a. I only
   b. I and II only
   c. II and III only
   d. I, II, and III

76. John Maynard Keynes advocated what?
   a. Supply-side economics
   b. Demand-side economics
   c. Laissez faire economics
   d. The Laffer Curve

77. If a society wants greater income equity, it will:
   a. impose a progressive income tax.
   b. impose high estate taxes.
   c. impose a gift tax.
   d. All of the above

78. Which of the following best defines American GDP?
   a. The value, in American dollars, of all goods and services produced within American borders during one calendar year
   b. The value, in American dollars, of all goods and services produced by American companies during one calendar year
   c. The total value, in American dollars, of all American household incomes during one calendar year
   d. The value, in American dollars, of a "market basket" of goods and services in one year divided by the value of the same market basket in a previous year multiplied by 100

79. Ivy loses her job because her skills as a seamstress are no longer required due to a new piece of machinery that does the work of a seamstress more quickly and for less money. Which type of unemployment is this?

a. Frictional
b. Structural
c. Cyclical
d. Careless

80. Which is considered part of the natural rate of unemployment?

I. Structural unemployment
II. Frictional unemployment
III. Cyclical unemployment

a. I only
b. II only
c. III only
d. I and II only

81. Which of the following is a supply shock likely to produce?

I. An increase in input prices
II. An increase in price levels
III. A decrease in employment
IV. A decrease in GDP

a. I and III only
b. II and IV only
c. I, II, and III only
d. I, II, III, and IV

82. Which of the following are true of the demand curve?

I. It is normally downward sloping
II. It is normally upward sloping
III. It is influenced by the law of diminishing marginal unity
IV. It is unaffected by the law of diminishing marginal unity

a. I and III only
b. I and IV only
c. II and III only
d. II and IV only

83. The price of fleece blankets goes up from \$10 to \$11. At the same time, demand goes down from 1,000 blankets to 800 blankets. Which of the following statements is true?

a. Demand is elastic
b. Demand is inelastic
c. The price elasticity quotient, or $E_d$, is less than 1
d. The price elasticity quotient, or $E_d$, is equal to 1

84. The price of oil drops dramatically, saving soda pop manufacturers great amounts of money spent on making soda pop and delivering their product to market. Prices for soda pop, however, stay the same. This is an example of what?

a. Sticky prices
b. Sticky wages
c. The multiplier effect
d. Aggregate expenditure

85. Which of the following will result if two nations use the theory of comparative advantage when making decisions of which goods to produce and trade?

a. Each nation will make all of their own goods
b. Both nations will specialize in the production of the same specific goods
c. Each nation will specialize in the production of different specific goods
d. Neither nation will trade with one another

86. Which of the following is most likely to benefit from inflation?

a. A bond investor who owns fixed-rate bonds
b. A retired widow with no income other than fixed Social Security payments
c. A person who has taken out a fixed-rate loan
d. A local bank who has loaned money out at fixed rate

*Consider the following table to answer Question 87:*

| Inputs | 1 | 2 | 3 | 4 |
|---|---|---|---|---|
| Output | 20 | 50 | 80 | 100 |

87. What does the data in this table most directly describe?

a. The Law of Diminishing Marginal Returns
b. Law of Increasing Opportunity Cost
c. Law of Demand
d. Consumer surplus

88. How do banks create money?

a. By printing it
b. By taking it out of the Federal Reserve
c. By loaning it out
d. By putting it into the Federal Reserve

89. Which of the following correctly states the equation of exchange?

a. MV = PQ
b. MP x VQ
c. MP / VQ
d. VP = MQ

90. Economics is best defined as the study of what?

a. Scarcity
b. Business
c. Trade
d. Supply and demand

## Constructed Response

1. During the latter half of the $19^{th}$ century, the United States changed into a more and more mobile society. We see this increased mobility in the settling of the West by people from the eastern part of the United States. For many people, this movement westward would bring new opportunities for economic growth; for others this movement meant conflict and the ending of a way of life.

Discuss two reasons why American settlers moved westward. Describe the effect of the railroads on life in the Western United States. Explain how this westward expansion impacted the lives of Native Americans.

2.

Selected Articles From the Articles of Confederation

Article I. "The Style of this Confederacy shall be "The United States of America."

Article II. "Each state retains its sovereignty, freedom and independence, and every power, jurisdiction, and right, which is not by this Confederation expressly delegated to the United States, in Congress assembled."

Article III. "The said States hereby severally enter into a firm league of friendship with each other, for their common defense, the security of their liberties and their mutual and general welfare, binding themselves to assist each other, against all force offered to, or attacks made upon them, or any of them, on account of religion, sovereignty, trade, or any other pretense whatever..."

According to the passage above, what form of government in the United States was established by the Articles of Confederation? Identify two advantages states had under this form of government and describe two reasons this form of government was later replaced by the United States Constitution.

3. A decades-long civil war in China ended in 1949, when a group of communist revolutionaries led by Mao Zedong overthrew Chiang Kai-shek's nationalist government and established the People's Republic of China.

Using your knowledge of world history, write an essay in which you:

- describe two consequences of the Chinese Revolution of 1949
- analyze how each of the consequences you have identified influenced the development of world history

## Answers and Explanations

1. D: Of those countries listed here, the two countries whose respective indigenous populations are not as large as the populations of the other countries are Argentina and Uruguay. Argentina's population is approximately 86.4% of European descent, roughly 8% of mestizo (of mixed European and Amerindian heritage), and an estimated 4% of Arab or East Asian ancestry. Uruguay's population is estimated to be 88% of European descent, 4% of African, and 2% of Asian, with 6% of mestizo ancestry in its rural northwest region Guatemala and Peru (a) have larger indigenous populations. Guatemala, in Central America, has approximately over 40% of its population as indigenous peoples. Peru, in South America, is estimated to have 45% indigenous peoples and 37% partly indigenous peoples for a total of 82%. Ecuador and Bolivia (b) in South America still have indigenous peoples. The population of Ecuador has an estimated 25% indigenous and 65% partly indigenous peoples, for a total of 90%. Paraguay in South America and Mexico in North America (c) both have sizeable indigenous populations. Paraguay's population is estimated to include 95% partly indigenous peoples. Mexico is estimated to have 30% indigenous and 60% partly indigenous peoples in its population for a total of 90%.

2. A: It is not true that England's defeat of the Spanish Armada in 1588 ended their war with Spain. It did establish England's naval dominance and strengthened England's future colonization of the New World, but the actual war between England and Spain did not end until 1604. It is true that Henry VIII's desire to divorce Catherine of Aragon strengthened English expansionism (b). Catherine was Spanish, and Henry split from the Catholic Church because it prohibited divorce. Henry's rejection of his Spanish wife and his subsequent support of the Protestant movement angered King Philip II of Spain and destroyed the formerly close ties between the two countries. When Elizabeth became Queen of England, she supported the Reformation as a Protestant, which also contributed to English colonization (c). Sir Francis Drake, one of the best known English sea captains during this time period, would attack and plunder Spanish ships that had plundered American Indians (d), adding to the enmity between Spain and England. Queen Elizabeth invested in Drake's voyages and gave him her support in claiming territories for England.

3. B: The Virginia Company of London was based in London, not Massachusetts. It had a charter to colonize American land between the Hudson and Cape Fear rivers (c). The other Virginia Company was the Virginia Company of Plymouth, which was based in the American colony of Plymouth, Massachusetts (a). It had a charter to colonize North America between the Potomac River and the northern boundary of Maine (d).

4. C: Hernando Cortes conquered the Mexican Aztecs in 1519. He had several advantages over the Indians, including horses, armor for his soldiers, and guns. In addition, Cortes' troops unknowingly transmitted smallpox to the Aztecs, which devastated their population as they had no immunity to this foreign illness. Vasco Nunez de Balboa (a) was the first European explorer to view the Pacific Ocean when he crossed the Isthmus of Panama in 1513. Juan Ponce de Leon (b) also visited and claimed Florida in Spain's name in 1513. Cabeza de Vaca (d) was one of only four men out of 400 to return from an expedition led by Panfilio de Narvaez in 1528, and was responsible for spreading the story of the Seven Cities of Cibola (the "cities of gold").

5. B: Peter Zenger was an 18th century journalist in New York who was charged with seditious libel after he published articles critical of New York governor William Cosby. His

subsequent acquittal in 1735 established a precedent for American freedom of the press. Options A, C, and D can all be rejected because they do not accurately describe the historical significance of Peter Zenger's trial. Although these options name other important freedoms or rights in American history, these rights or freedoms were not central to Peter Zenger's trial. In particular, note that while answers B, C, and D all list rights contained in the First Amendment to the United States Constitution, only B contains the particular right at issue in the Zenger case.

6. A: The attitudes of American colonists after the 1763 Treaty of Paris ended the French and Indian War were not a direct contributor to the American Revolution. American colonists had a supportive attitude toward Great Britain then, and were proud of the part they played in winning the war. Their good will was not returned by British leaders (b), who looked down on American colonials and sought to increase their imperial power over them. Even in 1761, a sign of Americans' objections to having their liberty curtailed by the British was seen when Boston attorney James Otis argued in court against the Writs of Assistance (c), search warrants to enforce England's mercantilist trade restrictions, as violating the kinds of natural laws espoused during the Enlightenment. Lord George Grenville's aggressive program to defend the North American frontier in the wake of Chief Pontiac's attacks included stricter enforcement of the Navigation Acts, the Proclamation of 1763, the Sugar Act (or Revenue Act), the Currency Act, and most of all the Stamp Act (d). Colonists objected to these as taxation without representation. Other events followed in this taxation dispute, which further eroded Americans' relationship with British government, including the Townshend Acts, the Massachusetts Circular Letter, the Boston Massacre, the Tea Act, and the resulting Boston Tea Party. Finally, with Britain's passage of the Intolerable Acts and the Americans' First Continental Congress, which was followed by Britain's military aggression against American resistance, actual warfare began in 1775. While not all of the colonies wanted war or independence by then, things changed by 1776, and Jefferson's Declaration of Independence was formalized.

7. C: Colonists did find that tea shipped directly by the British East India Company cost less than smuggled Dutch tea, even with tax. The colonists, however, did not buy it. They refused, despite its lower cost, on the principle that the British were taxing colonists without representation (d). It is true that the British East India Company lost money as a result of colonists buying tea smuggled from Holland (a). They sought to remedy this problem by getting concessions from Parliament to ship tea directly to the colonies instead of going through England (b) as the Navigation Acts normally required. Boston Governor Thomas Hutchinson, who sided with Britain, stopped tea ships from leaving the harbor, which after 20 days would cause the tea to be sold at auction. At that time, British taxes on the tea would be paid. On the 19th night after Hutchinson's action, American protestors held the Boston Tea Party, dressing as Indians and dumping all the tea into the harbor to destroy it so it could not be taxed and sold. Many American colonists disagreed with the Boston Tea Party because it involved destroying private property.

8. C: Massachusetts did set a valuable example for other states by stipulating that its constitution should be created via a special convention rather than via the legislature. This way, the constitution would take precedence over the legislature, which would be subject to the rules of the constitution. It is not true that twelve states had new constitutions by the end of 1777 (a). By this time, ten of the states had new constitutions. It is not true that Connecticut and <u>Massachusetts</u> retained their colonial charters minus the British parts (b). Connecticut and <u>Rhode Island</u> were the states that preserved their colonial charters. They

simply removed any parts referring to British rule. Massachusetts did not formalize its new constitution in 1778 (d). This state did not actually finish the process of adopting its new constitution until 1780.

9. D: The Louisiana Purchase actually increased the U.S.'s territory by 100% overnight, not 50%. The Louisiana territory doubled the size of the nation. It is true that Jefferson initially sent a delegation to Paris to see if Napoleon would agree to sell only New Orleans to the United States (a). It is also true that Napoleon, who expected America to encroach on Louisiana, decided to avoid this by offering to sell the entire territory to the U.S. (b). It is likewise true that America only had authority to buy New Orleans. Nevertheless, the delegation accepted Napoleon's offer of all of Louisiana (c).

10. B: Hamilton did not object to U.S. western expansionism, and Burr did not support it. There were certain Federalists other than Hamilton who opposed expansion to the west as a threat to their position within the Union, and these opponents did attempt to organize a movement to secede (a). To get Aaron Burr to champion their cause, they offered to help him run for Governor of New York (c). Hamilton did lead the opposition against Burr's campaign (d).

11. A: The U.S. did carry out a three-pronged invasion of Canada early in the war, but they did not succeed on two fronts. Instead, they lost on all three. Americans did win sea battles against the British early in the war, but were soon beaten back to their homeports and then blockaded by powerful British warships (b). Admiral Perry did defeat the British on Lake Erie on September 10, 1813 (c). Perry's victory allowed William Henry Harrison to invade Canada (d) in October of 1813, where he defeated British and Indians in the Battle of the Thames.

12. D: Political corruption was not an immediate effect of the rapid urban growth during this time. The accelerated growth of cities in America did soon result in services being unable to keep up with that growth. The results of this included deficiencies in clean water delivery and garbage collection, causing poor sanitation (a). That poor sanitation led to outbreaks of cholera and typhus, as well as typhoid fever epidemics (b). Police and fire fighting services could not keep up with the population increases, and were often inadequate (c).

13. D: All the laws (d) named were instrumental in spurring westward migration to the Great Plains. The Homestead Act (a), passed in 1862, gave settlers 160 acres of land at no monetary cost in exchange for a commitment to cultivating the land for five years. The Timber Culture Act (b), passed in 1873, gave the settlers 160 acres more of land in exchange for planting trees on one quarter of the acreage. The Desert Land Act (c), passed in 1877, allowed buyers who would irrigate the land to buy 640 acres for only 25 cents an acre. Thus, (d), all of these laws were instrumental in spurring westward migration to the Great Plains during that period, is correct.

14. B: Germany's declaration of war on Russia in 1914, following the assassination of Archduke Ferdinand (b), did not contribute to ending American neutrality in World War I. Once Germany declared war, England, France, Italy, Russia, and Japan joined as the Allied Powers against the Central Powers of Germany and Austria-Hungary, and US President Woodrow Wilson declared America's neutrality. When Germany designated the area surrounding the British Isles as a war zone in February 1913 (a), and warned all ships from

neutral countries to stay out of the zone, an end to American neutrality was prompted. President Wilson's responded to Germany's declaration by proclaiming that America would hold Germany responsible for any American losses of life or property. When Germany sank the British passenger vessel *Lusitania,* 128 American passengers were killed (c). This further eroded Wilson's resolve to remain neutral. In February 1917, Germany declared unrestricted submarine warfare on any ship in the war zone (d); this signified that ships from any country would face German attack.

15. A: The postwar conference that brought US-Soviet differences to light was (a) the Potsdam conference in July of 1945. The conference at Yalta (b), in February of 1945, resulted in the division of Germany into Allied-controlled zones. The Dumbarton Oaks conference (c) (1944) established a Security Council, on which with the US, England, Soviet Union, France, and China served as the five permanent members. Each of the permanent members had veto power, and a General Assembly, with limited power, was also established. The Tehran conference (d) included FDR's proposal for a new international organization to take the place of the League of Nations. This idea would later be realized in the form of the United Nations.

16. D: In 1956, Egypt did not attack Israel. On October 29, 1956, Israel attacked Egypt. England and France did join this war within two days. It is true that Egyptian President Gamal Abdul Nasser refused to take America's side in the Cold War (a). In reaction to his refusal, President Eisenhower's administration pulled its funding from the Aswan Dam project in Egypt (b). Nasser then nationalized the British-owned Suez Canal (c).

17. C: The person or group not instrumental in advancing civil rights and desegregation immediately after WWII was (c), Congress. As African American soldiers came home from the war, racial discord increased. President Harry Truman (a) appointed a Presidential Committee on Civil Rights in 1946. This committee published a report recommending that segregation and lynching be outlawed by the federal government. However, Congress ignored this report and took no action. Truman then used his presidential powers to enforce desegregation of the military and policies of "fair employment" in federal civil service jobs. The National Association for the Advancement of Colored People (NAACP) (d) brought lawsuits against racist and discriminatory practices, and in resolving these suits, the Supreme Court (b) further eroded segregation. For example, the Supreme Court ruled that primaries allowing only whites would be illegal, and it ended the segregation of interstate bus lines. The landmark civil rights laws were not passed by Congress until the 1960s.

18. B: Of the programs enacted by Johnson, the one most closely related to JFK's legacy was (b), the Civil Rights Act, which Johnson pushed through Congress using allusions to Kennedy's and his goals. While Kennedy received congressional backing for a raise in minimum wage and public housing improvements, his efforts regarding civil rights were thwarted by conservative Republicans and Southern Democrats in Congress. However, as the Civil Rights movement progressed through the campaigns of the Freedom Riders, Kennedy developed a strong commitment to the cause. The Economic Opportunity Act gave almost $1 billion to wage Johnson's War on Poverty. The Great Society (c) was Johnson's name for his comprehensive reform program which included a variety of legislation.

19. B: The GATT countries did agree to abolish or decrease many of their tariffs, but this agreement did not include only 57 countries. It was much larger, including a total of 117

countries. The GATT was approved by Congress in 1994 (a). In addition to having 117 countries agree to increase free trade, the GATT also set up the World Trade Organization (WTO) for the purpose of settling any differences among nations related to trade (c). Another instance of free trade policy established in the 1990s was the Senate's ratification of NAFTA. The negotiation of this agreement was originally made by the first Bush administration, with President Bush and the leaders of Canada and Mexico signing it in 1992 (d), but it still needed to be ratified.

20. B: There was not a reduction in military spending after the war. Although the manufacturing demand for war supplies and the size of the military decreased, the government had increased military spending from $10 billion in 1947 to more than $50 billion by 1953—a more than fivefold increase. This increase strengthened the American economy. Other factors contributing to the strengthened economy included the significantly higher birth rates during the Baby Boom (a) from 1946 to 1957, which stimulated the growth of the building and automotive industries by increased demand. Government programs, such as the GI Bill (the Servicemen's Readjustment Act of 1944), other veterans' benefits, and the National Defense Education Act all encouraged college enrollments, which increased by nearly four times (c). Additionally, larger families, increased mobility and low-interest loans offered to veterans led to suburban development and growth (d) as well as an increased home construction.

21. D: The statement that the 1986 Immigration Reform and Control Act reduced illegal Mexican immigration is not true. This legislation punished employers with sanctions for hiring undocumented employees, but despite this the illegal immigration of Mexicans to America was largely unaffected by the law. It is true that twice as many people immigrated to America in the 1980s than in the 1970s (a): the number reached over nine million in the 80s. It is true that the majority of immigrants were Latin American (b). In addition to Latin Americans, other large groups of immigrants in the 1980s were Asians and Caribbean inhabitants (c).

22. C: The Mississippi Freedom Democratic Party did attend the 1964 Democratic convention; however, they were unable garner Johnson's support to unseat the regular delegation from Mississippi. A riot did break out in Watts in 1965 (a), and in the following three years, more riots occurred in Newark, N.J. (b) and in Detroit, Michigan (d). These riots were manifestations of the frustrations experienced by blacks regarding racial inequities in American society.

23. A: The earliest written language in Mesopotamia was Sumerian. Ancient Sumerians began writing this language around 3500 B.C.E. Elamite (b), from Iran, was the language spoken by the ancient Elamites and was the official language of the Persian Empire from the 6th to 4th centuries B.C.E. Written Linear Elamite was used for a very short time in the late 3rd century B.C.E. The written Elamite cuneiform, used from about 2500 to 331 B.C.E., was an adaptation of the Akkadian (c) cuneiform. Akkadian is the earliest found Semitic language. Written Akkadian cuneiform first appeared in texts by circa 2800 B.C.E., and full Akkadian texts appeared by circa 2500 B.C.E. The Akkadian cuneiform writing system is ultimately a derivative of the ancient Sumerian cuneiform writing system, although these two spoken languages were not related linguistically. Aramaic (d) is another Semitic language, but unlike Akkadian, Aramaic is not now extinct. Old Aramaic, the written language of the Old Testament and the spoken language used by Jesus Christ, was current from c. 1100-200 C.E. Middle Aramaic, used from 200-1200 C.E., included literary Syriac

(Christian groups developed the writing system of Syriac in order to be able to write spoken Aramaic) and was the written language of the Jewish books of Biblical commentary (Namely, the Talmud, the Targum, and the Midrash). Modern Aramaic has been used from 1200 to the present.

24. C: The New Kingdom was the period during which no more pyramids were built in Egypt. The Pyramids were built between the years of 2630 and 1814 B.C.E., and the New Kingdom spanned from circa 1550-1070 B.C. As a result, the last pyramid was built approximately 264 years before the New Kingdom began. 2630 B.C.E. marked the beginning of the reign of the first Pharaoh, Djoser, who had the first pyramid built at Saqqara. 1814 B.C.E. marked the end of the reign of the last Pharaoh, Amenemhat III, who had the last pyramid built at Hawara. In between these years, a succession of pharaohs built many pyramids. The Old Kingdom (a) encompasses both the Third (d) and Fourth Dynasties; therefore, both choices encompass pyramid-building periods. Djoser's had his first pyramid built during the Third Dynasty (d). The Pharaohs Kufu, Khafre, and Menkaure, respectively, build the famous Pyramids of Giza during the Fourth Dynasty during their reigns at different times between circa 2575 and 2467 B.C.E., the period of the Fourth Dynasty. The Middle Kingdom (b) encompassed the 11th through 14th Dynasties, from circa 2080 to 1640 B.C.E.—also within the time period (2630-1814 B.C.E.) when pyramids were built by the Pharaohs.

25. B: It is not true that the Crusades succeeded at Christians' reclaiming the "holy land" (the Middle East) from Muslims. Despite their number (nine not counting the Northern Crusades) and longevity (1095-1291 not counting later similar campaigns), the Crusades never accomplished this purpose (a). While they did not take back the Middle East, the Crusades did succeed in exacerbating the decline of the Byzantine Empire (c), which lost more and more territory to the Ottoman Turks during this period. In addition, the Crusades resulted in Egypt's rise once again to become a major power (d) of the Middle East as it had been in the past.

26. D: All these events contributed to the Italian Renaissance. After the Black Death killed a third of Europe's population (a), the survivors were mainly upper classes with more money to spend on art, architecture, and other luxuries. The plague deaths also resulted in a labor shortage, thereby creating more work opportunities for the surviving people in lower classes (b). As a result, these survivors' positions in society appreciated. Once plague deaths subsided and population growth in Europe began to reassert itself, a greater demand existed for products and services. At the same time, the number of people available to provide these products and services was still smaller than in the past. Consequently, more merchants, artisans, and bankers emerged in order to provide the services and products people wanted, thereby creating a class of citizens between the lower class laborers and the upper class elite (c).

27. B: In order to prosper, a nation should not try to increase its imports. Mercantilism is an economic theory including the idea that prosperity comes from a positive balance of international trade. For any one nation to prosper, that nation should increase its exports (c) but decrease its imports. Exporting more to other countries while importing less from them will give a country a positive trade balance. This theory assumes that money and wealth are identical (a) assets of a nation. Mercantilism dictates that a nation's government should apply a policy of economic protectionism (d) by stimulating more exports and suppressing imports. Some ways to do accomplish this task have included granting

subsidies for exports and imposing tariffs on imports. Mercantilism can be regarded as essentially the opposite of the free trade policies that have been encouraged in more recent years.

28. C: It is not true that the English Civil Wars between 1641 and 1651 legalized Parliament's consent as a requirement for a monarch to rule England. These wars did establish this idea as a precedent, but the later Glorious Revolution of 1688 actually made it legal that a monarch could not rule without Parliamentary consent. The wars from 1641-1651 were all fought between Royalists who supported an absolute monarchy and Parliamentarians who supported the joint government of a parliamentary monarchy (a). Parliament was the victor (b) in 1651 at the Battle of Worcester. As a result of this battle, King Charles I was executed, and King Charles II was exiled. In the first of these civil wars, from 1642-1646, and the second, from 1648-1649, supporters of King Charles I (d) fought against supporters of the Long Parliament.

29. D: Resentment against the Protestant Reformation was not a cause given for the French Revolution. Choices (a), (b), and (c) are just a few among many causes cited for the war. Famines caused malnutrition and even starvation among the poorest people (a). Escalating bread prices contributed greatly to the hunger. Louis XV had amassed a great amount of debt from spending money on many wars in addition to the American Revolution. Military failures as well as a lack of social services for veterans exacerbated these debts. In addition, the Court of Louis XVI and Marie Antoinette spent excessively and obviously on luxuries even while people in the country were starving, and France's monetary system was outdated, inefficient, and thus unable to manage the national debt (b). Much of the populace greatly resented the Catholic Church's control of the country (c). However, there was not great resentment against the Protestant Reformation (d); there were large minorities of Protestants in France, who not only exerted their influence on government institutions, but undoubtedly also contributed to the resentment of the Catholic Church.

30. A: In the 1780s, the French national debt was very high. The French nobility adamantly resisted attempts by King Louis XVI to reform tax laws, which led to a high tax burden on the French peasantry. The French government spent almost 50% of its national expenditures on debt-related payments during the 1780s; thus it could not and did not spend almost 60% to finance luxuries for the French nobility. This eliminates choice B. King Louis XVI temporarily banned the guild system to bolster, rather than stifle, free trade. Because this system gave skilled craftsmen economic advantages, journeymen opposed ending the system. This eliminates choice D. Regardless of the status of guilds before the French Revolution, French society did not offer many opportunities for upward social mobility. Few peasants were able to advance. This eliminates choice C.

31. C: The only accurate statement about the end of WWI is that President Wilson had proposed that the nations of the world form a coalition to prevent future world wars. While he did not give the coalition a name, he clearly expressed his proposal that such a group form in the fourteenth of his Fourteen Points. The Treaty of Versailles (1919) did not bring peace among all countries involved in the war (a); Germany and the United States arrived at a separate peace in 1921. Furthermore, the Treaty of Versailles did not contain a clause for establishing the United Nations (b); it contained a clause for establishing the League of Nations. The League of Nations was created as dictated by the treaty, but when the Second World War proved that this group had failed to prevent future world wars, it was replaced

by the United Nations after World War II. President Wilson did not succeed in getting the USA to ratify the League of Nations (d).

32. A: Russian's involvement in World War I brought social tension in Russia to a head. Contributing factors included military defeats and civilian suffering. Prior to Russia entering the war, Russian factory workers could legally strike, but during the war, it was illegal for them to act collectively. This eliminates answer C. Protests continued during World War I, and the Russian government was overthrown in 1917. This eliminates answer D. Answer B can be rejected because World War I did not go well for the Russian Army; Nicholas III, therefore, had no successes upon which to capitalize.

33. A: The latest occurring decolonization event was the Eastern Bloc and Soviet Satellite states of Armenia, Azerbaijan, Estonia, Georgia, Kazakhstan, Kyrgyzstan, Latvia, Lithuania, Moldova, Russia, Tajikistan, Turkmenistan, Ukraine, and Uzbekistan all became independent from the Soviet Union in 1991. (Note: This was the last decolonization of the Cold War years, as the end of the Soviet Union marked the end of the Cold War.) Canada completed its independence from British Parliament via the Canada Act (b) in 1982. In the Caribbean, the Bahamas gained independence from the United Kingdom (c) in 1973. Algeria won its independence from France when the Algerian War of Independence, begun in 1954, ended in 1962 (d).

34. B: U.S. industrialization was confined to the Northeast until after the Civil War because the Northeast had faster-running rivers than the South. The earliest American factories used horse-drawn machines. When waterpower was developed and proved superior, the Northeast's faster rivers were more suited to water-powered mills than the South's slower rivers. The war did not delay the development of water power (a). Waterpower was developed before the Civil War in the late 1790s. Steam power, a more efficient alternative to water power, was developed after the Civil War and eventually replaced waterpower. With steam-powered engines, industry could spread to the South, since steam engines did not depend on rapidly running water like water-powered engines. While British emigré Samuel Slater's first cotton mill using horse-drawn production did lose a lot of money (c), this was not a reason for industrial delay. In fact, Slater's Beverly Cotton Manufactory in Massachusetts, the first American cotton mill, in spite of its financial problems, was successful in both its volume of cotton production and in developing the water-powered technology that ultimately would succeed the horse-drawn method. Slater's second cotton mill in Pawtucket, Rhode Island, was water-powered. Industrial delay was not because milling technology had not yet been invented (d). Slater learned of new textile manufacturing techniques as a youth in England, and he brought this knowledge to America in 1789. Resistance of Southern owners of plantations and slaves did not slow the spread of industrialism. Rather, as seen in (b) above, the South did not have the geographic capability to sustain waterpower. Once steam power was developed, the South joined in industrialization.

35. A: The inaccurate statement is the Puritans unconditionally supported the English Reformation. While they agreed with the Reformation in principle, they felt that it had not pursued those principles far enough and should make greater reforms. Similarly, they felt that the Church of England (or Anglican Church), though it had separated from the Catholic Church in the Protestant Reformation, still allowed many practices they found too much like Catholicism (b). The Puritans did become a chief political power in England because of the first English Civil War (c) between Royalists and Parliamentarians. The Royalists had a

profound suspicion of the radical Puritans. Among the Parliament's elements of resistance, the strongest was that of the Puritans. They joined in the battle initially for ostensibly political reasons as others had, but soon they brought more attention to religious issues. Following the Restoration in 1660 and the Uniformity Act of 1662, thereby restoring the Church of England to its pre-English Civil War status, the great majority of Puritan clergy defected from the Church of England (d).

36. D: It is not true that the Gilded Age is a term whose origins have not been identified clearly. In 1873, Mark Twain and Charles Dudley Warner co-authored a book entitled The Gilded Age: A Tale of Today. Twain and Warner first coined this term to describe the extravagance and excesses of America's wealthy upper class (b), who became richer than ever due to industrialization. Furthermore, the Gilded Age was the era of the "robber barons" (a) such as John D. Rockefeller, Cornelius Vanderbilt, J.P. Morgan, and others. Because they accumulated enormous wealth through extremely aggressive and occasionally unethical monetary manipulations, critics dubbed them "robber barons" because they seemed to be elite lords of robbery. While these business tycoons grasped huge fortunes, some of them—such as Andrew Carnegie and Andrew Mellon—were also philanthropists, using their wealth to support and further worthy causes such as literacy, education, health care, charities, and the arts. They donated millions of dollars to fund social improvements. Carnegie himself dubbed this large philanthropic movement the "Gospel of Wealth" (c).

37. A: It is not true that the founding fathers specifically stated in the Constitution that the USA would be a democracy. The founding fathers wanted the new United States to be founded on principles of liberty and equality, but they did not specifically describe these principles with the term "Democracy." Thus, the Declaration of Independence, like the Constitution after it, did not stipulate a democracy, although both did state the principles of equality and freedom (b). The Constitution also provided for the election of the new government (c), and for protection of the rights of some, but not all, of the people (d). Notable exceptions at the time were black people and women. Only later were laws passed to protect their rights over the years.

38. B: Preservatives such as salt were only introduced to the European diet after trade routes opened and these goods could be brought to Europe.

39. B: In 1792, when the French Revolution turned into European war, American traders conducted business with both sides. It is not true that Washington allied with the French (a) at this time. Washington issued a Proclamation of Neutrality in 1792 when the French went to war with European countries. While they did trade with both sides, American merchants profited the most from the French West Indies, not the British West Indies (c). The Spanish navy did not retaliate against America for trading with the French (d). Though Spain was an ally of Britain, it was the British who most often seized American ships and forced their crews to serve the British navy.

40. B: The Etruscans were from a kingdom to the north that seized control of Rome from the Latins in the mid-600s B.C. They began urbanizing the settlement, improving roads, adding drainage systems, etc. They were driven out of the region in 509 B.C. during an uprising of the Latins.

41. A: James Madison, John Jay, and Alexander Hamilton published The Federalist in the Independent Journal in New York. It was a response to the Anti-Federalists in New York,

who were slow to ratify the Constitution because they feared it gave the central government too much authority.

42. D: A practical application of content learned involves action, not merely knowledge. Options A and C, although they describe content that students would reasonably learn in a class or unit on the structure of the U.S. government, do not describe applications of content, or applications of a social studies education. Therefore options A and C can both be rejected. Option B does involve action and not merely the acquisition of knowledge. However, it is not as directly tied to learning the structure of the U.S. government as option D, informed participation in U.S. political processes. This is because informed participation in school elections is quite possible without knowing the structure of the U.S. government. Informed participation in U.S. political processes requires knowledge of the structure of the U.S. government (i.e., voting on an issue requires an understanding of where a given candidate stands on that issue).

43. C: A federalist system of government is a government under which power is shared by a central authority and sub-components of the federation. In the United States in particular, power is shared by the federal government and the individual states. Option A, that the legislative branch consists of two representative bodies (the House of Representatives and the Senate) is true, of course, but does not describe a uniquely federalist structure. Rather, it describes the concept of bicameralism. Option A may thus be eliminated. Option B, likewise, describes different types of democracy but not federalism. B can thus be eliminated. Regarding option D, this statement is also true (the U.S. Constitution shapes national legislation) but it is not a descriptive statement of the federalist system because the statement makes no mention that power is shared by the states.

44. D: Congress did not have the authority to levy taxes under the Articles of Confederation. Without the ability to levy taxes, there was no way to finance programs, which weakened the government.

45. A: The Age of Enlightenment was a time of scientific and philosophical achievement. Also called the Age of Reason, human thought and reason were prized.

46. C: The Constitution was not ratified immediately. Only five states accepted it in early 1788; Massachusetts, New York, Rhode Island, and Virginia were originally opposed to the Constitution. Rhode Island reluctantly accepted it in 1790.

47. B: James Madison was a close friend of Thomas Jefferson and supported a stronger central government. George Mason and Robert Yates were both against expanding federal authority over the states. Benjamin Franklin was a proponent of a strong federal government, but he was from Massachusetts.

48. D: Some of the men who helped frame the Constitution believed the central government needed to be stronger than what was established under the Articles of Confederation. Others were against this and feared a strong federal government. A system of checks and balances was established to prevent the central government from taking too much power. This arrangement is known as federalism.

49. A: The Senate and House of Representatives make up a bicameral legislature. The Great Compromise awarded seats in the Senate equally to each state, while the seats in the House of Representatives were based on population.

50. B: The Presidential Succession Act lists the Speaker of the House, President Pro Tempore of the Senate, and Secretary of State next in succession after the Vice President. However, anyone who succeeds as President must meet all of the legal qualifications.

51. C: The President has the power to veto legislation directly or use a pocket veto by not signing a bill within ten days after receiving it. Congress adjourns during this time period. A veto can be overridden if two-thirds of the House and the two-thirds of the Senate both agree. The President must veto a complete bill and does not have the authority to veto sections or lines.

52. C: The Civil Rights Act of 1964 affected the Jim Crow laws in the Southern states. Many minorities suffered under unfair voting laws and segregation. President Lyndon Johnson signed the Civil Rights Act of 1964 into law after the 1963 assassination of President Kennedy, who championed the reform.

53. B: Only the federal government has the power to give copyrights and patents to individuals or companies. The power to levy taxes, borrow money, and spend money (a) is a power shared by federal and state governments. The power to set the criteria that qualify individuals to vote (c) is a power given to state governments only. The power to ratify amendments proposed to the Constitution (d) is a power of only the state governments.

54. A: The action that needs a three-fourths majority vote is state approval of a proposed constitutional amendment. Proposing a constitutional amendment (b) requires a two-thirds majority vote. Ratifying presidential appointments in the Senate (c) also requires a two-thirds majority vote. Introducing charges for impeachment in the House of Representatives (d) requires a simple majority vote.

55. B: The term "Manifest Destiny" had not been used for many years before the 1830s. This term was coined in 1844. However, it is true that the idea this term expressed had been around for many years before that (a). It is also true that many Americans believed Manifest Destiny would mean America would ultimately encompass Canada and Mexico (c). Factors contributing to Manifest Destiny included the rise in nationalism that followed the War of 1812 and the population growth that increased that nationalism (d).

56. A: Presidential candidates are eligible for a match from the federal government (with a $250 per contribution limit) if they can privately raise $5,000 per state in twenty states. Candidates who accept public money agree to limit spending. Candidates who do not accept matching funds are free to use the money they raise privately.

57. D: America is a common law country because English common law was adopted in all states except Louisiana. Common law is based on precedent, and changes over time. Each state develops its own common laws.

58. D: The only answer choice that represents a possible absolute location for New Orleans is 30° N, 90° W. When a location is described in terms of its placement on the global grid, it is customary to put the latitude before the longitude. New Orleans is north of the equator, so

it has to be in the Northern Hemisphere. In addition, it is west of the prime meridian, which runs through Greenwich, England, among other places. So, New Orleans must be in the Western Hemisphere. It is possible, then, to deduce that 30° N, 90° W is the only possible absolute location for New Orleans.

59. B: On a political map, countries are represented in different colors, and countries that share a border are not given the same color. This is so that the borders between countries will be distinct. Political maps are used to illustrate those aspects of a country that have been determined by people: the capital, the provincial and national borders, and the large cities. Political maps sometimes include major physical features like rivers and mountains, but they are not intended to display all such information. On a physical, climate, or contour map, however, the borders between nations are more incidental. Colors are used on these maps to represent physical features, areas with similar climate, etc. It is possible that colors will overrun the borders and be shared by adjacent countries.

60. D: Around the world, the area around the equator is known for a relative lack of wind. Indeed, the equatorial belt is sometimes called the doldrums because the constant warm water encourages the air to rise gently. To the north and south, however, there are trade winds that can become quite violent. The equator only intersects three continents: Asia, Africa, and South America. It is in between the north and south horse latitudes, which are belts known for calm winds. Finally, the equator is located at 0° latitude, not longitude, though the 0° line of longitude does intersect the equator.

61. A: The apparent distance between Greenland and Norway will be greatest on a Mercator map. The Mercator map is a type of cylindrical projection map in which lines of latitude and longitude are transferred onto a cylindrical shape, which is then cut vertically and laid flat. For this reason, distances around the poles will appear increasingly great. The Mercator map is excellent for navigation because a straight line drawn on it represents a single compass reading. In a conic projection map, on the other hand, a hemisphere of the globe is transposed onto a cone, which is then cut vertically (that is, from rim to tip) and laid flat. The apparent distances on a conic projection will be smallest at the 45th parallel. A contour map uses lines to illustrate the features of a geographic area. For example, the lines on an elevation contour map connect areas that have the same altitude. An equal-area projection map represents landmasses in their actual sizes. To make this possible, the shapes of the landmasses are manipulated slightly, and the map is interrupted (divided into more than one part).

62. A: Symbols are not used to represent relief on a physical map. A physical map is dedicated to illustrating the landmasses and bodies of water in a specific region, so symbols do not provide enough detail. Color, shading, and contour lines, on the other hand, are able to create a much more complicated picture of changes in elevation, precipitation, etc. Changes in elevation are known in geography as relief.

63. D: A flow-line map describes the movement of people, trends, or materials across a physical area. The movements depicted on a flow-line map are typically represented by arrows. In more advanced flow-line maps, the width of the arrow corresponds to the quantity of the motion. Flow-line maps usually declare the span of time that is being represented. A political map depicts the man-made aspects of geography, such as borders and cities. A cartogram adjusts the size of the areas represented according to some variable. For instance, a cartogram of wheat production would depict Iowa as being much larger than

Alaska. A qualitative map uses lines, dots, and other symbols to illustrate a particular point. For example, a qualitative map might be used to demonstrate the greatest expansion of the Persian Empire.

64. B: The composite volcano, sometimes called the stratovolcano, is the most common type of volcano on earth. A composite volcano has steep sides, so the explosions of ash, pumice, and silica are often accompanied by treacherous mudslides. Indeed, it is these mudslides that cause most of the damage associated with composite volcano eruptions. Krakatoa and Mount Saint Helens are examples of composite volcanoes. A lava dome is a round volcano that emits thick lava very slowly. A shield volcano, one example of which is Mt. Kilauea in Hawaii, emits a small amount of lava over an extended period of time. Shield volcanoes are not known for violent eruptions. A cinder cone has steep sides made of fallen cinders, which themselves are made of the lava that intermittently shoots into the air.

65. C: After precipitation, the heat of the sun causes evaporation, a process by which water molecules change from a liquid to a gas, ultimately returning to the atmosphere. The other options describe processes that pertain to properties of water, but not to water's return to the atmosphere. Percolation is the process by which water moves down through soil. Cohesion (specifically, structural cohesion) is the property of matter by which the molecules in a single substance stay together. Condensation is the process by which matter changes from a gas to a liquid; after evaporation, molecules of water form rain droplets through condensation.

66. B: Metamorphic rock is formed by extreme heat and pressure. This type of rock is created when other rocks are somehow buried within the earth, where they are subject to a dramatic rise in pressure and temperature. Slate and marble are both metamorphic rocks. Metamorphic rocks are created by the other two main types of rock: sedimentary and igneous. Sedimentary rock is formed when dirt and other sediment is washed into a bed, covered over by subsequent sediment, and compacted into rock. Depending on how they are formed, sedimentary rocks are classified as organic, clastic, or chemical. Igneous rocks are composed of cooled magma, the molten rock that emerges from volcanoes. Basalt and granite are two common varieties of igneous rock.

67. A: The eye wall of a hurricane has the strongest winds and the greatest rainfall. The eye wall is the tower-like rim of the eye. It is from this wall that clouds extend out, which are seen from above as the classic outward spiral pattern. A hurricane front is the outermost edge of its influence; although there will be heavy winds and rain in this area, the intensity will be relatively small. The eye of a hurricane is actually a place of surprising peace. In this area, dry and cool air rushes down to the ground or sea. Once there, the air is caught up in the winds of the eye wall and is driven outward at a furious pace.

68. D: These are all geographically parts of Southeast Asia. The countries of Myanmar (Burma), Laos, Cambodia, and Thailand (a) are considered Mainland Southeast Asia, as are Vietnam and the Malay Peninsula (b). Brunei (b), East Malaysia, Indonesia, and the Philippines (c) are considered Maritime Southeast Asia, as are Singapore and Timor-Leste. The Seven Sister States of India are also considered to be part of Southeast Asia, geographically and culturally. (The Seven Sister States of India are Arunachal Pradesh, Assam, Nagaland, Meghalaya, Manipur, Tripura, and Mizoram, which all have contiguous borders in northeastern India.)

69. A: One example of the multiplier effect of large cities would be if the presence of specialized equipment for an industry attracted even more business. Large cities tend to grow even larger for a number of reasons: they have more skilled workers, they have greater concentrations of specialized equipment, and they have already-functioning markets. These factors all make it easier for a business to begin operations in a large city than elsewhere. Thus, the populations and economic productivity of large cities tend to grow quickly. Some governments have sought to mitigate this trend by clustering groups of similar industries in smaller cities.

70. D: The Sahel, a belt of grasslands just south of the Sahara Desert, has long been a focus of agricultural efforts in Africa. This semiarid region has provided sustenance to people and animals for thousands of years. In the last thousand years, stores of salt and gold were found there, giving rise to empires in Ghana and Mali. Changes in climate have expanded the Sahara, however, and pushed the Sahel farther south. The Qattara Depression is a low-lying desert in Egypt. The Great Rift Valley is a region of faults and rocky hills that extends along the southeastern coast of Africa. The Congo Basin is a repository of sediment from the Ubangi and Congo rivers. It is in the northern half of what is now called the Democratic Republic of the Congo.

71. B: To determine the shortest route between Lima and Lisbon, Tracy should use an azimuthal projection with Lisbon at the center. An azimuthal projection depicts one hemisphere of the globe as a circle. A straight line drawn from the center of the map to any point represents the shortest possible distance between those two points. Tracy could obtain her objective, then, with an azimuthal projection in which either Lisbon or Lima were at the center. If the North Pole were at the center, the map would not include Lima because this city is in the Southern Hemisphere. A Robinson projection approximates the sizes and shapes of landmasses but does distort in some ways, particularly near the poles.

72. B: North Korea and South Korea are separated by a geometric border, meaning that the boundary between the two nations is a straight line drawn on a map, without respect to landforms. Specifically, the boundary between the Koreas is the 38th parallel. Another example of a geometric border lies between the continental United States and Canada. The Turkish Cyprus–Greek Cyprus border is anthropogeographic, or drawn according to cultural reasons. The border between France and Spain is physiographic-political, a combination of the Pyrenees Mountains and European history. The Irish Sea separates England from Ireland.

73. D: More information is required to calculate the natural increase rate for Grassley County during this year. Natural increase rate is the growth in population measured as the surplus of live births over deaths for every thousand people. The calculation of natural increase rate does not take account of immigration or emigration. The natural increase rate for Grassley County cannot be calculated because the original population of the county is not given. As an example, if the beginning population of the county had been 10,000, the natural increase rate would be 40; 400 * 1,000/10,000 = 40.

74. A: North Africa is not one of the world's four major population agglomerations. These are eastern North America, South Asia, East Asia, and Europe. The largest of these is East Asia, which encompasses Korea, Japan, and the major cities of China. The second-largest population agglomeration is South Asia, which includes India and Pakistan. Most of the population in this area is near the coasts. The European agglomeration is spread across the

largest piece of land, while the much smaller agglomeration in eastern North America is primarily focused on the string of cities from Boston to Washington, DC.

75. D: It is true that scarcity causes producers (and other people) to make choices. Producers must choose what to produce with limited resources. It is also true that the choices a producer makes when faced with scarcity come with trade-offs. There are advantages and disadvantages to different production decisions. And, finally, calculating the opportunity cost of a choice provides a manner with which to measure the consequence of a choice and compare that against the consequence of other choices.

76. B: John Maynard Keynes argued that government could help revitalize a recessionary economy by increasing government spending and therefore increasing aggregate demand. This is known as demand-side economics.

77. D: If a society wants greater income equity, it will impose a progressive income tax, which taxes the wealthy at a higher rate; an inheritance tax, which prevents the wealthy from passing all their wealth on to the next generation; and a gift tax, which prevents the wealthy from simply giving their wealth away.

78. A: Answer B is a definition of gross national product, and answers C and D define other economic measures.

79. B: Structural unemployment is unemployment that results from a mismatch of job skills or location. In this case, Ivy's job skill—her ability to work as a seamstress—is no longer desired by employers. Frictional and cyclical are other forms of unemployment; economists do not use the term careless unemployment.

80. D: It is believed that some level of frictional and structural unemployment will always exist, and that the best economists (and politicians) can hope for is to reduce cyclical unemployment to zero. Therefore, frictional and structural unemployment are sometimes referred to as natural unemployment, meaning unemployment that naturally exists within an economy.

81. D: A supply shock is caused when there is a dramatic increase in input prices. This causes an increase in price levels and decreases in employment and GDP. A supply shock causes the AS curve to move to the left (in).

82. A: As people have more and more of something, they value it less and less. This is the law of diminishing marginal utility, and it is what causes the downward slope of the demand curve.

83. A: The change in demand is 20% (1,000 – 800 = 200), and the change in price is 10% ($11 - $10 = $1). Because the change in demand is greater than the change in price, the demand is considered elastic. In this case, the price elasticity quotient is greater than 1.

84. A: The phenomenon of "sticky prices" refers to prices that stay the same even though it seems they should change (either increasing or decreasing).

85. C: When a nation follows the theory of comparative advantage, it specializes in producing the goods and services it can make at a lower opportunity cost and then engages in trade to obtain other goods.

86. C: A person who has taken out a fixed-rate loan can benefit from inflation by paying back the loan with dollars that are less valuable than they were when the loan was taken out. In the other examples, inflation harms the individual or entity.

87. A: The input and output data illustrates the Law of Diminishing Marginal Returns, which states that as inputs are added during production, there eventually comes a time when increased inputs coincide with a decrease in marginal return.

88. C: Banks create money by giving out loans. For example, assume a person puts $100 into a bank. The bank will keep a percentage of that money in reserves because of the reserve requirement. If the reserve requirement is 10% then the bank will put $10 in reserves and then loan out $90 of it to a second person. The money total, which started at $100, now includes the original $100 plus the $90, or a total of $190. The bank creates $90 by loaning it.

89. A: The equation of exchange is MV = PQ. This means that M1 (a measure of the supply of money) multiplied by the velocity of money (the average number of times a typical dollar is spent on final goods and services a year) = the average price level of final goods and services in GDP x real output, or the quantity of goods and services in GDP.

90. A: Economics is defined as the study of scarcity, the situation in which resources are limited and wants are unlimited.

# Secret Key #1 - Time is Your Greatest Enemy

## Pace Yourself

Wear a watch. At the beginning of the test, check the time (or start a chronometer on your watch to count the minutes), and check the time after every few questions to make sure you are "on schedule." If you are forced to speed up, do it efficiently. Usually one or more answer choices can be eliminated without too much difficulty. Above all, don't panic. Don't speed up and just begin guessing at random choices. By pacing yourself, and continually monitoring your progress against your watch, you will always know exactly how far ahead or behind you are with your available time. If you find that you are one minute behind on the test, don't skip one question without spending any time on it, just to catch back up. Take 15 fewer seconds on the next four questions, and after four questions you'll have caught back up. Once you catch back up, you can continue working each problem at your normal pace.

Furthermore, don't dwell on the problems that you were rushed on. If a problem was taking up too much time and you made a hurried guess, it must be difficult. The difficult questions are the ones you are most likely to miss anyway, so it isn't a big loss. It is better to end with more time than you need than to run out of time.

Lastly, sometimes it is beneficial to slow down if you are constantly getting ahead of time. You are always more likely to catch a careless mistake by working more slowly than quickly, and among very high-scoring test takers (those who are likely to have lots of time left over), careless errors affect the score more than mastery of material.

# Secret Key #2 - Guessing is not Guesswork

You probably know that guessing is a good idea. Unlike other standardized tests, there is no penalty for getting a wrong answer. Even if you have no idea about a question, you still have a 20-25% chance of getting it right. Most test takers do not understand the impact that proper guessing can have on their score. Unless you score extremely high, guessing will significantly contribute to your final score.

## Monkeys Take the Test

What most test takers don't realize is that to insure that 20-25% chance, you have to guess randomly. If you put 20 monkeys in a room to take this test, assuming they answered once per question and behaved themselves, on average they would get 20-25% of the questions correct. Put 20 test takers in the room, and the average will be much lower among guessed questions. Why?

1. The test writers intentionally write deceptive answer choices that "look" right. A test taker has no idea about a question, so he picks the "best looking" answer, which is often wrong. The monkey has no idea what looks good and what doesn't, so it will consistently be right about 20-25% of the time.
2. Test takers will eliminate answer choices from the guessing pool based on a hunch or intuition. Simple but correct answers often get excluded, leaving a 0% chance of being correct. The monkey has no clue, and often gets lucky with the best choice.

This is why the process of elimination endorsed by most test courses is flawed and detrimental to your performance. Test takers don't guess; they make an ignorant stab in the dark that is usually worse than random.

## $5 Challenge

Let me introduce one of the most valuable ideas of this course—the $5 challenge:

- *You only mark your "best guess" if you are willing to bet $5 on it.*
- *You only eliminate choices from guessing if you are willing to bet $5 on it.*

Why $5? Five dollars is an amount of money that is small yet not insignificant, and can really add up fast (20 questions could cost you $100). Likewise, each answer choice on one question of the test will have a small impact on your overall score, but it can really add up to a lot of points in the end.

The process of elimination IS valuable. The following shows your chance of guessing it right:

| If you eliminate wrong answer choices until only this many remain: | Chance of getting it correct: |
|---|---|
| 1 | 100% |
| 2 | 50% |
| 3 | 33% |

However, if you accidentally eliminate the right answer or go on a hunch for an incorrect answer, your chances drop dramatically—to 0%. By guessing among all the answer choices, you are GUARANTEED to have a shot at the right answer. That's why the $5 test is so valuable. If you give up the advantage and safety of a pure guess, it had better be worth the risk.

What we still haven't covered is how to be sure that whatever guess you make is truly random. Here's the easiest way:

- *Always pick the first answer choice among those remaining.*

Such a technique means that you have decided, **before you see a single test question**, exactly how you are going to guess, and since the order of choices tells you nothing about which one is correct, this guessing technique is perfectly random.

This section is not meant to scare you away from making educated guesses or eliminating choices; you just need to define when a choice is worth eliminating. The $5 test, along with a pre-defined random guessing strategy, is the best way to make sure you reap all of the benefits of guessing.

# Secret Key #3 - Practice Smarter, Not Harder

Many test takers delay the test preparation process because they dread the awful amounts of practice time they think necessary to succeed on the test. We have refined an effective method that will take you only a fraction of the time.

There are a number of "obstacles" in the path to success. Among these are answering questions, finishing in time, and mastering test-taking strategies. All must be executed on the day of the test at peak performance, or your score will suffer. The test is a mental marathon that has a large impact on your future.

Just like a marathon runner, it is important to work your way up to the full challenge. So first you just worry about questions, and then time, and finally strategy:

## Success Strategy

1. Find a good source for practice tests.
2. If you are willing to make a larger time investment, consider using more than one study guide. Often the different approaches of multiple authors will help you "get" difficult concepts.
3. Take a practice test with no time constraints, with all study helps, "open book." Take your time with questions and focus on applying strategies.
4. Take a practice test with time constraints, with all guides, "open book."
5. Take a final practice test without open material and with time limits.

If you have time to take more practice tests, just repeat step 5. By gradually exposing yourself to the full rigors of the test environment, you will condition your mind to the stress of test day and maximize your success.

# Secret Key #4 - Prepare, Don't Procrastinate

Let me state an obvious fact: if you take the test three times, you will probably get three different scores. This is due to the way you feel on test day, the level of preparedness you have, and the version of the test you see. Despite the test writers' claims to the contrary, some versions of the test WILL be easier for you than others.

Since your future depends so much on your score, you should maximize your chances of success. In order to maximize the likelihood of success, you've got to prepare in advance. This means taking practice tests and spending time learning the information and test taking strategies you will need to succeed.

Never go take the actual test as a "practice" test, expecting that you can just take it again if you need to. Take all the practice tests you can on your own, but when you go to take the official test, be prepared, be focused, and do your best the first time!

# Secret Key #5 - Test Yourself

Everyone knows that time is money. There is no need to spend too much of your time or too little of your time preparing for the test. You should only spend as much of your precious time preparing as is necessary for you to get the score you need.

Once you have taken a practice test under real conditions of time constraints, then you will know if you are ready for the test or not.

If you have scored extremely high the first time that you take the practice test, then there is not much point in spending countless hours studying. You are already there.

Benchmark your abilities by retaking practice tests and seeing how much you have improved. Once you consistently score high enough to guarantee success, then you are ready.

If you have scored well below where you need, then knuckle down and begin studying in earnest. Check your improvement regularly through the use of practice tests under real conditions. Above all, don't worry, panic, or give up. The key is perseverance!

Then, when you go to take the test, remain confident and remember how well you did on the practice tests. If you can score high enough on a practice test, then you can do the same on the real thing.

# General Strategies

The most important thing you can do is to ignore your fears and jump into the test immediately. Do not be overwhelmed by any strange-sounding terms. You have to jump into the test like jumping into a pool—all at once is the easiest way.

## Make Predictions

As you read and understand the question, try to guess what the answer will be. Remember that several of the answer choices are wrong, and once you begin reading them, your mind will immediately become cluttered with answer choices designed to throw you off. Your mind is typically the most focused immediately after you have read the question and digested its contents. If you can, try to predict what the correct answer will be. You may be surprised at what you can predict. Quickly scan the choices and see if your prediction is in the listed answer choices. If it is, then you can be quite confident that you have the right answer. It still won't hurt to check the other answer choices, but most of the time, you've got it!

## Answer the Question

It may seem obvious to only pick answer choices that answer the question, but the test writers can create some excellent answer choices that are wrong. Don't pick an answer just because it sounds right, or you believe it to be true. It MUST answer the question. Once you've made your selection, always go back and check it against the question and make sure that you didn't misread the question and that the answer choice does answer the question posed.

## Benchmark

After you read the first answer choice, decide if you think it sounds correct or not. If it doesn't, move on to the next answer choice. If it does, mentally mark that answer choice. This doesn't mean that you've definitely selected it as your answer choice, it just means that it's the best you've seen thus far. Go ahead and read the next choice. If the next choice is worse than the one you've already selected, keep going to the next answer choice. If the next choice is better than the choice you've already selected, mentally mark the new answer choice as your best guess.

The first answer choice that you select becomes your standard. Every other answer choice must be benchmarked against that standard. That choice is correct until proven otherwise by another answer choice beating it out. Once you've decided that no other answer choice seems as good, do one final check to ensure that your answer choice answers the question posed.

## Valid Information

Don't discount any of the information provided in the question. Every piece of information may be necessary to determine the correct answer. None of the information in the question is there to throw you off (while the answer choices will certainly have information to throw you off). If two seemingly unrelated topics are discussed, don't ignore either. You can be confident there is a relationship, or it wouldn't be included in the question, and you are probably going to have to determine what is that relationship to find the answer.

## Avoid "Fact Traps"

Don't get distracted by a choice that is factually true. Your search is for the answer that answers the question. Stay focused and don't fall for an answer that is true but irrelevant. Always go back to the question and make sure you're choosing an answer that actually answers the question and is not just a true statement. An answer can be factually correct, but it MUST answer the question asked. Additionally, two answers can both be seemingly correct, so be sure to read all of the answer choices, and make sure that you get the one that BEST answers the question.

## Milk the Question

Some of the questions may throw you completely off. They might deal with a subject you have not been exposed to, or one that you haven't reviewed in years. While your lack of knowledge about the subject will be a hindrance, the question itself can give you many clues that will help you find the correct answer. Read the question carefully and look for clues. Watch particularly for adjectives and nouns describing difficult terms or words that you don't recognize. Regardless of whether you completely understand a word or not, replacing it with a synonym, either provided or one you more familiar with, may help you to understand what the questions are asking. Rather than wracking your mind about specific detailed information concerning a difficult term or word, try to use mental substitutes that are easier to understand.

## The Trap of Familiarity

Don't just choose a word because you recognize it. On difficult questions, you may not recognize a number of words in the answer choices. The test writers don't put "make-believe" words on the test, so don't think that just because you only recognize all the words in one answer choice that that answer choice must be correct. If you only recognize words in one answer choice, then focus on that one. Is it correct? Try your best to determine if it is correct. If it is, that's great. If not, eliminate it. Each word and answer choice you eliminate increases your chances of getting the question correct, even if you then have to guess among the unfamiliar choices.

## Eliminate Answers

Eliminate choices as soon as you realize they are wrong. But be careful! Make sure you consider all of the possible answer choices. Just because one appears right, doesn't mean that the next one won't be even better! The test writers will usually put more than one good answer choice for every question, so read all of them. Don't worry if you are stuck between two that seem right. By getting down to just two remaining possible choices, your odds are now 50/50. Rather than wasting too much time, play the odds. You are guessing, but guessing wisely because you've been able to knock out some of the answer choices that you know are wrong. If you are eliminating choices and realize that the last answer choice you are left with is also obviously wrong, don't panic. Start over and consider each choice again. There may easily be something that you missed the first time and will realize on the second pass.

## Tough Questions

If you are stumped on a problem or it appears too hard or too difficult, don't waste time. Move on! Remember though, if you can quickly check for obviously incorrect answer choices, your chances of guessing correctly are greatly improved. Before you completely give up, at least try to knock out a couple of possible answers. Eliminate what you can and then guess at the remaining answer choices before moving on.

## Brainstorm

If you get stuck on a difficult question, spend a few seconds quickly brainstorming. Run through the complete list of possible answer choices. Look at each choice and ask yourself, "Could this answer the question satisfactorily?" Go through each answer choice and consider it independently of the others. By systematically going through all possibilities, you may find something that you would otherwise overlook. Remember though that when you get stuck, it's important to try to keep moving.

## Read Carefully

Understand the problem. Read the question and answer choices carefully. Don't miss the question because you misread the terms. You have plenty of time to read each question thoroughly and make sure you understand what is being asked. Yet a happy medium must be attained, so don't waste too much time. You must read carefully, but efficiently.

## Face Value

When in doubt, use common sense. Always accept the situation in the problem at face value. Don't read too much into it. These problems will not require you to make huge leaps of logic. The test writers aren't trying to throw you off with a cheap trick. If you have to go beyond creativity and make a leap of logic in order to have an answer choice answer the question, then you should look at the other answer choices. Don't overcomplicate the problem by creating theoretical relationships or explanations that will warp time or space. These are normal problems rooted in reality. It's just that the applicable relationship or explanation may not be readily apparent and you have to figure things out. Use your common sense to interpret anything that isn't clear.

## Prefixes

If you're having trouble with a word in the question or answer choices, try dissecting it. Take advantage of every clue that the word might include. Prefixes and suffixes can be a huge help. Usually they allow you to determine a basic meaning. Pre- means before, post- means after, pro - is positive, de- is negative. From these prefixes and suffixes, you can get an idea of the general meaning of the word and try to put it into context. Beware though of any traps. Just because con- is the opposite of pro-, doesn't necessarily mean congress is the opposite of progress!

## Hedge Phrases

Watch out for critical hedge phrases, led off with words such as "likely," "may," "can," "sometimes," "often," "almost," "mostly," "usually," "generally," "rarely," and "sometimes." Question writers insert these hedge phrases to cover every possibility. Often an answer choice will be wrong simply because it leaves no room for exception. Unless the situation calls for them, avoid answer choices that have definitive words like "exactly," and "always."

## Switchback Words

Stay alert for "switchbacks." These are the words and phrases frequently used to alert you to shifts in thought. The most common switchback word is "but." Others include "although," "however," "nevertheless," "on the other hand," "even though," "while," "in spite of," "despite," and "regardless of."

## New Information

Correct answer choices will rarely have completely new information included. Answer choices typically are straightforward reflections of the material asked about and will directly relate to the question. If a new piece of information is included in an answer choice that doesn't even seem to relate to the topic being asked about, then that answer choice is likely incorrect. All of the information needed to answer the question is usually provided for you in the question. You should not have to make guesses that are unsupported or choose answer choices that require unknown information that cannot be reasoned from what is given.

## Time Management

On technical questions, don't get lost on the technical terms. Don't spend too much time on any one question. If you don't know what a term means, then odds are you aren't going to get much further since you don't have a dictionary. You should be able to immediately recognize whether or not you know a term. If you don't, work with the other clues that you have—the other answer choices and terms provided—but don't waste too much time trying to figure out a difficult term that you don't know.

## Contextual Clues

Look for contextual clues. An answer can be right but not the correct answer. The contextual clues will help you find the answer that is most right and is correct. Understand the context in which a phrase or statement is made. This will help you make important distinctions.

## Don't Panic

Panicking will not answer any questions for you; therefore, it isn't helpful. When you first see the question, if your mind goes blank, take a deep breath. Force yourself to mechanically go through the steps of solving the problem using the strategies you've learned.

## Pace Yourself

Don't get clock fever. It's easy to be overwhelmed when you're looking at a page full of questions, your mind is full of random thoughts and feeling confused, and the clock is ticking down faster than you would like. Calm down and maintain the pace that you have set for yourself. As long as you are on track by monitoring your pace, you are guaranteed to have enough time for yourself. When you get to the last few minutes of the test, it may seem like you won't have enough time left, but if you only have as many questions as you should have left at that point, then you're right on track!

## Answer Selection

The best way to pick an answer choice is to eliminate all of those that are wrong, until only one is left and confirm that is the correct answer. Sometimes though, an answer choice may immediately look right. Be careful! Take a second to make sure that the other choices are not equally obvious. Don't make a hasty mistake. There are only two times that you should stop before checking other answers. First is when you are positive that the answer choice you have selected is correct. Second is when time is almost out and you have to make a quick guess!

## Check Your Work

Since you will probably not know every term listed and the answer to every question, it is important that you get credit for the ones that you do know. Don't miss any questions through careless mistakes. If at all possible, try to take a second to look back over your answer selection and make sure you've selected the correct answer choice and haven't made a costly careless mistake (such as marking an answer choice that you didn't mean to mark). The time it takes for this quick double check should more than pay for itself in caught mistakes.

## Beware of Directly Quoted Answers

Sometimes an answer choice will repeat word for word a portion of the question or reference section. However, beware of such exact duplication. It may be a trap! More than likely, the correct choice will paraphrase or summarize a point, rather than being exactly the same wording.

## Slang

Scientific sounding answers are better than slang ones. An answer choice that begins "To compare the outcomes..." is much more likely to be correct than one that begins "Because some people insisted..."

## Extreme Statements

Avoid wild answers that throw out highly controversial ideas that are proclaimed as established fact. An answer choice that states the "process should used in certain situations, if..." is much more likely to be correct than one that states the "process should be discontinued completely." The first is a calm rational statement and doesn't even make a definitive, uncompromising stance, using a hedge word "if" to provide wiggle room, whereas the second choice is a radical idea and far more extreme.

## Answer Choice Families

When you have two or more answer choices that are direct opposites or parallels, one of them is usually the correct answer. For instance, if one answer choice states "x increases" and another answer choice states "x decreases" or "y increases," then those two or three answer choices are very similar in construction and fall into the same family of answer choices. A family of answer choices consists of two or three answer choices, very similar in construction, but often with directly opposite meanings. Usually the correct answer choice will be in that family of answer choices. The "odd man out" or answer choice that doesn't seem to fit the parallel construction of the other answer choices is more likely to be incorrect.

# Special Report: How to Overcome Test Anxiety

The very nature of tests caters to some level of anxiety, nervousness, or tension, just as we feel for any important event that occurs in our lives. A little bit of anxiety or nervousness can be a good thing. It helps us with motivation, and makes achievement just that much sweeter. However, too much anxiety can be a problem, especially if it hinders our ability to function and perform.

"Test anxiety," is the term that refers to the emotional reactions that some test-takers experience when faced with a test or exam. Having a fear of testing and exams is based upon a rational fear, since the test-taker's performance can shape the course of an academic career. Nevertheless, experiencing excessive fear of examinations will only interfere with the test-taker's ability to perform and chance to be successful.

There are a large variety of causes that can contribute to the development and sensation of test anxiety. These include, but are not limited to, lack of preparation and worrying about issues surrounding the test.

## Lack of Preparation

Lack of preparation can be identified by the following behaviors or situations:

- Not scheduling enough time to study, and therefore cramming the night before the test or exam
- Managing time poorly, to create the sensation that there is not enough time to do everything
- Failing to organize the text information in advance, so that the study material consists of the entire text and not simply the pertinent information
- Poor overall studying habits

Worrying, on the other hand, can be related to both the test taker, or many other factors around him/her that will be affected by the results of the test. These include worrying about:

- Previous performances on similar exams, or exams in general
- How friends and other students are achieving
- The negative consequences that will result from a poor grade or failure

There are three primary elements to test anxiety. Physical components, which involve the same typical bodily reactions as those to acute anxiety (to be discussed below). Emotional factors have to do with fear or panic. Mental or cognitive issues concerning attention spans and memory abilities.

## Physical Signals

There are many different symptoms of test anxiety, and these are not limited to mental and emotional strain. Frequently there are a range of physical signals that will let a test taker know that he/she is suffering from test anxiety. These bodily changes can include the following:

- Perspiring
- Sweaty palms
- Wet, trembling hands
- Nausea
- Dry mouth
- A knot in the stomach
- Headache
- Faintness
- Muscle tension
- Aching shoulders, back and neck
- Rapid heart beat
- Feeling too hot/cold

To recognize the sensation of test anxiety, a test-taker should monitor him/herself for the following sensations:

- The physical distress symptoms as listed above
- Emotional sensitivity, expressing emotional feelings such as the need to cry or laugh too much, or a sensation of anger or helplessness
- A decreased ability to think, causing the test-taker to blank out or have racing thoughts that are hard to organize or control

Though most students will feel some level of anxiety when faced with a test or exam, the majority can cope with that anxiety and maintain it at a manageable level. However, those who cannot are faced with a very real and very serious condition, which can and should be controlled for the immeasurable benefit of this sufferer. Naturally, these sensations lead to negative results for the testing experience. The most common effects of test anxiety have to do with nervousness and mental blocking.

## Nervousness

Nervousness can appear in several different levels:

- The test-taker's difficulty, or even inability to read and understand the questions on the test
- The difficulty or inability to organize thoughts to a coherent form
- The difficulty or inability to recall key words and concepts relating to the testing questions (especially essays)
- The receipt of poor grades on a test, though the test material was well known by the test taker

Conversely, a person may also experience mental blocking, which involves:

- Blanking out on test questions
- Only remembering the correct answers to the questions when the test has already finished

Fortunately for test anxiety sufferers, beating these feelings, to a large degree, has to do with proper preparation. When a test taker has a feeling of preparedness, then anxiety will be dramatically lessened.

The first step to resolving anxiety issues is to distinguish which of the two types of anxiety are being suffered. If the anxiety is a direct result of a lack of preparation, this should be considered a normal reaction, and the anxiety level (as opposed to the test results) shouldn't be anything to worry about. However, if, when adequately prepared, the test-taker still panics, blanks out, or seems to overreact, this is not a fully rational reaction. While this can be considered normal too, there are many ways to combat and overcome these effects.

Remember that anxiety cannot be entirely eliminated, however, there are ways to minimize it, to make the anxiety easier to manage. Preparation is one of the best ways to minimize test anxiety. Therefore the following techniques are wise in order to best fight off any anxiety that may want to build.

To begin with, try to avoid cramming before a test, whenever it is possible. By trying to memorize an entire term's worth of information in one day, you'll be shocking your system, and not giving yourself a very good chance to absorb the information. This is an easy path to anxiety, so for those who suffer from test anxiety, cramming should not even be considered an option.

Instead of cramming, work throughout the semester to combine all of the material which is presented throughout the semester, and work on it gradually as the course goes by, making sure to master the main concepts first, leaving minor details for a week or so before the test.

To study for the upcoming exam, be sure to pose questions that may be on the examination, to gauge the ability to answer them by integrating the ideas from your texts, notes and lectures, as well as any supplementary readings.

If it is truly impossible to cover all of the information that was covered in that particular term, concentrate on the most important portions, that can be covered very well. Learn these concepts as best as possible, so that when the test comes, a goal can be made to use these concepts as presentations of your knowledge.

In addition to study habits, changes in attitude are critical to beating a struggle with test anxiety. In fact, an improvement of the perspective over the entire test-taking experience can actually help a test taker to enjoy studying and therefore improve the overall experience. Be certain not to overemphasize the significance of the grade - know that the result of the test is neither a reflection of self worth, nor is it a measure of intelligence; one grade will not predict a person's future success.
To improve an overall testing outlook, the following steps should be tried:

- Keeping in mind that the most reasonable expectation for taking a test is to expect to try to demonstrate as much of what you know as you possibly can.
- Reminding ourselves that a test is only one test; this is not the only one, and there will be others.

- The thought of thinking of oneself in an irrational, all-or-nothing term should be avoided at all costs.
- A reward should be designated for after the test, so there's something to look forward to. Whether it be going to a movie, going out to eat, or simply visiting friends, schedule it in advance, and do it no matter what result is expected on the exam.

Test-takers should also keep in mind that the basics are some of the most important things, even beyond anti-anxiety techniques and studying. Never neglect the basic social, emotional and biological needs, in order to try to absorb information. In order to best achieve, these three factors must be held as just as important as the studying itself.

## Study Steps

Remember the following important steps for studying:

- Maintain healthy nutrition and exercise habits. Continue both your recreational activities and social pass times. These both contribute to your physical and emotional well being.
- Be certain to get a good amount of sleep, especially the night before the test, because when you're overtired you are not able to perform to the best of your best ability.
- Keep the studying pace to a moderate level by taking breaks when they are needed, and varying the work whenever possible, to keep the mind fresh instead of getting bored.
- When enough studying has been done that all the material that can be learned has been learned, and the test taker is prepared for the test, stop studying and do something relaxing such as listening to music, watching a movie, or taking a warm bubble bath.

There are also many other techniques to minimize the uneasiness or apprehension that is experienced along with test anxiety before, during, or even after the examination. In fact, there are a great deal of things that can be done to stop anxiety from interfering with lifestyle and performance. Again, remember that anxiety will not be eliminated entirely, and it shouldn't be. Otherwise that "up" feeling for exams would not exist, and most of us depend on that sensation to perform better than usual. However, this anxiety has to be at a level that is manageable. Of course, as we have just discussed, being prepared for the exam is half the battle right away. Attending all classes, finding out what knowledge will be expected on the exam, and knowing the exam schedules are easy steps to lowering anxiety. Keeping up with work will remove the need to cram, and efficient study habits will eliminate wasted time. Studying should be done in an ideal location for concentration, so that it is simple to become interested in the material and give it complete attention.

A method such as SQ3R (Survey, Question, Read, Recite, Review) is a wonderful key to follow to make sure that the study habits are as effective as possible, especially in the case of learning from a textbook. Flashcards are great techniques for memorization. Learning to take good notes will mean that notes will be full of useful information, so that less sifting will need to be done to seek out what is pertinent for studying. Reviewing notes after class and then again on occasion will keep the information fresh in the mind. From notes that have been taken summary sheets and outlines can be made for simpler reviewing.

A study group can also be a very motivational and helpful place to study, as there will be a sharing of ideas, all of the minds can work together, to make sure that everyone understands, and the studying will be made more interesting because it will be a social occasion. Basically, though, as long as the test-taker remains organized and self confident, with efficient study habits, less time will need to be spent studying, and higher grades will be achieved.

To become self confident, there are many useful steps. The first of these is "self talk." It has been shown through extensive research, that self-talk for students who suffer from test anxiety, should be well monitored, in order to make sure that it contributes to self confidence as opposed to sinking the student. Frequently the self talk of test-anxious students is negative or self-defeating, thinking that everyone else is smarter and faster, that they always mess up, and that if they don't do well, they'll fail the entire course. It is important to decreasing anxiety that awareness is made of self talk. Try writing any negative self thoughts and then disputing them with a positive statement instead. Begin self-encouragement as though it was a friend speaking. Repeat positive statements to help reprogram the mind to believing in successes instead of failures.

## Helpful Techniques

Other extremely helpful techniques include:

- Self-visualization of doing well and reaching goals
- While aiming for an "A" level of understanding, don't try to "overprotect" by setting your expectations lower. This will only convince the mind to stop studying in order to meet the lower expectations.
- Don't make comparisons with the results or habits of other students. These are individual factors, and different things work for different people, causing different results.
- Strive to become an expert in learning what works well, and what can be done in order to improve. Consider collecting this data in a journal.
- Create rewards for after studying instead of doing things before studying that will only turn into avoidance behaviors.
- Make a practice of relaxing - by using methods such as progressive relaxation, self-hypnosis, guided imagery, etc - in order to make relaxation an automatic sensation.
- Work on creating a state of relaxed concentration so that concentrating will take on the focus of the mind, so that none will be wasted on worrying.
- Take good care of the physical self by eating well and getting enough sleep.
- Plan in time for exercise and stick to this plan.

Beyond these techniques, there are other methods to be used before, during and after the test that will help the test-taker perform well in addition to overcoming anxiety.

Before the exam comes the academic preparation. This involves establishing a study schedule and beginning at least one week before the actual date of the test. By doing this, the anxiety of not having enough time to study for the test will be automatically eliminated. Moreover, this will make the studying a much more effective experience, ensuring that the learning will be an easier process. This relieves much undue pressure on the test-taker.

Summary sheets, note cards, and flash cards with the main concepts and examples of these main concepts should be prepared in advance of the actual studying time. A topic should never be eliminated from this process. By omitting a topic because it isn't expected to be on the test is only setting up the test-taker for anxiety should it actually appear on the exam. Utilize the course syllabus for laying out the topics that should be studied. Carefully go over the notes that were made in class, paying special attention to any of the issues that the professor took special care to emphasize while lecturing in class. In the textbooks, use the chapter review, or if possible, the chapter tests, to begin your review.

It may even be possible to ask the instructor what information will be covered on the exam, or what the format of the exam will be (for example, multiple choice, essay, free form, true-false). Additionally, see if it is possible to find out how many questions will be on the test. If a review sheet or sample test has been offered by the professor, make good use of it, above anything else, for the preparation for the test. Another great resource for getting to know the examination is reviewing tests from previous semesters. Use these tests to review, and aim to achieve a 100% score on each of the possible topics. With a few exceptions, the goal that you set for yourself is the highest one that you will reach.

Take all of the questions that were assigned as homework, and rework them to any other possible course material. The more problems reworked, the more skill and confidence will form as a result. When forming the solution to a problem, write out each of the steps. Don't simply do head work. By doing as many steps on paper as possible, much clarification and therefore confidence will be formed. Do this with as many homework problems as possible, before checking the answers. By checking the answer after each problem, a reinforcement will exist, that will not be on the exam. Study situations should be as exam-like as possible, to prime the test-taker's system for the experience. By waiting to check the answers at the end, a psychological advantage will be formed, to decrease the stress factor.

Another fantastic reason for not cramming is the avoidance of confusion in concepts, especially when it comes to mathematics. 8-10 hours of study will become one hundred percent more effective if it is spread out over a week or at least several days, instead of doing it all in one sitting. Recognize that the human brain requires time in order to assimilate new material, so frequent breaks and a span of study time over several days will be much more beneficial.

Additionally, don't study right up until the point of the exam. Studying should stop a minimum of one hour before the exam begins. This allows the brain to rest and put things in their proper order. This will also provide the time to become as relaxed as possible when going into the examination room. The test-taker will also have time to eat well and eat sensibly. Know that the brain needs food as much as the rest of the body. With enough food and enough sleep, as well as a relaxed attitude, the body and the mind are primed for success.

Avoid any anxious classmates who are talking about the exam. These students only spread anxiety, and are not worth sharing the anxious sentimentalities.

Before the test also involves creating a positive attitude, so mental preparation should also be a point of concentration. There are many keys to creating a positive attitude. Should fears become rushing in, make a visualization of taking the exam, doing well, and seeing an A written on the paper. Write out a list of affirmations that will bring a feeling of confidence, such as "I am doing well in my English class," "I studied well and know my material," "I enjoy this class." Even if the affirmations aren't believed at first, it sends a positive message to the subconscious which will result in an alteration of the overall belief system, which is the system that creates reality.

If a sensation of panic begins, work with the fear and imagine the very worst! Work through the entire scenario of not passing the test, failing the entire course, and dropping out of school, followed by not getting a job, and pushing a shopping cart through the dark alley where you'll live. This will place things into perspective! Then, practice deep breathing and create a visualization of the opposite situation - achieving an "A" on the exam, passing the entire course, receiving the degree at a graduation ceremony.

On the day of the test, there are many things to be done to ensure the best results, as well as the most calm outlook. The following stages are suggested in order to maximize test-taking potential:

- Begin the examination day with a moderate breakfast, and avoid any coffee or beverages with caffeine if the test taker is prone to jitters. Even people who are used to managing caffeine can feel jittery or light-headed when it is taken on a test day.
- Attempt to do something that is relaxing before the examination begins. As last minute cramming clouds the mastering of overall concepts, it is better to use this time to create a calming outlook.
- Be certain to arrive at the test location well in advance, in order to provide time to select a location that is away from doors, windows and other distractions, as well as giving enough time to relax before the test begins.
- Keep away from anxiety generating classmates who will upset the sensation of stability and relaxation that is being attempted before the exam.
- Should the waiting period before the exam begins cause anxiety, create a self-distraction by reading a light magazine or something else that is relaxing and simple.

During the exam itself, read the entire exam from beginning to end, and find out how much time should be allotted to each individual problem. Once writing the exam, should more time be taken for a problem, it should be abandoned, in order to begin another problem. If there is time at the end, the unfinished problem can always be returned to and completed.

Read the instructions very carefully - twice - so that unpleasant surprises won't follow during or after the exam has ended.

When writing the exam, pretend that the situation is actually simply the completion of homework within a library, or at home. This will assist in forming a relaxed atmosphere, and will allow the brain extra focus for the complex thinking function.

Begin the exam with all of the questions with which the most confidence is felt. This will build the confidence level regarding the entire exam and will begin a quality momentum. This will also create encouragement for trying the problems where uncertainty resides.

Going with the "gut instinct" is always the way to go when solving a problem. Second guessing should be avoided at all costs. Have confidence in the ability to do well.

For essay questions, create an outline in advance that will keep the mind organized and make certain that all of the points are remembered. For multiple choice, read every answer, even if the correct one has been spotted - a better one may exist.

Continue at a pace that is reasonable and not rushed, in order to be able to work carefully. Provide enough time to go over the answers at the end, to check for small errors that can be corrected.

Should a feeling of panic begin, breathe deeply, and think of the feeling of the body releasing sand through its pores. Visualize a calm, peaceful place, and include all of the sights, sounds and sensations of this image. Continue the deep breathing, and take a few minutes to continue this with closed eyes. When all is well again, return to the test.

If a "blanking" occurs for a certain question, skip it and move on to the next question. There will be time to return to the other question later. Get everything done that can be done, first, to guarantee all the grades that can be compiled, and to build all of the confidence possible. Then return to the weaker questions to build the marks from there.

Remember, one's own reality can be created, so as long as the belief is there, success will follow. And remember: anxiety can happen later, right now, there's an exam to be written!

After the examination is complete, whether there is a feeling for a good grade or a bad grade, don't dwell on the exam, and be certain to follow through on the reward that was promised...and enjoy it! Don't dwell on any mistakes that have been made, as there is nothing that can be done at this point anyway.

Additionally, don't begin to study for the next test right away. Do something relaxing for a while, and let the mind relax and prepare itself to begin absorbing information again.

From the results of the exam - both the grade and the entire experience, be certain to learn from what has gone on. Perfect studying habits and work some more on confidence in order to make the next examination experience even better than the last one.

Learn to avoid places where openings occurred for laziness, procrastination and day dreaming.

Use the time between this exam and the next one to better learn to relax, even learning to relax on cue, so that any anxiety can be controlled during the next exam. Learn how to relax the body. Slouch in your chair if that helps. Tighten and then relax all of the different muscle groups, one group at a time, beginning with the feet and then working all the way up to the neck and face. This will ultimately relax the muscles more than they were to begin with. Learn how to breathe deeply and comfortably, and focus on this breathing going in and out as a relaxing thought. With every exhale, repeat the word "relax."

As common as test anxiety is, it is very possible to overcome it. Make yourself one of the test-takers who overcome this frustrating hindrance.

# Additional Bonus Material

Due to our efforts to try to keep this book to a manageable length, we've created a link that will give you access to all of your additional bonus material.

Please visit http://www.mometrix.com/bonus948/nesincmgsocsci to access the information.

MW00772753

# NEW CHINESE ARCHITECTURE

# NEW CHINESE ARCHITECTURE

## TWENTY WOMEN BUILDING THE FUTURE

Austin Williams

*Foreword by* Zhang Xin

With over 370 illustrations

On the cover: Youth Hotel in iD Town by Jiang Ying
(see page 86). Photo credit: Chaos.Z
Page 2: Ding Xiang Eco-Village by Dong Mei
(see page 42). Photo credit: Zhang Yong

First published in the United Kingdom in 2019
by Thames & Hudson Ltd, 181a High Holborn,
London WC1V 7QX



British Library Cataloguing-in-Publication Data
A catalogue record for this book is available from the British Library

ISBN 978-0-500-34338-8

Printed and bound in China by Reliance Printing (Shenzhen) Co. Ltd.

Contents

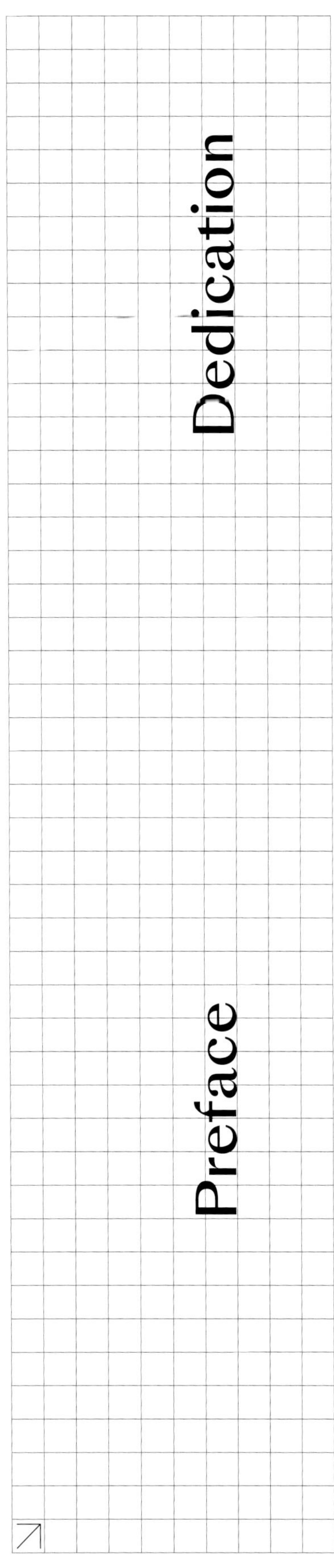

## Dedication

Zaha Hadid had kindly agreed to write the foreword to this book but sadly died at the beginning of the project. We dedicate this book in her honour.

Her work in China has undoubtedly been a huge influence on the new generation of architects: from Ma Yansong at MAD Architects, who has called her his 'mentor',[1] to Zhang Di's parametric designs for WAA, as well as numerous Chinese copycat developers who have emulated her work.

Hadid's architectural legacy in China extends from her unbuilt proposal for the Peak Leisure Club in Hong Kong, through her first completed work at Guangzhou Opera House completed in 2010, to the world's biggest terminal building at Beijing International Airport. From these three examples alone, it is clear that her social legacy is equally worthy of admiration, with the Peak Leisure Club being described by Vincent Ng as 'an inspiration for Hong Kong architects',[2] the Opera House helping in the cultural rejuvenation of the nation, and an airport that literally facilitates the mobility of millions.

Her contemporary, architect Eva Jiřičná, sums it up: 'If we can eliminate the practice of talking about female architects, it would be the greatest tribute we could give her.'[3] Indeed, her death was a tragedy for architecture globally, not because she was a female architect but because she was a great architect.

## Preface

This book examines twenty female Chinese architects who are the founders or leaders of their practices and who are delivering significant construction projects. It is important to understand that they are architects who, for the purposes of this book and in the spirit of Hadid, just happen to be female. Consequently, this book is not a polemical statement in praise of Western-style diversity theory, nor is it a patronizing inclusion agenda, nor a call for a Women in Architecture special pleading award. The story of China and the personal recollections of these architects present a far more interesting and complex story. This is a book that acknowledges the work of these architects on its own terms.

**Naming conventions:** Chinese names have been rendered in the traditional order (family name first), except for the architects Rossana Hu and Doreen Heng Liu, as they are most widely known, whose names are rendered in the traditional Western order.

# Foreword

ZHANG XIN 张欣
Co-founder and CEO, SOHO China

As a property developer in China since 1995, I have had a unique position in observing China's evolution as the country became increasingly globalized, which has in turn given birth to a new generation of Chinese architects who draw their inspiration from China as well as from design influences around the world. An addition to this trend is the exciting emergence of female architects in China, who are now active in designing impressive projects across the country. This book is a celebration of their work.

Over the last decade or so, China's women architects, whether academic or practitioner, have proved themselves to be talented, confident, hard-working and successful. These are new young female designers stepping onto the world stage. Their work is innovative and challenging. Whether traditional or contemporary, small- or large-scale, their projects show China to be a place of real creative possibilities for male and female architects alike.

As CEO of SOHO China, I had the pleasure of commissioning and working with Zaha Hadid, one of the most talented architects of our time. Zaha created her own design language, revolutionizing the world of architecture. We commissioned her repeatedly because she was the best, not because she was a woman. It is my deepest wish that Chinese women architects will strive to rise to Hadid's stature, elevating the discussion of architecture to focus on quality and innovation, regardless of gender.

# Introduction

AUSTIN WILLIAMS 奥斯汀·威廉姆斯

This book details the lives, achievements and ambitions of twenty Chinese architects living and working in China today. The practices variously deal with small-scale and mega-scale, residential and commercial, and urban and rural developments. The featured architects are those who have made a significant impact on the national scene. Mostly they are emerging talents in the architectural firmament, but we have also included one or two more established architects to indicate some of the continuity as well as the changes that have affected this country in the recent past.

Architects in China are keenly engaged in trying to understand the changing nature of this vast country as it metamorphoses from a predominantly rural economy into an urbanized nation faster than any other country in history. Chinese architects are responding to real social and political changes, changes that are having an enormous impact on the way architecture and urban design are practised.

Although many of their names will be relatively unknown in the Western world, each of them is part of a social transition that is affecting the most populous country on earth. These are architects of considerable influence who are diligently getting on with producing important and challenging work to transform the skyline but at the same time transforming social reality on the ground.

This volume presents a series of articles taken from interviews with each architect and featuring several examples of their built work, including photographs and drawings as well as sketches and technical details. We hope that the collection of projects on display will go some way to highlight some of the talent and skill currently available in China.

With China increasingly in the news, it is time to appreciate its diverse architecture and to learn from the creative ambitions of some of its best practitioners.

↗

In 1949, at the foundation of the People's Republic of China, the country was home to a total of 120 cities. Today it has 684 cities. In ten years, it will have 926, more than half of which will contain over one million people. Admittedly, Chinese statistics are not always reliable, but there has without question been an urban explosion in China the like of which the world has never before seen. Back in 1992, for example, Shenzhen comprised a series of villages housing around 30,000 people; now it is a vast sprawling metropolis of 14 million residents, reflecting an average population growth of 30 per cent per annum over the past three decades.[1]

Over a period of just forty years, China's urban population has grown from 14 per cent in 1980 to 59 per cent today. Within the next twenty years, China will have another 400 million city dwellers. In other words, in the past two decades there has been a flow of people into China's cities greater than the entire population of the United States. In the next two decades, it will happen again. It is a remarkable transition. This book takes a look at some of the architects and urbanists who have been engaged in that process.

It is worth looking back to see the magnitude of the changes wrought. After the formation of the People's Republic of China in 1949, architecture was nationalized. Private architects, many of whom had studied in the West, had their offices seized and were forced to work for state-owned 'design institutes'. With centrally planned targets set by the Communist Party, architects had to produce a huge number of new buildings, new towns, new cities.

To achieve such a rapid rise in urbanization, technical assistance was sought from the Soviet Union to set the standards for construction, to train Chinese workers in new design methods, and to churn out the results. These were socialist cities: their layouts were founded on a basic Soviet model of repetitive building blocks. Frankly, it was monotonous architecture befitting a rather monotonous social structure.[2] In the early days of Communist rule, architecture and urban design was either functional or symbolic. City centre buildings and plazas had to be designed to glorify the socialist state, cities had to prioritize manufacturing above all else, and workers' houses existed merely to service that industry.[3] As such, new cities found expression in a tedious grid of uniformity. The demand for more and more towns inevitably resulted in a significant reduction in the quality of those urban areas. In this period of rapid construction, architecture qua architecture was in short supply.

Architectural researcher Sylvia Chan notes that architectural writing at that time appeared in the mainstream press only on rare occasions. What architectural journalism there was, was solely for the dissemination of state policy. She writes that 'it was impossible to engage...in a debate about architectural principles'. Almost parodying Ayn Rand's dystopian novel *Anthem*, architectural journals at this time spoke only of the collective 'we'; individual architects were seldom named. Articles were not allowed to critique but simply to support and announce the government's next design requirement. Debate – insofar as it existed – was merely about *how* to successfully implement the rules, not whether the rules were any good.[4]

At the beginning of the 1960s, during the brutality of the Great Leap Forward, Mao proclaimed that 'women hold up half the sky'. Such a statement was meant to enforce the idea not only that women should play an equal part in the reconstruction of the nation, but also that they should embody the kind of physical toughness and socialist dedication needed to hold their own in a man's world.

During this period, women were encouraged to join the workforce as productive labour to add to the manpower needed to transform the economy. Not only were the 1960s seen as a 'revolutionary puritan period' in which boys and girls were not allowed to mix in schools,[5] but gender inequality was antithetical to the new socio political order. As a consequence, women were often dragooned into heavy industries.[6]

The heroic poster of Liang Jun typifies this moment. Born into a peasant family and entered into an arranged marriage when she was twelve, she became the first

↗ 1

↗ 2

female tractor driver of the socialist state. Liang was the Chinese equivalent of the iconic US World War II female industrial icon Rosie the Riveter, supposedly shown in the famous 'We Can Do It!' poster (although Norman Rockwell's painting for the cover of the *Saturday Evening Post*, 29 May 1943, is a more specific depiction of Rosie).[7] Both Liang and Rosie were patriotic emblems intended to encourage women to take an active role in the workforce, as symbols of independent female empowerment. The difference, of course, was that Liang's role was to build a socialist republic that would rival and surpass America. There were many other Chinese socialist heroines from that time, from Fu Wenying, the first female steam-engine driver, to Tang Sixiao, the first female director of a steel coking works.

Difficult though much of this work was, the release that it brought from domesticity challenged the framework of social relations. It led to women's greater autonomy and participation so that women were exercising political authority and holding high-ranking office far more visibly than in the West at that time.[8] But the majority of women were only notionally liberated, so that they could join the growing army of labour. Similarly, in education, the motto was 'whatever men can do, woman comrades can do too',[9] even though, for the state, education was often just a tactical policy for economic development.

Chairman Mao died in 1976, and within a few years Deng Xiaoping initiated economic reforms leading to a market economy. The pace of social change quickened and more opportunities presented themselves, although without the protective state, discriminatory practices began to flourish. The old dogmatic communist social relations were undercut by a more pragmatic capitalism. Anyone, young or old, male or female, could and should find work, though it was not always as easy as it sounded.

This was China's 'opening up' to the world that began tentatively in 1978. It meant the end of collectivization and the introduction of the profit motive; and importantly, it allowed students to return to universities. Indeed, one of the many criticisms of Mao's reign is that education was denied to an entire generation, many of whom were sent down to the countryside to labour in the fields instead.

While some universities in the early 1970s had permitted select party loyalists to attend, by the end of the decade universities introduced an entrance examination to allow everyone to apply. Intellectuals and aspiring intellectuals freed from manual labour returned to the cities, throwing themselves into university education with gusto. Women were among them.[10] In 1980, 23 per cent of all university students were women; by 1999 women comprised 41 per cent of the student body, and today the figure is 48 per cent.[11] There are '25 per cent more university-educated urban women now than there were in 2000'.[12] The implications have been significant.

Writer Michelle Che is one of the new generation. 'I went to the US to study because American education is higher quality...I'd describe myself as a very independent career woman. I think I'm lucky that I'm not married and I don't have children. I have my own life goal, I have my own job, I can support myself, and I learned to be emotionally independent. I can take care of myself very well'.[13]

Journalist Brook Larmer interviewed many aspirational female school students in China who planned to go to university precisely because it provided an escape. One says, 'I am drowning in sameness...in an environment in which individualism is not valued... This is not what I want.'[14] Unsurprisingly, young women want a break from the constraints of tradition. As with all developing economies (as China calls itself), people are seeking a route out of poverty, a means to escape, a way to progress.

Beijing-based photographer Luo Yang has been documenting young, free-spirited women across China for a number of years for a project called simply 'Girls'. She describes it as an exploration of Chinese females who are 'independent, free and [who] dare to dream'. She says that 'Chinese girls are now living through a time of change and sometimes conflict. They are constantly trying to find ways to express themselves.' She adds an important rider: 'I am not trying to pursue some kind of gender equality. This project is not about patriarchal society. It's just focusing on the girls' world.'[15]

Of course, options may be easier for some than for others. Poor migrant workers seldom have the luxury of expressing themselves through lavish consumer choices. Sadly, even today there is still a persistent notion among more traditional Chinese families that an educated woman will be an unattractive marital catch. But, against the odds, the trend continues for young women to move away from home for life experiences, economic advancement and the bright lights.

Leslie Chang's acclaimed book *Factory Girls* explores everyday life in factories in the industrial town of Dongguan in southern China, where one third of the migrant workers are female. Women such as these are prepared to travel further, they are younger, they stay away longer and they are motivated to improve themselves. They value migration for its life-changing possibilities. Chang notes that, counterintuitively, 'to some extent...deep-rooted sexism worked in women's favour...young women – less treasured, less coddled – could go far from home and make their own plans. Precisely because they mattered less, they were freer to do what they wanted.'

This ability to transform oneself, to make oneself into someone else, is clearly an unintended consequence of social marginalization and unfair practices. For example, controversial new research suggests that the one-child policy, and the subsequent lavish attention placed on the only child, has benefited girls who might otherwise have been marginalized by traditional parents had they been in competition with a male sibling.[16] If these factors are advantageous, it is a precarious advantage.

3

Chang sees positives in the bleakest of circumstances, but she is simply reflecting on the migrant women's own appetite for a better life:

'The migrant women I knew never complained about the unfairness of being a woman. Parents may favour sons over daughters, bosses prefer pretty secretaries, and job ads discriminate openly, but they took all these injustices in their stride – over three years in Dongguan, I never heard a single person express anything like a feminist sentiment. The divide between countryside and city was the only one that mattered. Once you crossed that line, you could change your fate.'[17]

The opportunities that migration to urban centres provides – such as material gain and increased autonomy – are frequently hindered by the fact that 'most jobs available to women require few skills, offer little pay, and are full of physical and emotional hazards'.[18] But for millions of young people, this does not matter: economic independence, however meagre, is still a way out. For the affluent few, however, new, better and more meaningful opportunities are opening up. One of the clearest expressions of this has been the tendency of students to study abroad.

From the early 1950s to the mid-1970s there were just eight architecture schools in China. At the time of writing, there are sixty-nine validated schools and about 281 other architecture programmes, producing around 16,000 qualified undergraduates every year. The original eight architecture schools had such names as the Harbin Institute of Building Technology, Chongqing Institute of Building Engineering and Xi'an Institute of Metallurgical Building Engineering, clearly emphasizing their science and engineering bent. Chinese architecture has long tended to defer to technical skills rather than the arts. Even today, all architecture schools accredited by the Ministry of Education deliver B. Eng. degrees and are considered to be an engineering discipline.

Until the first decade of the new millennium, engineering was deemed to be a core skill for China's rapid urbanization and development. After all, until only a few years ago, the Central Politburo of the Communist Party were all engineers, as their aim was to rebuild the nation. Recently, China has entered an era of creativity and innovation that requires a softer edge to its skills-based educational provision. Now art, philosophy, history and design-led courses are increasingly becoming a first option for undergraduates. At the moment, Western education is still seen in China as something of a gold standard precisely because it helps in the 'cultivation of creative talents'. It is revered predominantly for its encouragement of experimentation: and architecture, perhaps more than most other subjects, encourages students to use their initiative, and to travel in order to better appreciate different cultures, buildings, people and contexts. More and more Chinese students with sizeable disposable incomes are taking advantage of more liberal visa policies and the availability of international flights, and are jetting off to universities in Europe and the USA.

Chinese men and women are travelling the world, learning English and also learning the language of creative and critical thinking. After absorbing some of the Western ways of doing things students are returning to China to act as a critical bridge between East and West. After the death of Chairman Mao in 1976, China's first private architectural practice, Atelier FCJZ, was not founded until 1993. It was only 1999 when such architects as Wang Shu, Liu Xiaodu, Dong Yugan and even Ma Yansong were being hailed as the new Chinese avant garde – the 'experimental' set.[19] Now, in less than a generation, Chinese architecture is entering on to the world's stage.

The newly emerging young female talents – together with a couple of grandes dames – explored in this book should be seen as evidence of the normalization of female architectural practice in China. Ironically, these female Chinese architects haven't yet been praised in the West, maybe because they aren't reflecting the contemporary western feminist discourse. These are architects who happen to be women. When Dang Qun, principal partner at Beijing's MAD Architects, was asked about the differences between male and female practitioners, she simply retorted: 'It's not an issue.'[20]

A book entitled *New Chinese Architecture* that featured only men might not be unusual, and we want the featuring of twenty females to be similarly unremarked upon. If at all, these twenty architects should be remarkable solely for the merits of their work.

1. 'We are proud of participating in the founding of our country's industrialization', poster, Shanghai, 1954.
2. Detail from the 1943 'We Can Do It!' poster produced by J. Howard Miller.
3. Female migrant labour in Suzhou.

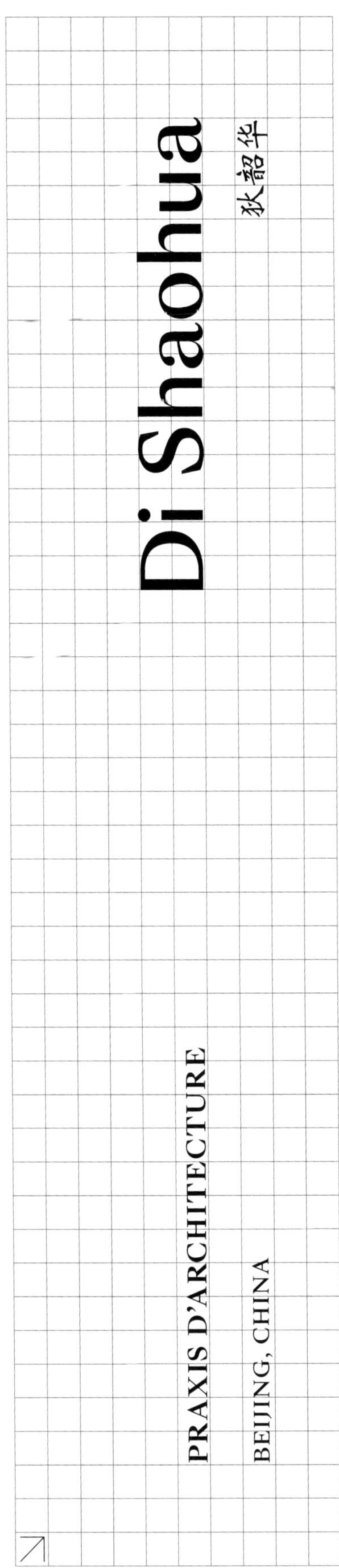

Di Shaohua's home town is Wuxi in Jiangsu Province. At an early age she moved with her family to Beijing, relocating to the industrial heartland of Lanzhou in Gansu when she was ten years old.

As a youngster, watching her grandmother make clothes for the family, her dream was to become a tailor or a fashion designer. She set her heart on attending the Beijing Institute of Fashion Technology, China's leading design and technology university. Chinese universities often reserve many of their places for students with local *hukou* (residency status), and, unfortunately, the year that Di took the National College Entrance Examination, Beijing's fashion programme was not accepting applicants from her part of the country.

Fashion's loss has been architecture's gain. As a desperate second option, Di applied to study architecture at Tianjin University, with no idea of what she was getting into. It was the only course she could find that provided her with some exposure to art and creativity. From such humble and unintended beginnings began an impressive architectural journey.

After graduating from Tianjin in 1995 she moved to the United States, where at the Massachusetts Institute of Technology (MIT) she gained a master's degree in architecture, followed by a Master of Science in Architecture, specializing in Urbanism, a course that engages in contemporary debates about good city design. Her student experience and her professors have clearly influenced her ways of working and thinking, as she has developed a wide range of interests, from Chinese traditional architecture to philosophy and even performance art.

Most of all, she appreciates the fact that her tutors encouraged her to find her creative confidence, her self-belief and an ability to trust her own instincts. In 2003, she received the Francis Ward Chandler Prize from MIT, awarded for outstanding achievement in architectural design. She founded PRAXiS d'ARCHITECTURE in 2009.

When Di graduated, the Chinese market was dominated by government-owned design institutes. Private companies were rare. A few successful ones were considered to be the movers and shakers of Chinese architecture at the time, but even they, she says, were not making much money because the market was still quite closed. Twenty years later, independent architectural practices occupy a large section of the market, thanks in part to globalization and the rapid pace of Chinese urbanization. The market has become much more open and diverse. 'Today it is possible to be famous and also have a good business.'

Chinese architects, Di says, are now in a healthy transition period, moving from 'Made in China' to 'Designed in China'. It is a period in which clients (and society more generally) are recognizing the need for a more creative sector. In other words, more people are realizing the added-value economic benefits of good design.

This kind of pragmatic bottom line seems to influence many of Di's professional decisions, and a concern for efficiency is a strong thread running through her practice's considerations. For example, she claims to be inspired by the Japanese architect Kazuyo Sejima because, she says, Sejima prioritizes all the functional and practical requirements 'and the last thing that [Sejima] considers is how to make it beautiful'. Di says that the very nature of the profession is to 'solve problems'.

One of her early heroes was Louis Kahn but she admires Zaha Hadid too, less for her architectural forms than for the way she demonstrated such resolve and self-confidence. It was this that gave Hadid the power to turn ideas into form. And for Di, 'every project has its uniqueness. The process of discovery is the most intriguing part of design for me.'

Di clearly respects the potential of Western design education in the way that it privileges individuality and self-awareness. For her, these are fundamentally important conceits that allow architectural students and professionals to 'externalize their internal world'. As a result, her intellectual energies are engaged with what she calls the 'cultural resonances between ancient Chinese styles and modern Western design'. Even though China is a huge market for architectural practices, she wants people outside the field of architecture to be guided to understand what good architecture is.

Meanwhile, China is changing fast. There have been many places in and around her offices in Beijing that have now been demolished and their lively cultural and commercial scenes lost. 'The constant replacement of the old with the new generates a huge amount of construction – which is fine – but it also dilutes people's memory about the meaning of an "authentic Beijing".' In PRAXiS d'ARCHITECTURE's recent Ying Gallery renovation, located near the 798 Art Area, PRAXiS has extended rather than demolished the existing structure so as to halt the sense of constant transformation along the periphery of Beijing city. It is a small building on a very small budget and with difficult site constraints.

Generally speaking, Di acknowledges that there are more female architects now than ever before, but it is still largely a male-dominated field. This, she says, is because realizing a project requires dedication and often long working hours, for which women still regularly pay the price, expected as they are to take on the bulk of childcare duties. Asked about her greatest achievement, she does not have to think twice: 'Simply that when I became a mother of two, I managed to keep my studio.'

↗ 1

**Page 15** Dongrun Apartments façade

**Architect:** Di Shaohua
**Project:** Dongrun Apartments
**Location:** Songzhuang, Beijing
**Completion:** 2012

Songzhuang is known as an 'art colony' of more than 2,000 artists who have, to a large extent, transformed the area. It is now a well-known independent – almost countercultural – zone. Like the area itself, Dongrun Apartments is a project funded and managed by multiple private interests rather than being a government-backed scheme. Di Shaohua intends for its management style to be made manifest in its design, shedding light on the building's local cultural setting. The building is 110m (360ft) long x 20m (65ft) deep. The structure and the side-by-side arrangement of its apartments opens the building to the possibilities of flexibility. Indeed, residents may select one or more standard units according to their living or working needs and are free to create a wide-open space by removing the partitions between units, which do not bear any structural weight. The largest structural overhang protrudes 3.6m (12ft) in accordance with the economic efficiencies of framed shear wall structures.

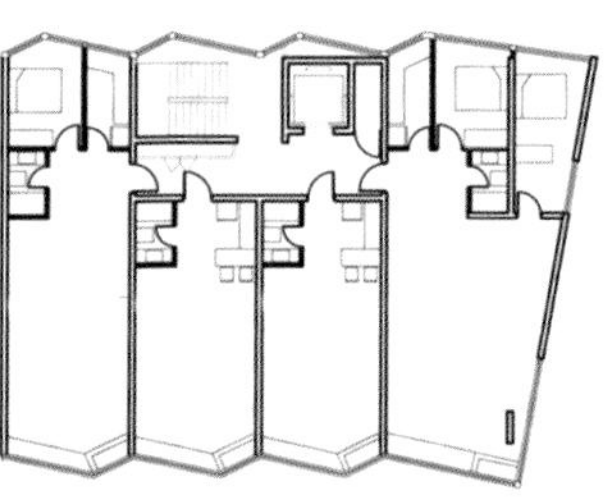

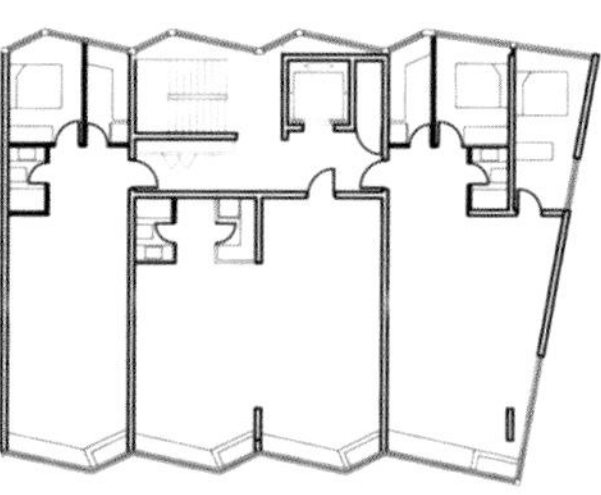

↗ 3

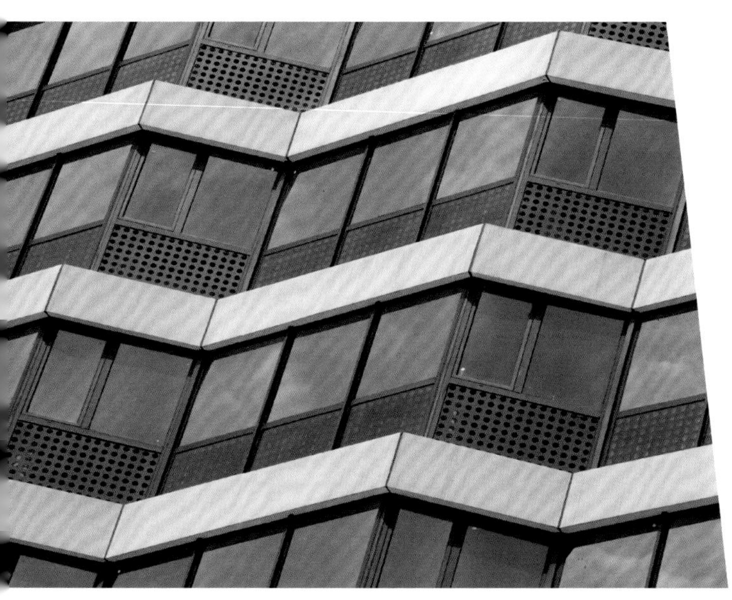

↗ 2

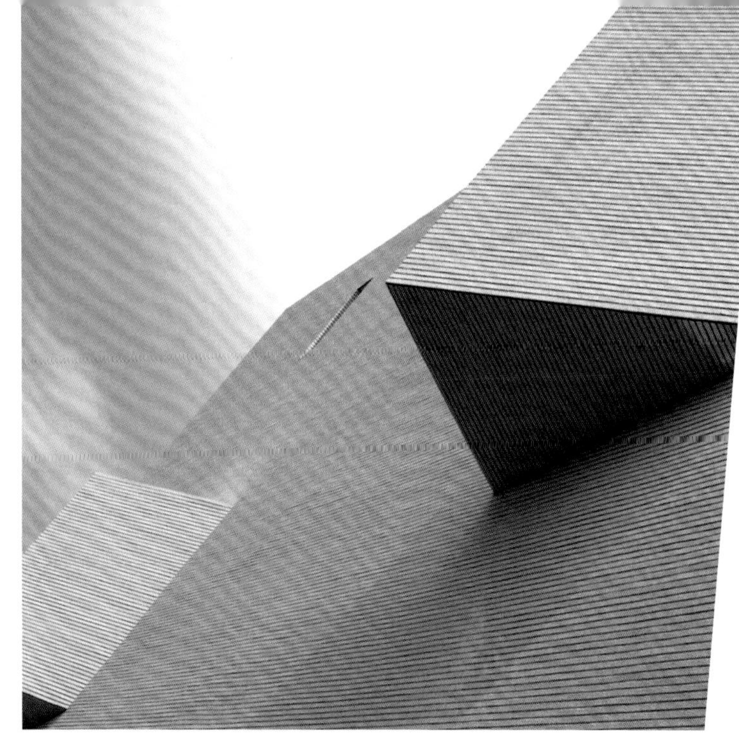

↗ 1

**Architect:** Di Shaohua
**Project:** Spring Art Museum
**Location:** Songzhuang, Beijing
**Completion:** 2015

In the art district of Songzhuang, the architect has made an attempt to reflect on local three-sided buildings, recalling the traditional residential courtyards. The roof comprises a series of stepped terraces, and the height difference allows daylight into the major exhibition spaces. These spaces have a ceiling profile that corresponds to that of the roof. Views are revealed through a few precious protruding windows in the major exhibition space. The exterior wall surface is composed of rather economical wall tiles that are readily available in the local market.

↗ 2

↗ 3

↗ 4

↗ 5

↗ 6

↗ 1

**Architect:** Di Shaohua
**Project:** Ying Gallery
**Location:** Caochangdi, Beijing
**Completion:** 2016

This art gallery has been formed by the renovation of a residual building. The gallery space is meant to be used for five years only, so the construction cost was limited to be 1000RMB (£90) per square metre. Since the yard wall had to be retained, the architect sandwiched it between the interior fit-out and an exterior layer of polycarbonate panels, both lightweight and economical. To increase its durability and achieve the desired visual quality, a layer of reflective membrane was applied to it at the back, giving the surface a metallic look. A DIY ceiling lamp is composed of more than 30 'flowers' made from non-woven fabrics, filtering blue or red light into the space. The design intended the Ying Gallery to be like a fresh flower, temporary and transient, but exuding freshness and energy, in the hope of contributing to better surroundings.

↗ 2

'I really didn't want to become an architect. I loved maths and engineering and wanted to get into computer science,' says Ding Wowo, reminiscing about her early life. Like many others in this collection, Ding's story records how, by sheer hard work and application – kick-started by a random choice of university degree programme – she is now dean of the prestigious School of Architecture at Nanjing University and a member of the National Supervision Board of Architectural Education.

It was her father who suggested architecture. He was one of the first generation of professional engineers in China. He became fascinated by observing architects who seemed to design buildings through sketches and drawings rather than with numbers and calculations. As a result, he recommended the subject to her by suggesting that 'architecture is obviously very playful'. Like many students wanting to relax after the stress of the National College Entrance Examination, she did not need to be asked twice.

She studied at Nanjing Institute of Technology (now Southeast University) and admits to not being a very good undergraduate student. Like many, she became frustrated with a subject that seemingly offered no right or wrong answers.[1] Open-endedness is confusing for Chinese students who are used to a repetitive diet of rote learning and definitive answers. She muddled along by following the teachers' instructions: 'I did what I was told. I did what they wanted to see.'

Her modesty belies the fact that she completed her studies, winning first prize for her thesis on the markets in Nanjing's Confucius Temple, gained an outstanding

designation for her Jiangsu provincial urban and rural planning design work, and went on to complete her doctorate at the Swiss Federal Institute of Technology (ETH) in Zurich in 2001.

Along the way, she began to challenge the notion that architecture, in Chinese language and education, was not considered to be a meaningful subject but was often regarded as the mere application of technology. Architecture was never included in discussions about art, and even today is often regarded as a subset of engineering or science, rather than a humanities or social sciences subject.

It was while being taught by the generation of architects who had experienced Western architecture at first hand in the 1930s (such as Yang Tingbao, architect of the Art Deco Dahua Cinema in Nanjing) that Ding was introduced to Western architectural theory. 'At the time,' she says, 'it was like learning a dictionary. These ideas were, I thought, just words with no application to design.' But in those early days – so soon after the reform and opening-up of China that began in 1978 – she remembers that many people were worried that China would blindly follow the West. Ding was less concerned. 'Western theory is based on their cognition, which is totally different to China. Western logic and methods need to be learned, because they can help us to analyse and understand ourselves.'

Another tutor, Professor Zhong Xunzheng (who joined the university in 1954, and is still there) did not approve of theory – and so taught her the relationship between structure and form. 'He taught me about urbanism. How to build, and the relationship with the site and context.' Combining the influences of these two tutors in particular, Ding now specializes in urban design and theory.

She believes that one of the most important issues for China's urban condition is how to use land more efficiently. Sprawl must be contained and architects must learn how to design well using smaller spaces.

## Sprawl must be contained

Good architecture, Ding asserts, is that which is 'built in the most beautiful, most suitable and most reasonable way'.

Speaking about working practices in China, she criticizes the practice of paying foreign firms a lot more than Chinese architectural practices. Foreign architects should be encouraged to work in China, she says, but the Chinese cannot just commission foreigners for all the major projects and ignore home-grown talent. 'We should compete fairly and, let me tell you, if a Chinese architectural practice loses in a competitive tender situation, have no doubt that it will learn a lesson and win next time.'

When asked about the position of women architects in China, she is characteristically feisty. 'Listen,' she says, 'if you are a woman and you are excellent, then you will be praised and the men will take second place. Actually, if you are a woman and you are excellent you will get *more* compliments than the men at the same level.'

The problem for Chinese women, she says, is determined by traditional gender roles. When a woman has children her career will take a back seat and 'to a certain extent, she'll give up'. Ding says: 'I'm very lucky because my family have always stood behind me in terms of my studies and career. The reason that there aren't more famous female architects is that they have given in. It is not because of gender-motivated injustices in the political system.'

She is on a roll. 'Some male architects are expected to get massively drunk with clients. But women can't. If I am told to meet a horrible client, I'll stay as far away as I can. I just can't do it. Basically, architecture is a service industry and if I'm honest it's one of the reasons that I became a teacher. In this job I don't need to talk and work with people I dislike.'

**Page 23** The façade of Suzhou Garden Museum New Building

**Architect:** Ding Wowo
**Project:** Suzhou Garden Museum New Building
**Location:** Suzhou, Jiangsu Province
**Completion:** 2007

The museum is separated from the Humble Administrator's Garden by an old wall, and Ding considered that while the old buildings should be renovated, the outline of the ancient traditional garden should remain untouched, as should the footprint of the buildings. Ding has attempted to make the architectural form fade away into the landscaping. Perspective and glimpsed views change naturally while walking through the traditional Chinese corridor and mirrors help to fade the materiality of the project. It has been described as creating a 'mystical illusion'.

↗ 1

↗ 2

↗ 3

↗ 4

↗ 5

↗ 6

↗ 1

↗ 2

**Architect:** Ding Wowo
**Project:** People's Hall
**Location:** Jiangyin, Jiangsu Province
**Completion:** 2010

Changjing Ancient Town is a typical river town south of the Yangtze River. The People's Hall, built in the 1970s, is an emblem of collective history. Here the façades literally present memory and context, whereby coated glass panels reflect the old building and surrounding residential area. 'Like our memory, the image flickers,' says Ding.

↗ 3

↗ 4

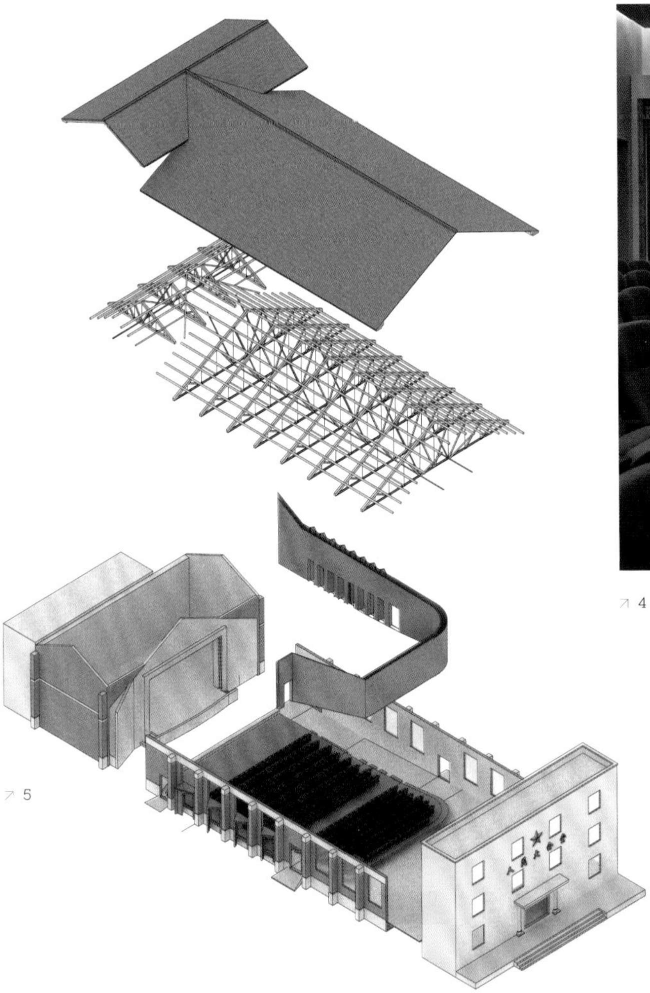

↗ 5

↗ 6

# Dong Mei 东梅

BIECHU KONGJIAN ARCHITECTS

BEIJING, CHINA

Dong Mei's father was a professor of philosophy and social sciences, her mother a scientist specializing in space technology, both based at China's foremost research university, Beihang, in Beijing. Dong's dream was to be a doctor, but she was put off, at the age of eighteen, when told that she would have to memorize Latin words, whereas if she studied architecture she could supposedly simply travel, paint and relax. She enrolled at the Nanjing Institute of Technology, one of the most traditionalist architecture schools in China, where she realized she would actually have to work. Here, construction is taught as a rational process, where economic practicality is the most important factor of any design decision. 'Aesthetics,' she says, is dealt with as a matter of 'self-cultivation'.

After graduating in 1989, Dong began work in Beijing at a small design institute owned by a large state-run construction company. She worked primarily on housing projects and won the Outstanding Design Award of Beijing in 1993 for her Beijing Daxing Zaoyuan residential project. She was offered more responsibility, and stayed for eleven years, working on commissions for primary schools and office buildings, and qualifying as a professional architect in the process. She also got married and had a child.

Life was normal. But one day in the late 1990s, Dong's husband brought home a copy of *A+U*, a Japanese architecture and urbanism magazine, featuring projects by Renzo Piano, Jacques Herzog and Rem Koolhaas; then she saw an article in *World Architecture* about Luis Barragán. When she read that he did not care about 'fashion' but only about 'aesthetics' and 'emotion', she

was so upset that she started crying at her desk. She realized that she 'had an ordinary life, in the same city where I was born, and I had already passed my thirtieth birthday. I felt lost.'

In 2000, Dong travelled to Europe, 'to see the world', and then, that same year, won her first individual project, a commission for the Peking University Agriculture Garden Cafeteria. It was the first time that she had used contemporary design to deal with a historical site. Unable to completely shake off her Nanjing training, she says that this project 'successfully optimized the distribution of meals', but then describes how it focused on the quality and diversity of the dining area, completely changing the traditional floor-plan layout of a student cafeteria in China. It gained a silver medal at the China Architectural Awards.

In the spring of 2004, Dong founded BieChu KongJian (Other Space) architects office with her husband, Liu Xiaochuan. The pair re-evaluated their architectural philosophy, which became 'using life to think about space, rather than space to think about life'. The company took on several prestigious commissions that focused on the harmonious effects of comprehensive energy conservation. 'This was before China's public building energy-efficiency standards came out. We did a lot of theoretical investigation and practical research on how to simplify the building volumes, improve natural ventilation, and so on.' Environmental friendliness became her design principle. Subsequently, Dong's Hangxing Technology Centre in Beijing was awarded a LEED silver rating by the US Green Building Council.

In May 2008, the Sichuan (or Wenchuan) earthquake struck, killing nearly 70,000 people and displacing millions more. Dong bought a booklet called *Harmonious Homeland Reconstruction* and took its ideas of sustainable development to the earthquake zone. Respecting the local people's culture and self-esteem, she tried to provide them with the information to reconstruct their homeland using environmentally friendly and sustainable disciplines.

Dong considers travelling as a 'deep, relaxing breath' between different projects. Her domestic and international travel experiences fundamentally changed how she views the world. 'I not only pay attention to the architecture of a city but also to its people and culture. I have found myself turning the firm's business into a "travelling journey" rather than "a pursuit of commercial success".'

Using this experience, she has lectured on comparisons between Eastern and Western culture, considering the differences in traditional architectural construction and cultural habits. 'I think the real difference is not only the external representation but rather the way of thinking and philosophy. When I look back on the journey I have been through, I found the big difference to be my Western rational education.'

In 2012, she spent a year researching in preparation for her Shuiguang Christian Church project, which will be sited on a hillside beside the Liangzi Lake in Hubei province. 'The sunlight reflecting off the water will give the altar a living beauty,' Dong says. Construction of the church began in 2017. She also completed a Buddhist temple project in the spring of that year. The Feitianshan Shoufo Buddhist Temple is located on the top of a mountain in Chenzhou in Hunan province. 'Comparing the locations of both projects, we found that the church reflects the idea of China's traditional "hidden" *shan shui* landscape design concept. In contrast, the Buddhist temple's location reflects a Western "positive expressive" design concept. The Eastern and Western design concepts have been swapped in these projects. I consider this the real embodiment of Eastern and Western cultural exchange.'

As a female architect with her own firm, she finds she can be very independent compared to female architects who work for China's architectural institutions. 'I need to take care of every

# Environmental friendliness became her design principle

detail in the firm's business. In order to succeed, I think the most important things are a strong, determined mind and the ability to communicate with others. From my point of view, architecture is a representation of ponderous artistic expressions. It not only requires rational, logical construction to provide structural support for human beings but also a cultural and conceptual support to protect the inner self.' She thinks that China has developed too fast over the past thirty years, preventing people from slowing down and thinking about their ideas. 'We are building buildings as if we were "doing detailed needlework while running".'

As her career has progressed, she has come to understand that architecture is not just a design skill, but also a way to see the world. Running her own firm has meant facing the challenge of a lack of human resources and project opportunities, and it took a long time to build up her own business circle. But she believes it has been worth it. 'Since setting up the firm, I've received more independent opportunities to think and express my own architectural ideas.'

As China's economy develops, more people are paying attention to the value of a cultural education and to quality of life. As such, she says, this will 'provide more and more job opportunities, with more women architects joining the field'. Dong is keen that gender should not be considered a factor in the evaluation of an architect's work. 'Men and women share the same professional standards in this field, but of course women are under more pressure than men since they are expected to work and take good care of their family at the same time.'

She is not able to quickly select the project that she is most proud of out of all the work she has done. 'Somewhere deep in my heart I am still expecting something new and different. Maybe in the future, when my inner world has expanded further, I hope I can still create and think independently.'

↗ 1

↗ 2

↗ 3

**Page 33** Beijing Badaling Forest Experience Centre

**Architect:** Dong Mei
**Project:** Beijing Badaling Forest Experience Centre
**Location:** Qinglong Valley, Badaling, Yanqing County, Beijing
**Completion:** 2014

The Badaling forestry area was founded in 1958. Situated in the Qinglong Valley, this forest experience museum has been designed to educate people about the need to preserve natural woodlands and to propagate forestry knowledge. It comprises a reception area, four exhibition halls, a conference hall, a multifunctional lounge, a workshop, offices, etc. The thirty-three poplar trees on the site were retained and incorporated into the design of the building (the foundations were spread between the trees to protect the roots). The building uses recoverable and recyclable material such as steel and wood, and thanks to the canopy of poplar trees, the indoor space stays cool in summer.

↗ 5

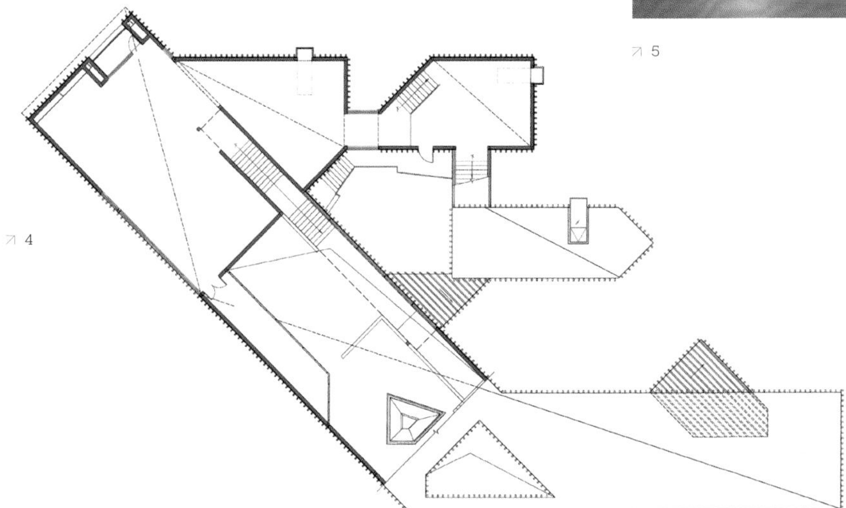

↗ 4

↗ 6

↗ 7

八达岭
森林体验馆

↗ 1

**Architect:** Dong Mei
**Project:** Hei Hu Primary School
**Location:** Hei Hu Township, Maoxian, Sichuan Province
**Completion:** 2012

The scenery couldn't be more dramatic, although it is also deadly as this is the post-disaster reconstruction of Hei Hu (Black Tiger) primary school, which was severely damaged in the Sichuan earthquake of 2008. The reconstruction started in 2010 to create a new, green school but also to retain the Qiang cultural heritage of this particular area. The new school provides teaching space for 320 young students, cafeterias, student dormitory (for boarders), offices, and so on. Dong says: 'It was particularly difficult to solve the contradiction between local masonry building materials and the need for a reliable anti-seismic structure.' This was resolved by incorporating structural columns in the fabric of the walls and using reinforcing mesh throughout. The architect has also introduced rainwater harvesting, biogas digesters, solar panels, double glazing and thermal insulation boards made from rice husk.

↗ 2

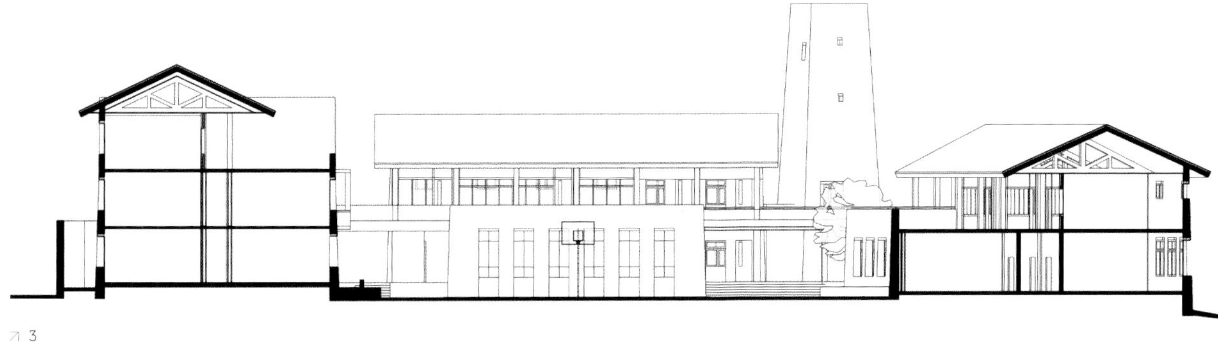

↗ 3

↘ 4

↘ 5

↗ 1

↗ 2

**Architect:** Dong Mei
**Project:** Ding Xiang Eco-Village
**Location:** Badaling, Beijing
**Completion:** 2016

This project is located approximately 80 kilometres (50 miles) northwest of Beijing, near the most visited section of the Great Wall, in the lush vegetation and mountain ranges of Badaling. The site is renowned for its clove fragrance in summer and its brightly coloured leaves in autumn. This project is a high-end eco-hotel comprising forty chalets, designed to respect and protect the surrounding natural environment and save energy. These timber outcrops, on a steel frame with bamboo screens, manage to blend into the setting in both summer and winter months.

↗ 3

↗ 4

↗ 5

↗ 6

↗ 7

↗ 8

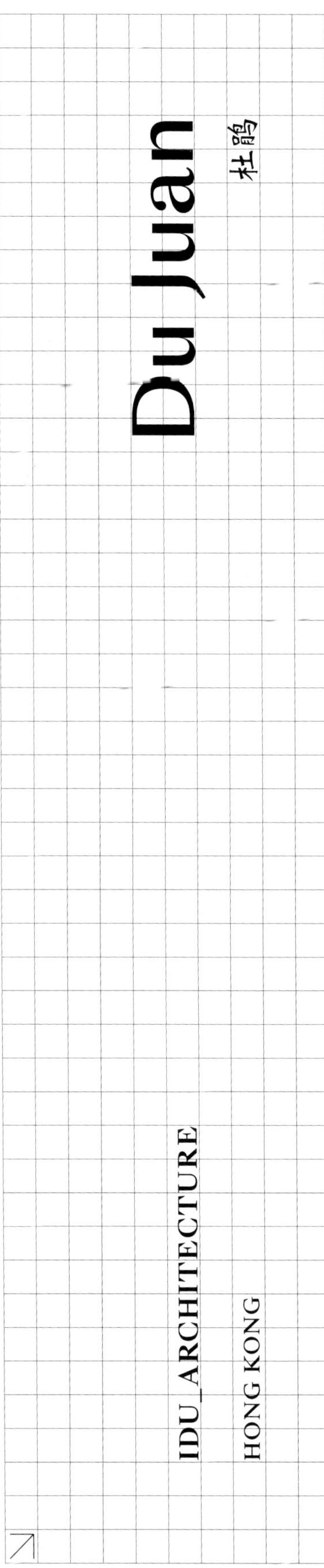

Du Juan is associate dean of the Faculty of Architecture at the University of Hong Kong. She also heads up IDU_architecture, a design and research office that was formed in 2006 to promote socially and environmentally responsible practice. Du has worked extensively in the USA, Europe and China as an academic, theoretician and practitioner, having taught at the Department of Architecture at Massachusetts Institute of Technology, explored modern Dutch architectural practice with Christine Boyer, and taught urban studies at the Graduate Centre of Architecture at Peking University.

Her international journey turned full circle with a Ruskin travel grant that she used to turn her interest in Chinese landscape gardens into a research and cultural speciality. Over the course of her studies, she explored Palladio and Carlo Scarpa in Venice in order to read buildings and landscape, 'to discover architecture that transcends cultural context and nationality'.

Du Juan was born in China (her family is from northern Jinan) and in her early years she displayed a talent and enthusiasm for painting and history, although she acknowledges that she enjoyed 'elements of everything'. Such eclecticism ultimately directed her to architecture: a subject, she says, that 'lets you see all the world in a material sense but also with intellectual and critical depth'.

While she was growing up, her family lived for a time in Beijing, until the turmoil surrounding the Tiananmen Square pro-democracy protests in 1989 inspired them to leave for the United States. Here her father pursued a second PhD, while she became the first Chinese

student to enrol in her school in Ohio. From there she went to college in Florida – an immigrant state, as she calls it (80 per cent of the state's population growth results from net migration[1]) – before moving on to her postgraduate studies at Princeton, completed in 2004.

Du worked for some time in the United States, notably for Mack Scogin Merrill Elam Architects in Atlanta, Georgia – an experience that she said 'shaped her to see the possibilities of unconventional practice and the joy of working with people'. Then, after spending a working summer vacation in Paris at the offices of Santiago Calatrava, she landed a Fulbright scholarship that brought her back to China for the first time as a professional. The year was 2003, and she spent twelve months in Shanghai and Suzhou examining the meaning and influence of the Chinese garden in a historical and contemporary context, exploring what Du calls the essential interrelationship between landscape and architecture.

Suzhou was a logical place for Du to settle, not only because its ancient, classical gardens and canals are world-famous and UNESCO-protected, but also because it resembles her old home town of Jinan. In both locations, huge areas have been destroyed by rapid urbanization, but she felt that her research would have been coloured by nostalgia if she had gone back to Jinan. Even in Suzhou she is emotionally engaged in her subject, confessing that on her first garden visit she wept at its centuries-old beauty and sophistication.

In 2005, her travels took her to Shenzhen, where she 'accidentally ran into an "urban village"'. This was at the time when the mayor of this explosively expanding city had called for the 'eradication of the cancer of urban villages'. She became obsessed. 'I found that in a newly emerging planned city, 50 per cent of the population lived in illegal settlements... and the more I learned, the more I saw the contradictions.'

Her interests then as now reveal a fascination with the transformations of the contemporary Chinese city, but also a concern for the consequences of those transformations; she explores how cities can move forward while still respecting the history and heritage of the built fabric and the people who inhabit those forgotten spaces. Her mission – her contribution – has become one of engaging in the Chinese city while, rather than after, decisions are made.

Anyone seriously interested in cities ought to take a look at Shenzhen. Admittedly, hidden within are some dark realities of slum residences and exploited and disenfranchised workers, but there is also a vitality to this remarkable city that should not be ignored and could be consciously directed in a more progressive direction.

Du's work has been exhibited internationally, including at the Venice Architecture Biennale and the Brazil International Exhibition of Architecture and Urbanism. But it was as the assistant curator, in 2005, of the first Shenzhen Biennale of Urbanism/Architecture that Du created a meaningful legacy project, with a significant intervention in the policies and practices of the city. She speaks of the privilege of having space to be idealistic and of trying to make a difference in a city that, for many people, is moving too fast.

She is currently working on a book focused on the extended urban history of Shenzhen and the role of the city's informal urbanism, which she characterizes as an 'informal intelligence of everyday life that we have to be open-minded about in order to learn from'. She is also working with poor families in tiny apartments in super-dense housing blocks in order to provide space-saving solutions and something resembling a quality of life. Quietly, stealthily, hopefully, she has steered local discussion and influenced a wider national discourse towards learning from, and caring about, how people live.

Page 47 Open House interior

**Architect:** Du Juan & Chad McKee
**Project:** Open House
**Location:** Sai Ying Pun, Hong Kong
**Completion:** 2010

Open House is a preservation and adaptive reuse project of a 1940s four-storey residential building in Hong Kong's historic Sai Ying Pun area, nestled between imposing high-rise residential towers. After extensive repair work, the simple beauty of the original architecture inspired the design of an open volume whereby the urban and the natural are brought into the living spaces. With careful attention to environmentally responsible materials, natural lighting, passive ventilation and an insulating garden roof, the project has respectfully adapted a traditional dwelling type into an environmentally modern response to its history.

↗ 1

↘ 2

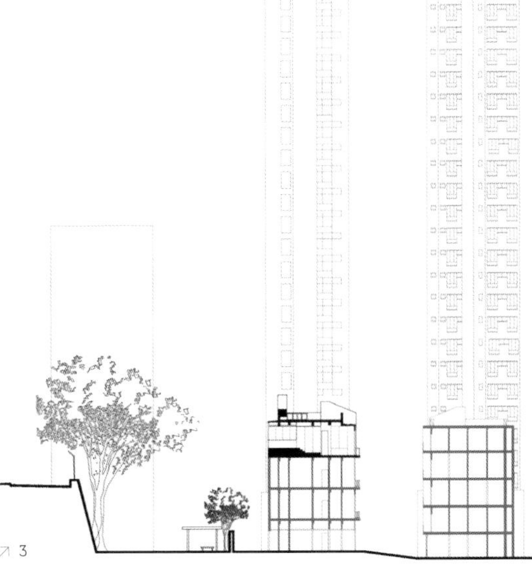

↗ 3

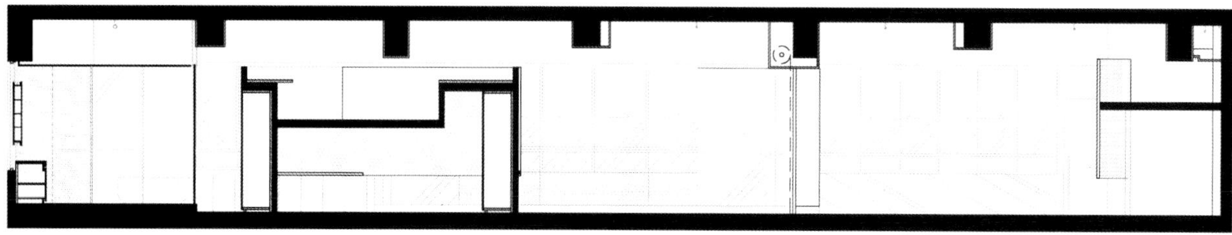

↗ 1

↗ 2

**Architect:** Du Juan & Chad McKee Urban Ecologies Design Lab
**Project:** Room with a Changing View
**Location:** Chai Wan, Hong Kong
**Completion:** 2013

Located in a mid-rise industrial building, Room with a Changing View is an adaptive reuse project converting a storage warehouse into a contemporary live-work space for an artist and her friends and family. With panoramic views of the surrounding harbour, landscape and city, it presents a unique way of understanding and reconsidering the ever-changing context. Sliding windows, glass panels and mirrored surfaces carefully wrap the structure and create illusions of continuity, spatial extension and contraction. Glass, perforated metal screens, and translucent and transparent materials ensure the continuous flow of natural light and air throughout the project.

↗ 3

↗ 4

↗ 5

↗ 1

↗ 2

**Architect:** Du Juan and HKU Urban Ecologies Design Lab
**Project:** Project Home Improvements
**Location:** Subdivided Units, Aberdeen District, Hong Kong
**Completion:** 2017–

Hong Kong has a large population living with substandard housing conditions, predominantly in subdivided units (SDU). These ones are regular 43.5m² (468ft²) apartments subdivided to accommodate several families, some of multiple generations. The project aims to improve the indoor living conditions of SDUs through small-scale architectural interventions, at the same time collecting much-needed empirical knowledge on SDUs in Hong Kong. This is a co-creation process with students, residents and social workers. A key challenge is that the team is working with renters, and not owners, to avoid the possibility of rental increases. Furthermore, the design interventions may not change the structures or the general layout and have to be at a scale that does not further overwhelm the limited space.

↗ 1

**Architect:** Du Juan
**Project:** House with a Borrowed Landscape
**Location:** Hong Kong
**Completion:** 2017

This is a house refurbishment and reconfiguration of a property in a ravine-like site, boxed in by walls and rockfaces. By opening up the windows and embracing the proximity of the facing wall strewn with plants and mosses, it brings light streaming in but also provides a high-level garden scene. Daylighting is accentuated by the glazed partitions and pristine white interiors. Mirrors, a popular device of Juan's, also increase the sense of space, which is at a premium in Hong Kong.

↗ 2

↗ 3

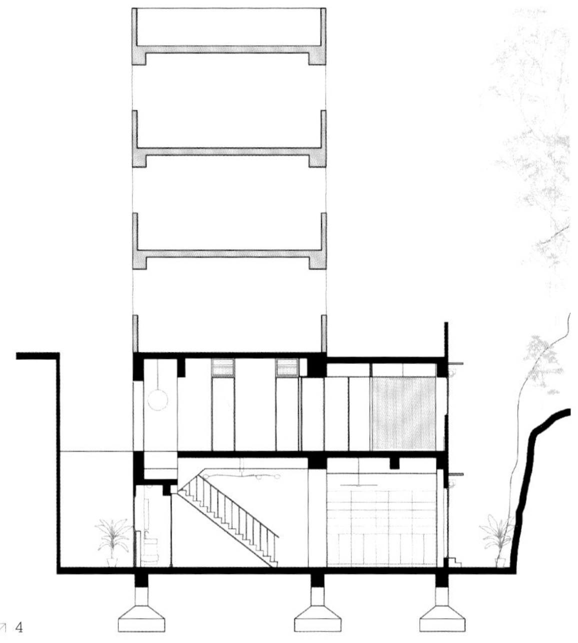

↗ 4

↗ 5

↗ 6

↗ 7

Fan Beilei is a co-founder of genarchitects in Shanghai, a company that she started in 2013 with her partner, Kong Rui. The company name is difficult to translate, but the Chinese word *gèn* refers to an intangible element or energy that permeates the whole of existence. It is a reflection of Fan's spiritual belief in the serene origins of the universe. Such a worldview has been influenced by her professors, employers and peers, but also inspired by her travels and experiences.

Born in Huainan, a poor town in Anhui province, she applied to Tongji University to study physics but failed the entrance examination. As a result she had to turn to Plan B, which was to sign up to architecture.

Having effectively fallen into the subject by accident, it was only when she met her tutor Professor Wang Fangji during her late undergraduate studies that she really began to see architecture as a valid option. By bringing in a variety of external practitioners, he taught her to see architecture as a real-world profession, focusing on construction, materials and details rather than concepts and abstraction.

Fan worked for a while at Atelier Deshaus in Shanghai, a practice that offered her a modern apprenticeship-style education. She describes three passionate architects there who, on a daily basis, enthusiastically organized discussions about architecture. This effective pupillage was, she says, 'a hugely rewarding period, which gave me a lot of strength'.

After a few years, she won a scholarship to complete her master's degree at Tongji with a dual degree option to study at the Technische Universität in Berlin (TUB). It seems that she

relished the opportunity to acclimatize somewhat to a European lifestyle. She explains that, when not in class, she would travel around France, Belgium, Switzerland and Italy. 'In every city,' she says, 'I liked to dine at the same restaurant to imagine that I was living as a local.'

One of the TUB design projects was based in Ahmedabad, India. During a site visit, she found work as an intern at HCP Design, Planning and Management, a practice that prides itself on elegant solutions to practical problems. Her experiences in India 'completely overturned [her] perception of the world'. On the one hand, it was the poverty and resilience of the poor that shocked and humbled her; on the other hand the trip brought her into contact with the work of Louis Kahn. She describes her first visit to Ahmedabad's Indian Institute of Management in almost poetic terms: 'At that moment I felt the tranquillity of architecture, a timelessness and a beauty beyond words.'

Her extensive travels made her consider the quotidian but also the culturally different ways that we appreciate the meaning of life. European students, she says, have the freedom, self-assurance and time to develop their ambitions, whereas Chinese students are always on a treadmill. Reflecting back on her experiences, she believes that she has learned how to take things a bit more easily, to prioritize and to appreciate life.

By the end of 2011, Fan and her partner were given a commission by a couple of friends to design a retreat in Moganshan near Hangzhou. Designed together (Kong moved there for a year to supervise construction), this became the inaugural project for their newly independent office. 'It was this project above all else that made us realize where our passion lay. For us, the practice of architecture is about the pursuit of beauty.'

In some ways, the glory days of small start-up architects' practices getting large commissions had already come to an end in China by 2013. No longer could a new firm pick up work easily. Commissions for new-build projects particularly were being directed by well-established developers who had their own tried and tested networks. As a result, genarchitects found it difficult to get substantial, new or prestigious projects: instead, they made their name as renovation architects of old derelict industrial and commercial premises.

This kind of remodelling project is complicated, but it was precisely because of the time-consuming nature of the work that design institutes were not particularly interested in doing it. This left the field open for Fan – who had been schooled in the practical detailing of architecture – to seize the opportunity. Genarchitects had their foot in the door.

Fan recounts her first experience. Facing a worn-out building that had previously undergone a wide range of uses and prior modifications – from hotels to fast-food restaurants, as well as illegal additions – forced her to rigorously appraise the merits of the architecture. 'How does the building interact with the city and with history? How will the building be used in the future? The resolution of these two questions determines whether we can reconfigure the building to provide a new quality of life.'

Winning contracts is always difficult and the times are getting more challenging in China. But she is clear in her ambitions: 'It is not about having no jobs or finding it hard to survive, but it is always about how to realize satisfying architecture. All I can do is be true to myself, insist on my ideas and my beliefs, and push as hard as I can to achieve the highest possible standards.' She continues: 'Whether in today's context or in the past, the most important part is not to think of being a female architect, but of becoming a great architect.'

**Page 57** Baggy Treehouse

**Architect:** Fan Beilei
**Project:** Baggy Treehouse
**Location:** Xiuning, Anhui Province
**Completion:** 2016

This village project has been built at Mount Huangshan, a gently sloping natural landscape densely coated with pine trees. The Baggy Treehouse is a free-standing architectural prototype, able to adapt to different terrains with minimal design variations. The design concept aims to imitate a primitive cave or nest.

It is in fact a hotel standing among the pine groves on the mountainside, overlooking the valley from above the tree canopy. Guests enter through a darkened vestibule and emerge in a bright corner, from which views of the mountains unfold.

↗ 1

↗ 2

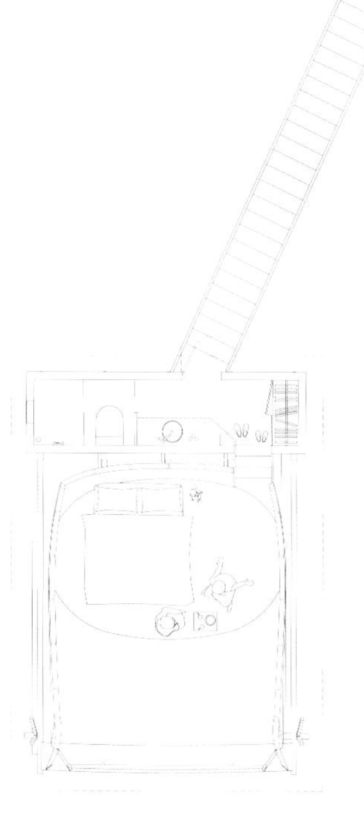

↗ 3

↗ 4

↘ 5

↗ 6

**Architect:** Fan Beilei
**Project:** Original Homestay
**Location:** Deqing, Zhejiang Province
**Completion:** 2013

This retreat lies in a narrow site set in a valley planted with bamboo and tea and alongside a small brook. A single mass is dispersed into five components and spread along the site at varying heights. The double-pitch, black-tile roof is retained as an echo of local housing: a response to the shape of the surrounding mountain and a representation of a primary school that was originally there. The black brick wall – the local architectural material – brings a sense of scale.

↗ 1

↘ 2

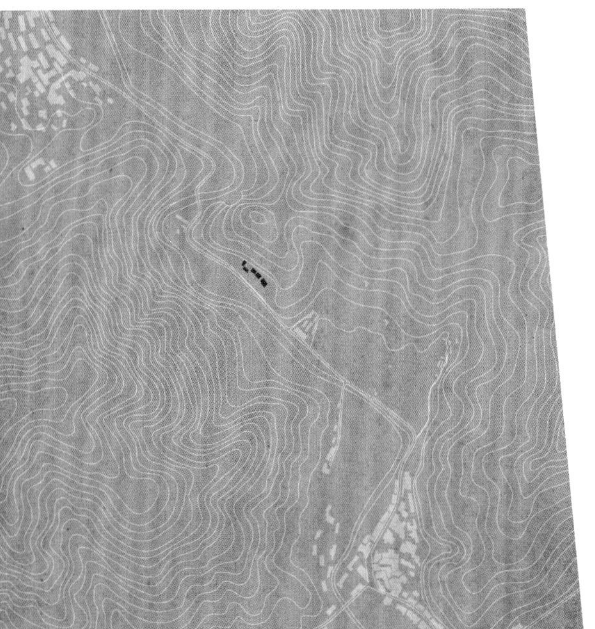

↘ 3

↗ 4

↗ 5

↗ 6

↗ 1

**Architect:** Fan Beilei
**Project:** Shangsi'an Retreat
**Location:** Changxing, Zhejiang, China
**Completion:** 2016

Shangsi'an village is located on the west shore of Taihu Lake. One of its inlet creeks runs through the site, with a stone bridge connecting the north and south banks. This project transforms six different buildings – including a Qing dynasty timber house, a warehouse, three two-storey buildings with tile façades and a newly built archaized exhibition hall – into a distributed village retreat. Working with the structural reality of what they found, the architects demolished and replaced derelict buildings while simply strengthening the timber house. A light pavilion has been constructed as an outdoor public space for both guests and villagers.

↗ 2

↗ 3

↘ 4

↗ 5

Rossana Hu, also known as Hu Rushan, is a founding partner of Neri&Hu Design and Research Office, an architectural practice with a growing reputation and an increasingly international client base. She and her husband, Lyndon Neri, opened the office in Shanghai in 2004 and now have more than 100 staff. By 2010, they had won the Architectural Review Award for Emerging Architecture, and soon afterwards they opened a new, smaller office in London. The practice provides an interdisciplinary service including interiors, furniture and lighting design as well as their architectural staple.

Hu claims that she studied architecture by default rather than by design, saying that as a schoolchild she enjoyed both arts and sciences. In a characteristically – or perhaps stereotypically – Chinese way she says, 'I found that mathematics was very easy for me and so I took all the really hard calculus classes', while she also excelled in social sciences. She went on to study at Princeton and the University of California, Berkeley (as did her husband), and from there moved to New York to work in the offices of Michael Graves & Associates and Skidmore, Owings & Merrill. It was while working on Graves's refurbishment of the Union Building on the Shanghai Bund that Hu and Neri decided to settle in the city and try their luck in private practice.

Hu's international exposure has provided her with a wealth of experience, allowing her to balance Western and Eastern modes of thinking and working. Indeed, she professes an interest in challenging the creeping architectural homogenization that comes with globalization: something that is, she argues,

1

adversely affecting many Chinese architects. Famously, in an interview several years ago, she claimed that 'all architects in China are lost', asserting that they have no real belief in what they are doing. For Hu though, architecture is always about subtlety, intuition, passion and keeping an open mind.

Some people observing China from a distance may think that this desire for open-mindedness is counter-intuitive – surely China is a country little renowned for creativity and open discussion? But Hu is adamant. She suggests that it is, in many ways, the Western architects arriving in China who are the ones with preconceived ideas. It is they who cannot handle such a fervid atmosphere in which exploration and experimentation are commonplace – 'where people have the freedom to be bad'.

In such a rapidly changing country, architects clearly face pressures to deal with alterations imposed on their designs, learning that things might not go their own way. While this is frustrating, Hu looks positively on the fact that this teaches architects – some architects, at least – patience and humility. For her, these are important qualities. But that humility should be balanced with the professional confidence to exercise one's judgment. She says that personal and professional development is not about what we know but rather what we do not know, which in turn forces us to know more. Such an approach is reflected in her office's working practices.

Using designers and artists to complement Neri&Hu's architectural services has resulted in a section of the company that now designs and produces high-end furniture for leading brands. The product range, known simply as 'objects', includes furniture, light fittings, glassware, ceramics and various tableware products, with commissions from leading global retailers. Working closely with allied creative practitioners, sharing expertise and skills in-house, is something that few Chinese practices do. Hu says, 'Without our product design team, all of our furniture would look like boxes, like buildings, so they bring a different scale to the details.'

The architectural arm of the practice is firmly interested in respecting the history of a city. This, too, is something new both for Shanghai and for China. It is a way of working best exemplified by the Waterhouse Building renovation project in Shanghai, completed in 2010. This scheme did more than transform a disused warehouse; it also transformed Neri&Hu's fortunes. The project catapulted them to world renown as thoughtful and contemporary practitioners.

With this project, an old industrial building that had been used as a military headquarters by the Japanese Army in the 1930s was recreated as a

**in China, people have the freedom to be bad**

boutique hotel and restaurant. It retained much of the dilapidated fabric but ensured that there remained a clear distinction between original and new – reminiscent of David Chipperfield's Neues Museum in Berlin (completed a year earlier). It is apparent that Neri&Hu's architectural approach to this project, and to heritage-inspired designs generally, seeks to apprehend 'the beauty of the passing of time'. This aspect, Hu says, is something that she cannot artificially create, and so she must capture it in the original and use it.

Hu has great ambitions for the practice. When asked about what it means to be a woman architect in China, she laughs. 'Honestly, I barely think about my gender,' she says, but notes that the outlook for women architects in China is much better than it was. She adds, 'Actually, in our practice we have more female architects than men. That's not a conscious policy, it's just turned out that way. We simply have really great female architects.'

**Page 69** The interior of Rachel's Burger

**Architect:** Neri&Hu
**Project:** Rachel's Burger
**Location:** Shanghai
**Completion:** 2015

Clearly inspired by 1950s American burger bars, this kerb-side restaurant is designed to be a porous space, blurring the edges of inside and outside. The external wall shutters can be opened fully to create a real sense of external space, or closed to create intimacy, security and weather protection. When fully closed, a combination of clear, textured and mirrored glass is used to great effect to visually extend the boundaries of the space while bringing light, views and streetscape deep inside. The dematerialization of the walls emphasizes the horizontal planes where the roof structure seemingly floats above the space. Integrated communal tables with pivoting benches are suited for individual or group dining needs.

↗ 1

↗ 2

↗ 1

**Architect:** Neri&Hu
**Project:** The Waterhouse
**Location:** South Bund, Shanghai
**Completion:** 2010

The Waterhouse is a four-storey, nineteen-room boutique hotel that has been created from an old industrial building on the southern bank of Shanghai Bund. Its refurbishment reflects the evolutionary process of Shanghai over the last century. In the 1930s, the building was used as the military headquarters of the Japanese occupying forces and so it has a chilling history that is not lost in its fortified, prison-like appearance. An extra floor added to the original three-storey construction creates a juxtaposition of contrasting old and new, with the original concrete textures supplemented with Cor-Ten steel. The courtyards are revealed and wooden casement windows of different sizes puncture the walls, emulating some of the longtang (alley housing) of old Shanghai.

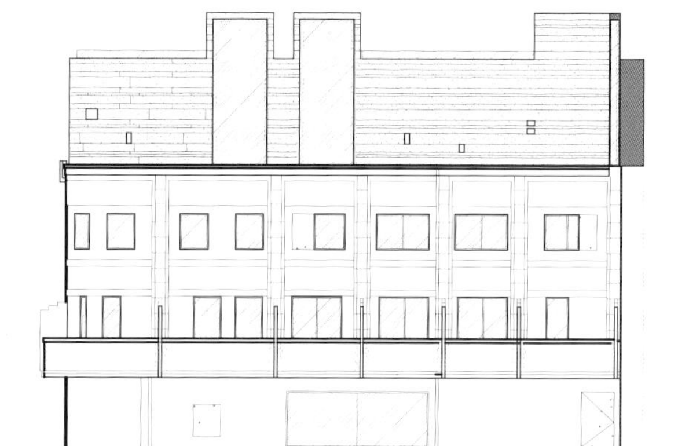

↗ 2

↗ 3

↗ 1

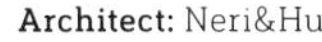

**Architect:** Neri&Hu
**Project:** Sulwhasoo Flagship Store
**Location:** Gangnam-gu, Seoul, South Korea
**Completion:** 2016–17

The lantern is highly significant in Asian history and myth – it leads you through the dark, shows the way and indicates the start and the end of a journey. Neri&Hu's radical transformation of an existing five-storey building originates from three core themes – identity, journey and memory – aspiring to create a space that appeals to all the senses. The concept of the lantern generated a continuous brass structure that ties the whole store together, leading customers to explore the full extent of the space. Through a series of voids and openings in the building, visitors experience the transition from the dark brick basement spa with warm timber floors, to a lighter material palette that becomes more open as you move up the building. The journey culminates in a roof terrace with its free-flowing brass structure canopy that frames the views of the surrounding city.

↗ 2

↘ 3

↘ 4

↗ 1

**Architect:** Neri&Hu
**Project:** Le Méridien Zhengzhou
**Location:** Zhengzhou, Henan Province
**Completion:** 2013

To showcase Henan's art history, the architect conceived of the building as an 'archive' of new and old artefacts. Externally the archives are expressed as cantilevered stacked boxes, each carefully composed with subtle ins and outs to break down the bulky proportions of the original structure. The twenty-five-storey building consists of a five-storey podium of public functions and a tower of 350 private guest rooms, with inspiration from the nearby historic Longmen Caves. The project has strong verticals, including its hanging lights, the forest of columns at the entrance and the internal dividing slats.

↗ 2

↗ 3

↗ 4

↗ 5

↗ 6

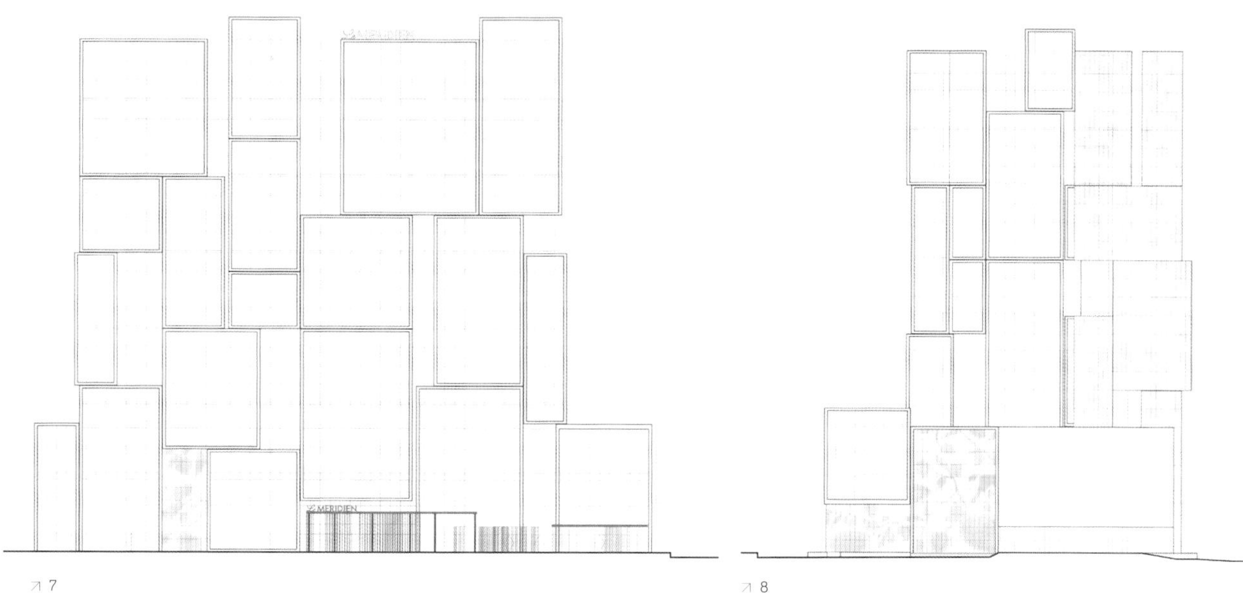

↗ 7

↗ 8

↘ 9

↘ 10

Jiang Ying says that she was born into architecture. Her father was an architect, and her childhood memories are of a house full of architectural magazines and photograph albums of buildings. Her mother, a nurse, would work most evenings, and Jiang describes growing up in her father's architectural design studio. 'There were always 2B pencils and worn triangular rulers scattered around, so I took to doodling.'

Her home town is Nanning, the capital of Guangxi province. After completing her undergraduate degree in the School of Architecture of the South China University of Technology (SCUT), she was selected, along with fifteen other students, to join the French exchange programme '100 Architectes Chinois en France'. She relocated to L'École Nationale Supérieure d'Architecture de Versailles on a President Chirac Scholarship, from where she graduated as an *architecte* DPLG (registered architect) in 2004.

Jiang decided to stay on in Europe for a while, joining the huge multidisciplinary consultancy AREP in Paris as a project architect on a wide range of large-scale international projects, including Gare de Schuman in Brussels as well as Xizhimen Station in Beijing and Shanghai South Station. She also worked with the German architectural practice von Gerkan, Marg and Partners on Nanning International Convention and Exhibition Centre, using the opportunity to examine the state of cooperation between

China and other countries and 'better get to know the design environment'.

By 2005, she had joined the Belgium-based practice of Buro2, liaising on the Guangzhou Baiyun International Convention Centre, a governmental project. Jiang acted as the design representative, while the primary architect was He Jianxiang, now her husband. He had studied at KU Leuven university in Belgium some years earlier and by this time was the chief architect for the China International Trust and Investment Corporation (CITIC) Design Institute in South China.

Jiang says that they both wanted more independence, but also wanted to right some of the wrongs of ill-considered and inappropriate architectural interventions in their own country, and so she returned to China in 2007 to help He. The two founded their own practice, O-office Architects, in Guangzhou. The practice is rooted in the southern China experience: 'The fast development of the Pearl River Delta over the last thirty years has smashed traditional architecture into pieces. We are constantly thinking about how we can rectify it.'

Clearly, they can do little about the fact that China is in a rapidly changing period when projects, even their own, are subject to all kinds of alterations. But 'architecture is constantly being amended, distorted and decomposed... and as architects, we need to look for our own way out in this process of rapid change, creatively responding to these changes while maintaining our independent critical thinking.'

O-office sees this as an opportunity to intervene in the practical realities of urban transition to create new functions. But more than that, it is an opportunity to be part of a city's history. Jiang sees renovation projects as an opportunity to rewrite a new narrative on to abandoned spaces. She says, 'Careless renovation is architectural violence. It has the same irreversibly disruptive power as demolition. We pride ourselves on carefully talking to the site, letting our new urban specimen incise the city memory, blending in the thinking and longing of its new participants.'

Some of her exemplary projects are shown here. One uses the abandoned Honghua Dyeing Factory, located in Shenzhen East, to create a youth hostel. The machinery was removed but the architects tried to minimize the new intervention and maintain the originality of the building. The second project is the Silo Reconversion at the Shenzhen Architectural Biennale, which repurposed the empty shell of the Guangdong Float Glass Factory into a space to display exhibitions, hold debates and conduct workshops. After the biennale was over it could easily morph into 'postindustrial workspaces for local creatives'. These themes of recycling and reuse can be found in Jiang and He's own office building – the conversion of the oldest beer factory in Guangzhou into a giant concrete penthouse-style office.

This elevated working environment appears to have given her some distance from which to reflect on life. Here, in this floating commune, she says that family and work are not necessarily opposites. Her studio partner is also her husband, and 'we don't separate work and family. Architects require long working hours, so we have kitchens and relaxing café bars in our office. We have planted all kinds of fruit trees and flowers on the balcony and when the sun is shining there are wonderful shadows from the greenery next to our desks. Sometimes our colleagues bring children to the office when we're working overtime.'

She continues, 'The classification of a "female architect" is a false proposition. Any differences are merely the differences that you might find between any individual architects. Compared to the old days, modern females have more choices and possibilities. Although the shackles on women are everywhere in terms of social values, I never really pay attention to what others think. Whether it is work or family, design or life, it is what it is. There is no point in adopting external labels to define yourself. Just get on with it.'

**Page 81** Inside the Silo Reconversion

**Architect:** Jiang Ying
**Project:** Silo Reconversion
**Location:** Nanshan District, Shenzhen
**Completion:** 2013

This huge factory silo – repurposed as exhibition and workshop space for the Shenzhen Architectural Biennale – is the key landmark on the entire site, located between the production hall and the sand storage warehouse. The building is 78m (256ft) long and is divided into three parts: two steel silos of 5.4m (18ft) diameter at the western edge, four 14m (46ft) diameter silos in the middle, and a rectangular building containing vertical transportation. The monumentality of these industrial relics is a potent symbol of China's recent past.

↖ 1

↗ 2

↗ 3

↗ 4

↘ 5

↗ 1

**Architect:** Jiang Ying
**Project:** Youth Hotel in iD Town
**Location:** Shenzhen
**Completion:** 2014

In an abandoned factory complex on the east coast of Shenzhen, this building was originally industrial workers' staff quarters and now has been converted into a youth hostel. Jiang was inspired by this working history and has attempted to root new functions into the ruined shell of the original. The ground floor is a community space comprising reception, rest area, café and open kitchen. The second floor to the fourth floor are guest rooms, following the basic structural divisions of the workers' dormitories. The ground-floor feature windows are designed to emulate a series of cabins in the woods.

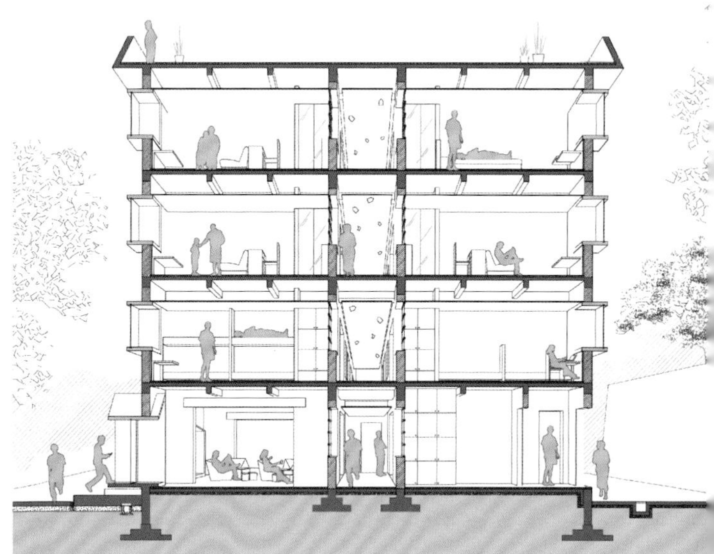

↗ 2

↗ 3

↗ 4

↗ 5

↗ 6

↘ 7

↘ 8

**Architect:** Jiang Ying
**Project:** Z Gallery
**Location:** Dapeng New District, Shenzhen
**Completion:** 2014

The Honghua Dyeing Factory was built in the 1980s and was O-office's first renovation project. It transformed the existing ruined workshop into a series of art studios. The gallery space is designed as a series of black steel boxes sitting on the ruins of previous equipment foundations, and containing exhibition functions, meeting rooms and receptions. The façade is made up of rotating doors and sliding glass doors. Seven grey boxes – artists' studios – zigzag throughout the factory, and even extend out into the site.

↗ 1

↗ 2

↗ 3

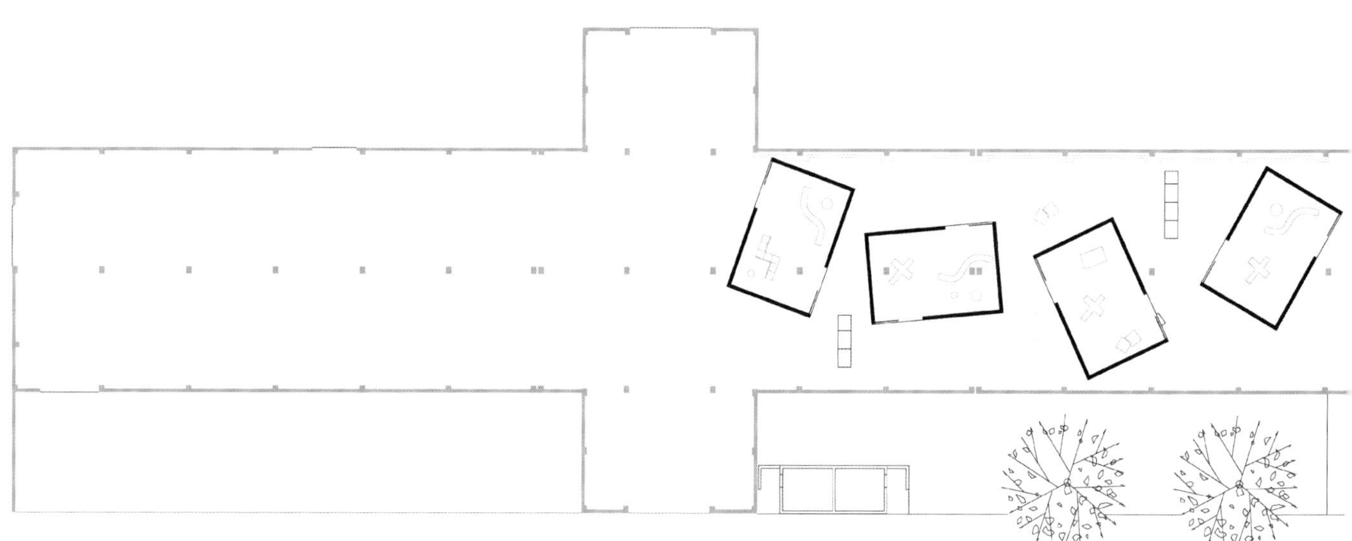

↗ 4

 5

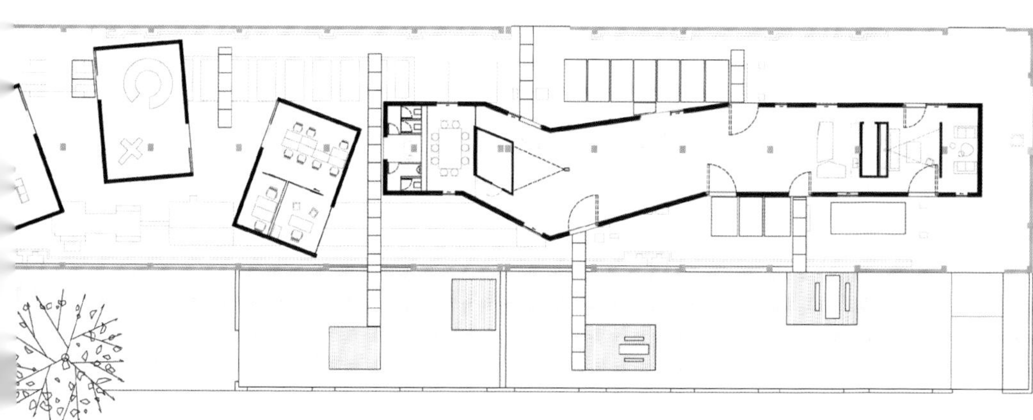

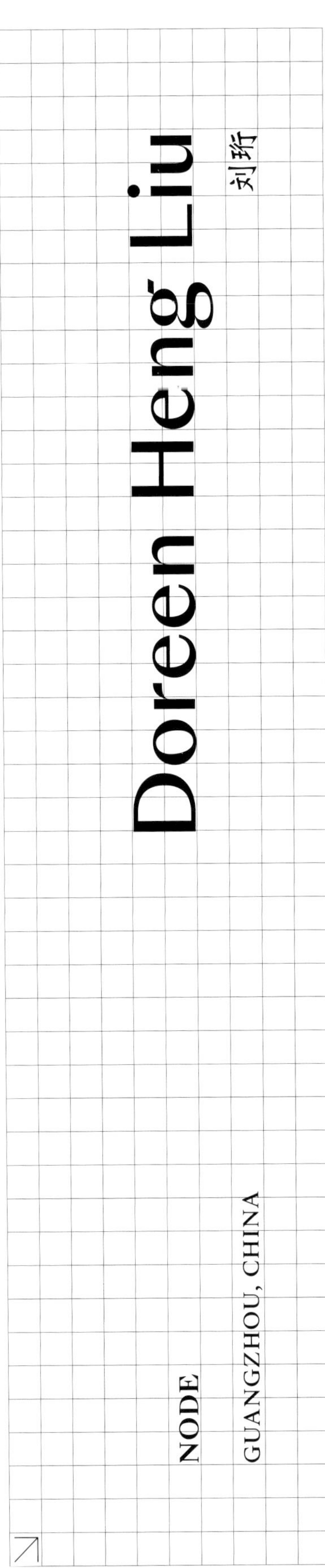

# Doreen Heng Liu 刘珩

NODE

GUANGZHOU, CHINA

Doreen Heng Liu chose architecture very early on in life. At school, a friend told her that the subject combined her two loves, science and art, and from that moment she was hooked. Matter-of-factly, she explains that her childhood influences at that time were Albert Einstein and Jorge Luis Borges, so she clearly was not lacking in confidence, intellectual drive and scholarly ambition.

Precocious she may have been, but she was also smart enough to be accepted to study at Huazhong University of Science and Technology and the top-tier Tongji University in Shanghai, both without having to take the usual National College Entrance Examination. After graduation she moved to the United States and gained a master's degree from the University of California, Berkeley, and a PhD from Harvard Graduate School of Design.

After living and working in San Francisco for a few years, Liu eventually returned to her home town of Guangzhou, where in 2004 she set up her architectural practice, NODE (Nansha Original Design). The name refers to Nansha district, a region of Guangzhou that was once bleak enough to be known as 'the Siberia of the Pearl River Delta'. It has now been transformed by the foresight – and massive investment – of the Fok Ying Tung Group, Hong Kong investors who seized on the potential arising out of the reunification of China and Hong Kong in 1997.

This development zone is untypical in many ways, not least because rather than a piecemeal approach to Chinese urbanism, it is an experiment in a more considered approach towards the city, with Liu acting as the Fok Group's chief architectural consultant.

In this role, she has completed several high-profile architectural projects in Nansha and orientated her office into a research-based practice that seeks to understand the complexities of China's urban revolution. In 2009, in line with her growing reputation and her knowledge of the area, she established a studio in neighbouring Shenzhen, a mega-city of fifteen million.

Liu's work focuses on what she calls the 'basics of architecture', which she uses to counter the tremendous speed and size of this region's frenetic urban growth. The Pearl River Delta already houses forty-two million people and such changes can sometimes be disorientating. Hers is a plan for an urban renewal that can retain a sense of place and a sense of history, without denying the future or romanticizing the past.

Liu is clearly frustrated that the pressure to build fast results in a design and construction industry that is incoherent and anarchic. Very often, she says, it seems that 'the only rational person is the architect'. Her Western training has taught her to do things systematically, but unfortunately 'this is not important in China nowadays. Often everything changes, and there is a high probability of having to redo the design. The whole industry is neither professional nor rational and sometimes you feel that you are the only one seriously contributing to the project. This is a big problem.'

But such difficulties have only strengthened her resolve. Tenacity is a quality that she says is required of all architects who wish to succeed in China – this, combined with strong idealism. 'You have to have a dream to support yourself,' she says.

Referring to the problems that she encounters in the construction industry – a lack of care or consideration for quality – she admits that she sometimes thinks about quitting. But 'when I realize that the project is worthwhile, that it can facilitate a new lifestyle or reflect specific values, I regain the resolve to stick to my work even if I have to lose something.' It is an admirable trait and one that too few in China possess. Too many, it seems, find it easier to acquiesce.

Her sacrifices have driven her on to persevere. Such steadfastness, she suggests, is a by-product of being a female architect in China. Her personal sacrifice is that – unusually for China – she neither married nor had children. 'I spend so much energy on my career that if I had a family, I wouldn't have any time to dedicate to it. The sacrifice for me, and for female architects generally, is time. Life.'

Her work life is everything, and Liu is as comfortable in her position as adjunct associate professor at the Chinese University of Hong Kong as she is in her visiting professorial role at the Swiss Federal Institute of Technology (ETH) in Zurich, or curating work at the Venice and Shenzhen biennales. In 2011, her practice was named as one of the five rising international architectural practices by the influential Audi Urban Future Initiative Awards. Liu clearly bridges cultures.

She is well placed to compare the differences in Western and Chinese architectural education and practice. 'Chinese education actually misses a lot,' she says. 'In the West, students learn professional skills and judgment safe in the knowledge that their basic humanistic values have been developed as a matter of course. But in China, our social education is very poor and we consider architecture to be just a skill or an application of technology.' She continues, 'Fortunately, I benefited from a Western education and accepted its universalist values. But, sadly, that means that on architectural projects in China, what I care about is not necessarily what they care about.'

Railing at the proliferation of merely technical solutions, she defers to the artistic side of her character. 'I am a very free person and I want that level of creativity for everyone. I want to take us beyond just our daily lives. I simply want to make life poetic.'

**Page 95** Yong-chong River Water Infrastructure

**Architect:** Doreen Heng Liu
**Project:** Yong-chong River Water Infrastructure
**Location:** Bao'an, Shenzhen
**Completion:** 2015

Doreen Heng Liu enjoys integrating unlikely infrastructure into her work, turning something that is often regarded as purely engineering into a benefit for urban public life. Her first built project was Yong-chong River Water Infrastructure. The heavy concrete sluice gate is clearly a bridge across the river but, because of the various pieces of technical machinery, it was impossible to cross. To enable citizens to engage with it on a more human scale, a metal staircase, bridge and zigzag path were installed to weave across the sluice gate. A simple, vivid and ingenious pathway over the river.

↗ 1

↗ 2

↗ 3

↗ 4

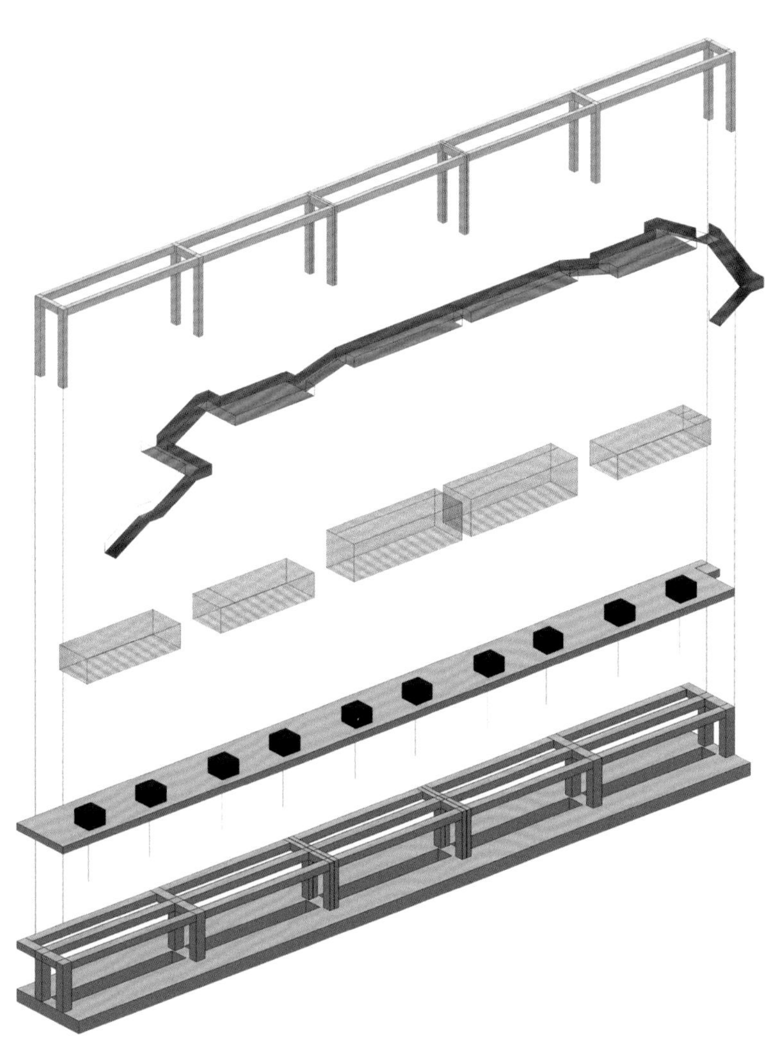

↗ 5

↗ 1

**Architect:** Doreen Heng Liu
**Project:** No.7 Da-Ban-Jie Hutong Renovation
**Location:** Shichahai, Beijing
**Completion:** 2016

This regeneration project is an exhibition held in a short and narrow *hutong* (alleyway) in Beijing. The architect wanted to display the life of the community, but also to engender a sense of community, by designing facilities that were an extension of the city – scaffolding materials representing dismantled buildings, hemp ropes as screens and vertical metal sheets dividing the spaces. In this project, Doreen Heng Liu experimented with common materials to create an experience that might enrich poor local people's sense of place and fire their imaginations.

↗ 2

↗ 3

↘ 4

↗ 5

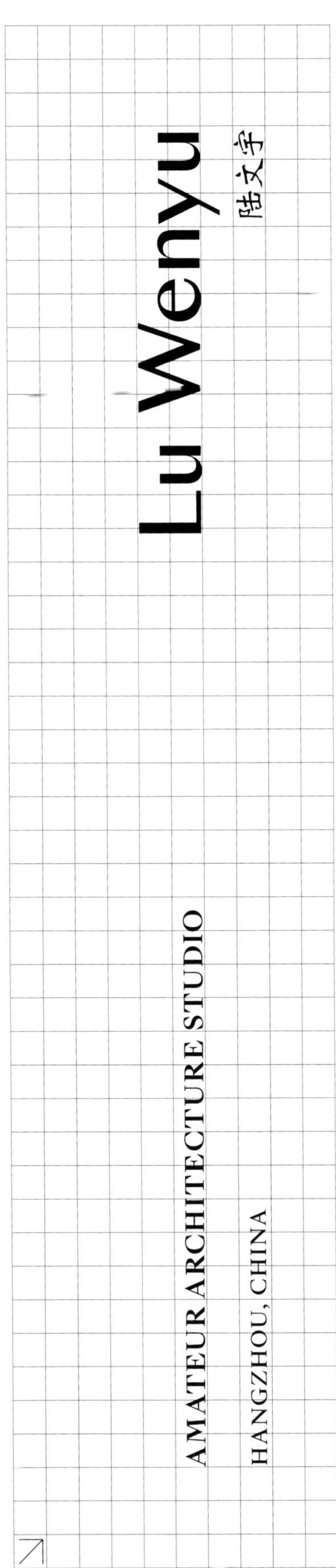

Lu Wenyu is a talented architect and designer, a leading academic and an experienced practice manager. An intensely private person, she describes her attitude to life as 'peaceful', saying, 'I don't want the public to know more about me'.

Like so many in this book, she became an architect by accident. As a youngster, Lu was taken to Ürümqi in the far west Xinjiang region of China when her family was relocated. Her schoolteacher was an architect who taught her to draw and encouraged her in the arts but, rebelliously, she applied to study biological sciences. By some twist of fate, she changed her mind and ended up in Nanjing Institute of Technology (now Southeast University) to study architecture. The journey to college from Xinjiang took four days and was the first time that she had left her home town.

After graduating in 1985, she took up her first job in 1989 in a state-owned institute. Her husband is architect Wang Shu (who went on to win the Pritzker Prize), and in the early years of their partnership, he was training himself in craft-based skills and construction techniques, so that it fell upon Lu to subsidize his reclusive lifestyle. By 1997, they were ready to set up Amateur Architecture Studio in Hangzhou...and the rest is history.

Unlike Wang, Lu has managed to shun the limelight, although her globetrotting is making it harder for her to stay in the background. 'After Wang Shu won the Pritzker Prize,' she says, 'his private life disappeared, but I wanted mine. I want my life.' Indeed, when Wang was singly named as the Pritzker Prize winner, many condemned the fact that she didn't get equal plaudits.

Many others criticized her for not demanding parity. But she says that 'to assume that I – or anyone – merit acclaim simply by being a woman is wrong'. Besides, she adds, 'I prefer privacy'.

Both she and Wang now teach at the prestigious China Academy of Art in Hangzhou, where they have devised and run a unique pedagogical experiment. Here first-year students learn crafts such as woodwork, bricklaying or rammed earth, followed by Chinese calligraphy, sketching and drawing, for a whole year. It is meant to give the students a feel for the materials to enable them to relate to those materials' possibilities. At the 2017 departmental show, her 'mountain of chairs' (shown in her photograph) comprised her pupils' handmade timber chairs in a 10-metre (33-foot) high display.

Hers is a recognition of the merits of good old-fashioned craftsmanship. 'I believe that architectural design is based on drawing,' says Lu, 'so it is essential to know that different lines represent different materials like bamboo, wood, metal, concrete, bricks and earth. Our academy might be the only one in China that allows students to spend a year working with different materials and literally feeling them.' Architects, she says, must learn to think for themselves and explore the many complex relationships in architecture, not only structure, philosophy and poetics but also materials and tradition.

However, she is not a classic traditionalist and she understands the limitations of the past as well as the essence of the cultural identity embodied within it. Her techniques are rooted in Chinese traditions, but she insists that historical knowledge should be a springboard to explore new and inventive ideas, constantly seeking to broaden her horizons – 'to embrace everything'. The intention is to retain Chinese identity but within an international frame of reference.

Lu clearly extols craft-based practice, working with locals, with the community and with materials. This is time-consuming, and in a country hallmarked for its speed of construction, it can lead to tensions. Several of the company's projects have not been built in accordance with the drawings as clients push for more rapid closure. Speaking of the practice's Vertical Courtyard outside Hangzhou, for example, Lu explains that 'the building you see now is not the one that was originally designed. It was altered and adjusted by the developer to attract customers in a recessionary climate.'

Similarly, she says, 'when we designed the Ningbo History Museum, we had conflicts with the exhibition commissioners and designers, who wanted to change our design. Finally we made a compromise: they controlled the interior, and we controlled the outside.' Indeed, building designs come under regulatory guidance of the Ministry of Construction, while

## I prefer privacy

exhibitions come under the Ministry of Culture. 'This is the reality of China.'

So she is no stranger to architectural challenges. She is Wang's most incisive critic. But more importantly, she designs and orchestrates her own work and plays a major role on site. This is something that is fundamental to the success of her practice.

Asked about her favourite project, she replies that she is proud of all their work. But she works in CAA's Xiangshan Campus so has an emotional connection to that project. She relates how 'we didn't have money to plant trees. But several years later, there are willows growing along the lake planted by seeds dropped by birds. Nature is so fantastic and the project changes every day in ways we couldn't have imagined.'

She is self-effacing. 'The world is big, and within it there are only a few people – men or women – with great ability. Really, I am not so talented.'

↗ 1

**Page 103** Ningbo Contemporary Art Museum

**Architect:** Lu Wenyu and Wang Shu
**Project:** Ningbo Contemporary Art Museum
**Location:** Ningbo, China
**Completion:** 2005

Ningbo's Port area became available for development thanks to the decline and relocation of the shipping industry. The heritage protection plan to retain the original block had to be rethought when it was found that the building could not meet contemporary building regulations. It was demolished to make way for the new building, albeit one that attempts to reconnect to the site. The grey brick in the foundation and lower portions is the main construction material of the former building, while the steel and timber in the upper parts is the main material of the port and ships.

↗ 1

↗ 2

**Architect:** Lu Wenyu
**Project:** The Ceramic House
**Location:** Jinghua City, Zhejiang Province
**Completion:** 2006

This remarkable structure takes tectonics and materiality as its starting and end points. The staggered site lent itself to a sunken or tiered building. The rectilinear façades belie the sloping interior roof hidden within, bringing light to a glazed rear wall. The surfaces are coloured ceramic fragments embedded in concrete, with protruding white slips and regular pocket recesses. This 100m$^2$ (1,075ft$^2$) tea-shop looks out over a balcony and a reflective pool. In the other direction, one can look up the slope, through the newly planted trees to the 'infinity beyond'.

↘ 3

↗ 4

↗ 1

↗ 2

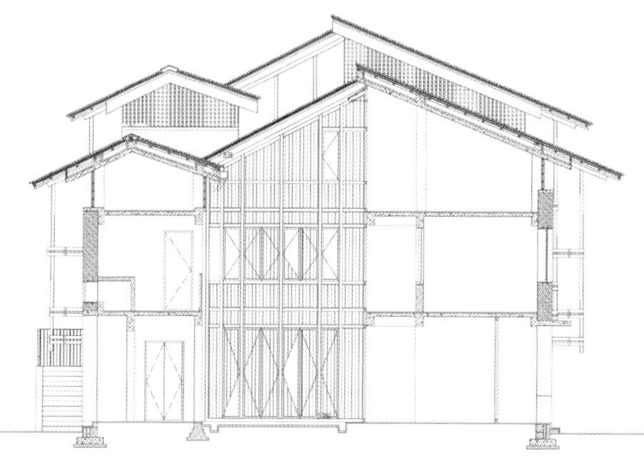

↗ 3

**Architect:** Lu Wenyu
**Project:** Renovation of Wencun Village
**Location:** Fuyang, near Hangzhou, Zhejiang Province
**Completion:** Ongoing

This is a project to reconstitute a traditional village sitting on the banks of the Heshan Stream, in an attempt to breathe life into decaying rural areas. It is intended to modernize people's homes (providing decent infrastructure, comfort and amenities) while halting the decline within the social and built fabric of rural society. Lu liaises with craftspeople and builders almost every day to promote this combined social and architectural vision. Lu and Wang's conception of this rural renaissance chimes with the government's desire to promote countryside renewal. Lu says that the project is intended 'to change the perception of the local people and the officials'.

Peng Lele was born in Anqing, Anhui province. She studied architecture at Nanjing Architectural and Civil Engineering Institution, graduating in 1990, and, as many young architects had done before her, she worked for some time at her local architecture design institute. In 1996, she moved to Beijing and began work at Huamao Architecture Design; then, after a few years she started at Atelier Feichang Jianzhu. (The practice's name, which is commonly abbreviated to FCJZ, translates as 'Unusual Architecture'.)

Moving to Atelier FCJZ in 1999 was significant. The first private practice in China, it was set up by Yung Ho Chang in 1993, and is a ground-breaking office that, with others, was at the forefront of so-called 'experimental architecture' that allowed them to freely express their own ideas.[1] For Peng, the experience of working alongside Chang, who had been a professor at Massachusetts Institute of Technology for fifteen years – was invaluable, not only opening up design opportunities but also helping to develop her ambition to create her own independent studio.

Within two years of joining FCJZ, in 2001, Peng founded Atelier 100s+1 in Beijing. Eight years later, one of her projects – the design for the G-Dot Art Space in Songzhuang artists' community in eastern Beijing's Tongzhou district – was chosen by the influential magazine *Urban Environment Design* as one of the most exceptional museums in Asia.

Peng has found a niche designing art spaces and galleries, and has even settled in the Songzhuang art district herself, where her family home nestles on the edge of the lake and doubles

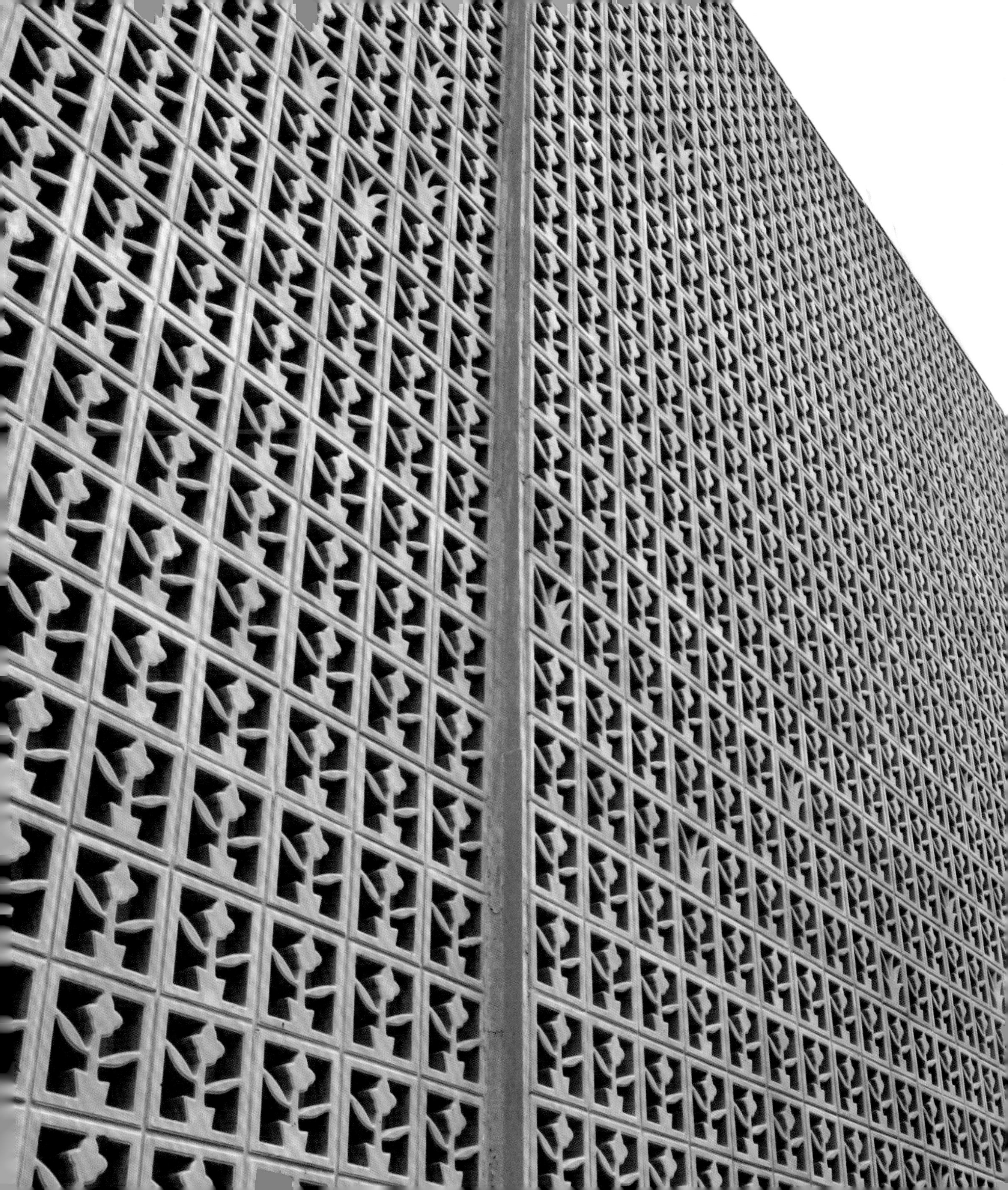

as her office. She describes living in the studio as 'the most efficient lifestyle for me, as an architect'.

The house is a series of independent brick boxes at the basement level with a glass dining area and architect's studio above. It is a complex arrangement with courtyards, and a brick-walled garden that wends into the centre of the house, enclosing the stairs, secret lofts and independent rooms for guests. The house is unmistakably modern but borrows from traditional culture and the vernacular.

Peng explains that during the time she worked at FCJZ, especially with her mentor Yung Ho Chang, she was taken to construction sites, where she observed how people really worked with materials and made designs into a reality. Consequently, she now ensures that young students who are working at her atelier regularly go on to construction sites so that they get 'intuitional instruction and a first-hand experience of how things are built'.

Peng's education – academically as well as in her early architectural training – focused primarily on construction and materials. She suggests that it was because of this grounding that she developed a sensitivity to details and an appreciation of tectonics, which, she says, has been the biggest influence on her architectural career.

She cites Swiss architect Peter Zumthor as the person who has given her the most inspiration, but there are clear resonances of other contemporary and Western architects. Her design for the X+Q Sculpture Studio, for example, shows her mastery of brick and is often strongly reminiscent of Louis Kahn's use of geometry and light.

Indeed, Peng is deft at using brick perforations for ventilation and subtle shading, also using chamfers and differently textured bricks to transform rather monumental façades into sculptural forms. Floors, walls and façades are carefully differentiated to bring a potentially unforgiving material to life. An earlier example, the Snake Wall at the house of art critic Li Xianting, displays a playfulness with the material and a curvature not usually associated with the material. It is a form that then repeats in a number of Peng's buildings, externally, internally, as dividing walls or even as installations and design concepts.

**Living in the studio is the most efficient lifestyle for me**

When asked about her position as a leading female architect in China, Peng says that she does not believe that being female confers any special meaning. 'Admittedly,' she says, 'I am an architect and I am female – but I design as an individual person.' Her single-minded character and independent spirit are typified by her ambition to 'keep working in architecture...but to always have my freedom'.

Peng is proud (and fortunate) to have taken on projects one by one: in other words, she has not had to divide her time between various competing projects and clients. As a result, she has accrued a portfolio of completed projects that have a clear design integrity as well as a construction quality with which she admits to being very pleased. She explains that the rapid turnover of architecture for most architects in China creates such a limited time for design and construction that it is a constant battle for them to take control of either the design quality or the construction quality. 'This,' she says, 'is China's challenge.'

**Page 111** G-Dot Art Space façade

**Architect:** Peng Lele
**Project:** G-Dot Art Space
**Location:** Songzhuang Town, Tongzhou, Beijing
**Completion:** 2010

This building, which is principally used for exhibitions, is situated in Songzhuang and features some of its local art and design, such as the feature flower-pattern tiles. It manifests the separation between public and private spaces using subtle demarcations provided by natural light, allowing the works of art to be displayed to their best effect.

↗ 1

↗ 2

↗ 3

↖ 4

↗ 5

↘ 6

↗ 1

↗ 2

↗ 3

**Architect:** Peng Lele
**Project:** Atelier 100s+1
**Location:** Songzhuang Town, Tongzhou, Beijing
**Completion:** 2011

This is where Peng Lele and her colleagues live and work, with the divide between the two functions creating an important distinction in the architecture and using a configuration often seen in Chinese ancient gardens. By the contrasting use of different partition heights, the play of virtual and real, revealing and hiding, the functions of space are separated from but also interrelated to each other.

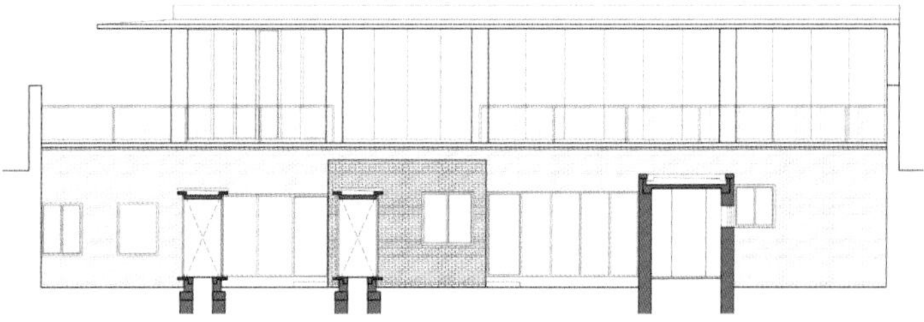

↗ 4

↗ 5

↗ 1

↗ 2

↙ 3

**Architect:** Peng Lele
**Project:** S+Q Sculpture Studio
**Location:** Tongzhou, Beijing
**Completion:** 2013

The volume of this building has been transformed - seemingly lightened - by courtyards, where daylight and natural ventilation flows remould the volume into a series of spaces. The curved paths, the buildings of different heights, and the solid and hollowed-out walls help the architecture to demarcate different functions.

↙ 4

↗ 5

↘ 6

↗ 7

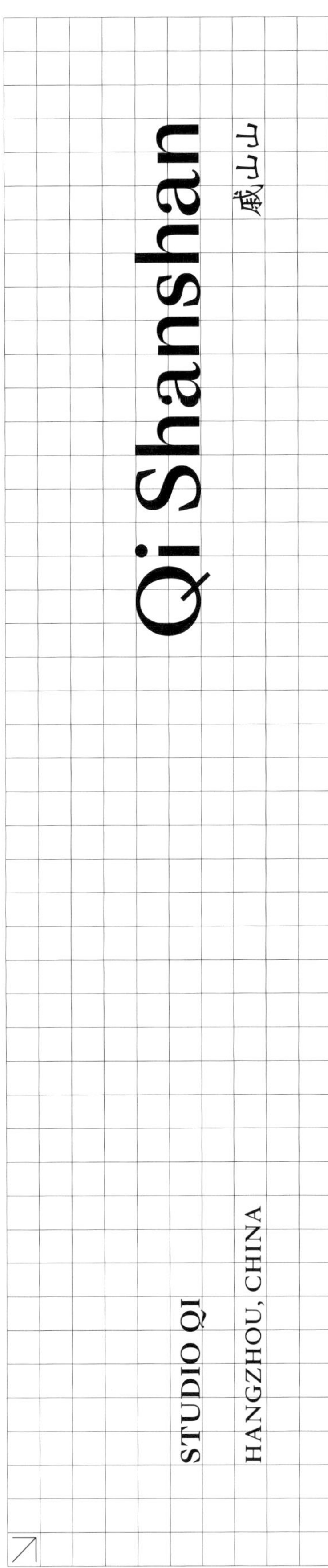

In 2013, almost 24,000 Chinese schoolchildren – nationals of China – had been enrolled by their parents in American private schools. These youngsters were being sent abroad to gain an early advantage in the battle to enter a high-ranking American university. By 2014, the figure was almost 40,000.

Just ten years earlier, in 2005, US Department of Homeland Security statistics confirm that a mere sixty-five Chinese students were enrolled to study in American high schools. Qi Shanshan was one of the youngsters from that earlier, pioneering period, leaving home when she was just fourteen years old. She eventually returned to China when she was twenty-nine.

Her years abroad are a catalogue of success, from graduating top of her class from a US Air Force boarding school to gaining a top degree in architecture (with a minor in economics) from Columbia University followed by a master's from Harvard. She was also the only student in her year to be offered an internship at Renzo Piano, and she then worked at Foster + Partners in New York, where she was responsible for its China division. Returning to China in 2012, she set up her own architectural practice, Studio Qi, based in her home town of Hangzhou.

The office started life as a rather inauspicious industrial building, which became her first substantive project. It is located on the ground floor of an old

concrete-framed film production campus not far from Hangzhou's West Lake. The ground-floor façades have been removed and the finishes stripped back to brutalist concrete basics. The thin floor-to-ceiling glazing brings daylight deep into the main office space and allows the interior to connect with the neighbouring external vegetation. The office is thus a weightless glass box, flooded with light. It is essentially a Studio Qi display case that ignores the chaos of the building's upper floors. It is an exercise in simple design principles.

Indeed, Qi was taught that 'architecture is a way of thinking'. It is not really about architecture itself, she says, 'but about seeing the world *through* architecture'. This approach was nurtured in discursive modules at university that allied rigorous analytical skills with courses that played 'an even more important role' in her education, including philosophy, art history and social sciences. 'All of those subjects based in Western philosophy and sociology, in the broadest sense, influenced my overall approach to architecture.'

Her abiding enjoyment of the process of intellectual discovery was fired up by university tutors such as Karen Fairbanks – architect, mentor and the woman who oversaw the merger of the Barnard College and Columbia Architecture programmes. With clear role models and an ambition to learn more, Qi has recently taken up a PhD placement at the China Academy of Art (CAA), under resident professor and Pritzker Prize-winner Wang Shu.

Qi now teaches modules at Zhejiang University and at the CAA, and is bringing a touch of Western abstraction to their architectural syllabuses. She revels in a pedagogical and design approach that cuts across cultural stereotypes, explaining that her work seeks to challenge interpretations of traditional cultures that portray them as if they are set in aspic. Instead, she is looking for what she calls the 'culture gene', something that transcends the status quo. Indeed, she says that architecture 'questions the known and challenges the unknown'.

## Architecture is a way of thinking

Her most important project to date is Nine House in the ancient water town of Xitang, Zhejiang. This is a boutique hotel and gallery located in the heart of a protected historic environment. It is a bold intervention that has evolved from an understanding of the spatial configurations of the town at both the urban and the architectural scale. Its scale, colours, horizontal and vertical movement, and 'spatial excitements' blend a modernist form into the organic surrounding fabric. Nine is not a building, Qi says, but a building community.

Her favourite commission is White House, another boutique hotel, this time on the shore of Erhai Lake in Dali, Kunming. (Qi's book *Escape: Designing the Modern Guest House* [2016] has already become something of a reference book for designers of this oeuvre.) She notes that this particular parametric form is a response to the cultural quality of this area, where the local Bai minority people make their living from fishing in the lake. For the Bai, white is considered to be a sacred colour of purity. Qi's white walls reflect Erhai Lake and bring a mottled landscape into the building.

Studio Qi is currently 90 per cent female, although Qi says that this is purely coincidental, as staff are hired on merit. However, she acknowledges that architecture is still a male-dominated profession and that to be a female architect means that one 'has to be strong'. Describing herself as 'a citizen, an architect and an educator', she falls back on her philosophical training – both Socratic and Confucian – to assert that 'architecture is about sensibilities. Before becoming a great architect, you first have to be a good human being.'

↗ 1

**Page 123** Nine House interior

**Architect:** Qi Shanshan
**Project:** Nine House
**Location:** Xitang, Zhejiang Province
**Completion:** 2016

The project is a boutique villa and gallery, winning the award for China's Most Charming Boutique Villa in 2016. Set in Xitang, a historic water town famous for its dense neighbourhoods, the architecture adapts itself to the traditional housing styles while introducing modern elements: a more permeable interpretation. The building has private residences on the ground floor, with public areas on the first floor providing views and interactions across the whole architecture. Internal, external and covered pathways between residences connect with the other levels. The architect wants this to be a place for an organic community to evolve.

↘ 2

↗ 3

↗ 4

↗ 5

↗ 6

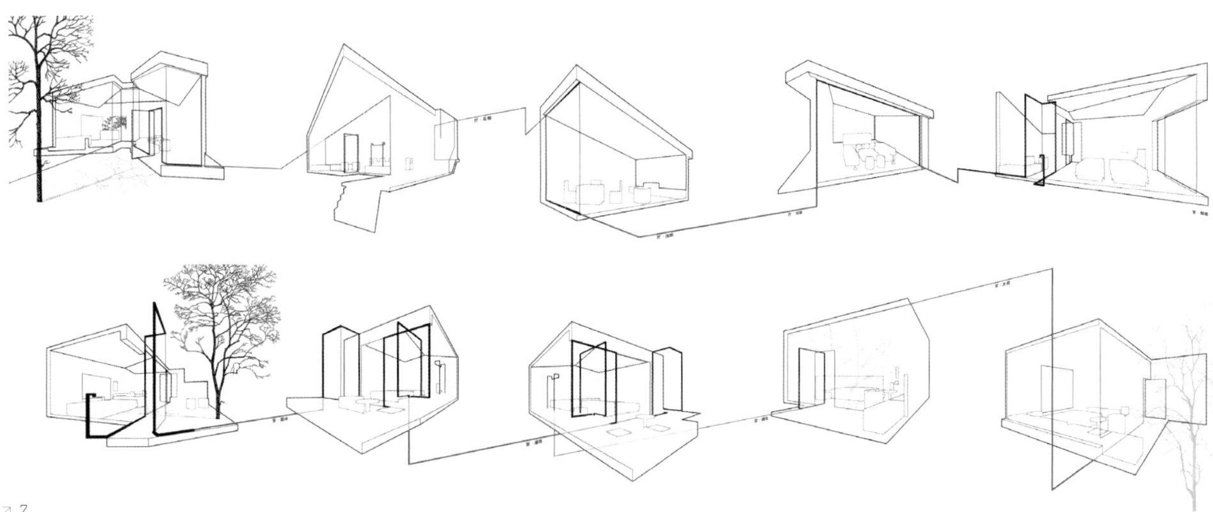

↗ 7

↗ 8

**Architect:** Qi Shanshan
**Project:** Studio Qi Office No. 1
**Location:** Hangzhou, Zhejiang Province
**Completion:** 2015

The first project of Studio Qi was to transform the former Zhejiang Filming Company, situated on the ground floor of an office building, into their own studio space. In the process, Studio Qi succeeded in solving three main problems: giving a visual focus to their office façade, unifying the diverse internal spaces, and breaking through the low and narrow interior space. By opening up the floor plan and adding glass curtain walling, the office now functions well as an architectural studio.

↗ 1

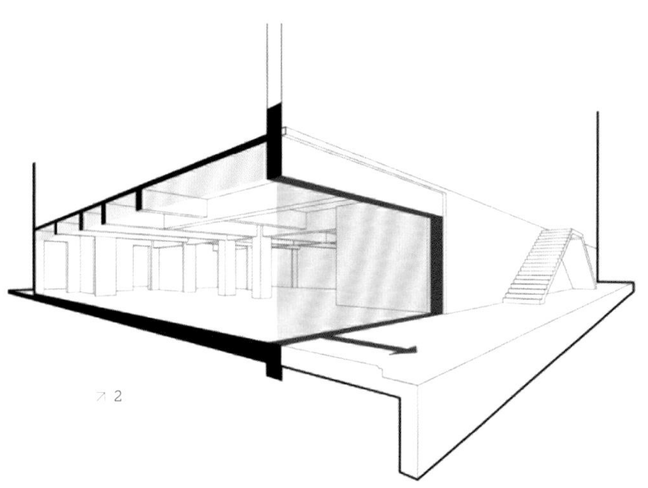

↗ 2

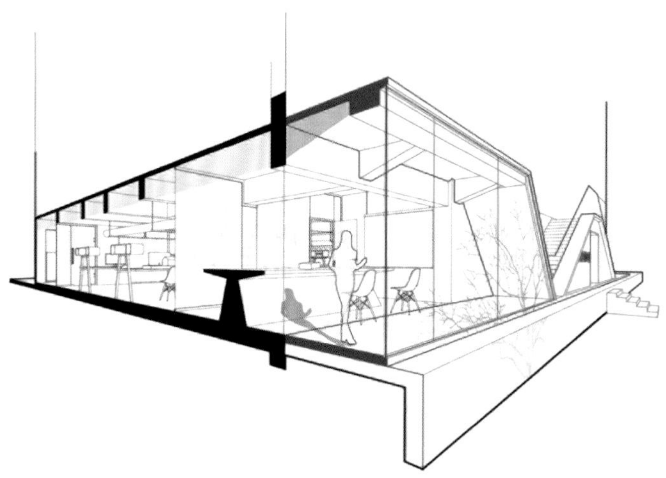

↗ 3

↗ 4

↘ 5

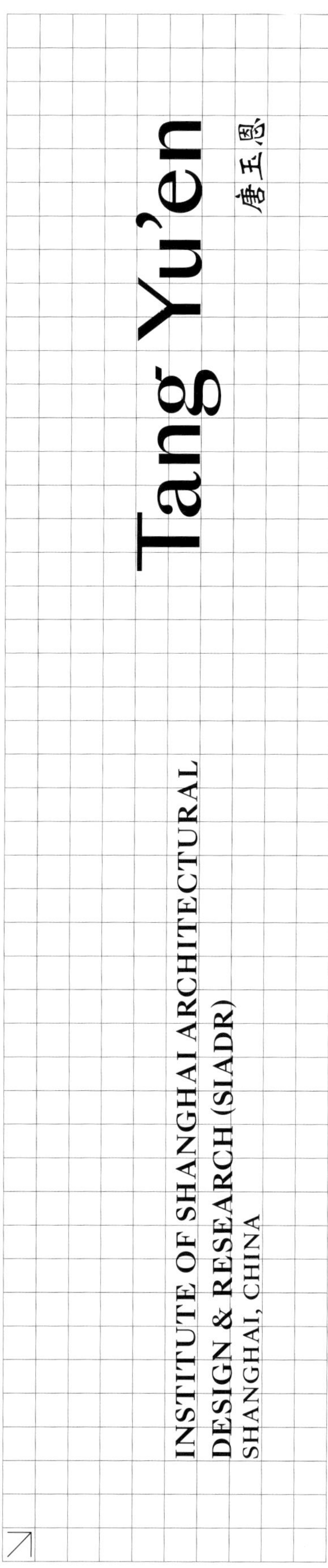

Born in 1944, Tang Yu'en completed her undergraduate studies at Beijing's Tsinghua University in 1967. After a hiatus during the Cultural Revolution, she returned to her architectural studies as soon as universities in China reopened and was admitted to Tongji University as a postgraduate in 1978.

She describes the reopening of the universities in 1978 as a period full of positive atmosphere. She was taught by a number of respected scholars, and everyone – staff and students alike – was enthusiastic to make up for lost time. This liberating experience planted the seeds of her enthusiasm for, and her dedication to, architectural design in the following decades.

After her graduation in 1981, she went to work at the Institute of Shanghai Architectural Design & Research (SIADR), where she still works to this day. Her early years with the company coincided with China's era of rapid development. Coincidentally, she had been researching the problems of high-rise hotel design at the very time that China began constructing its own high-rise hotels to cater for the influx of 'Western guests'. Under the instruction of what she calls 'old experts', she took part in the design of high-rise hotels, and went to Hong Kong to learn about hotel design and construction standards, coming back to Shanghai to take charge of many important tall-building developments that started to define the skyline of the city.

In the late 1980s, Shanghai started to build large-scale public cultural buildings such as museums, libraries and theatres. At this time, Tang was presented with the opportunity to design the new Shanghai Library. This 84,000$m^2$ (904,000$ft^2$) super-scale public library

containing fourteen million books is located in the western area of Shanghai, surrounded by historical buildings such as the Shanghai Community Church and Shanghai American School. Tang's design adapts to this cosmopolitan environment, its modern design reflecting Shanghai's 'fusion of Eastern and Western cultures'. She proceeded to design several municipal and provincial public libraries, university libraries and Zhejiang Shaoxin Museum. In 1999 she became the chief architect of SIADR, a design institute of more than a thousand people, and in 2004 she was awarded the title of Chinese engineering 'Design Master'.

She says: 'The internationalization and modernization of the city are not necessarily in contradiction with the desire to respect local history and culture. To a certain degree, by experiencing other cultures, people might actually cherish and respect their local culture even more...Culture needs to be accumulated to demonstrate how creative and confident a city is. The greater the depth of that historical culture the more we reveal the soul of that city.'

She regularly seeks to address historical and cultural tensions such as those expressed in the design of the Shanghai Library, and she takes intellectual delight in resolving – or harmonizing – paradoxical issues. Usually, this takes the form of an exploration between preservation and restoration, between past and future, authentic and inauthentic, all of which are live dilemmas for many in China. Her expertise in reconciling these issues is exemplified by the renovation of two key buildings in Shanghai's rich architectural heritage. The first is the 1929 Art Deco Fairmont Peace Hotel on the Bund. The second is the Shanghai Sihang Warehouse, a project to repair and upgrade part of a battle-scarred industrial building to form a war memorial and museum.

The defence of the warehouse against Japanese attack in 1937, when a single battalion halted the Japanese advance, is a proud moment in Chinese history. Through careful research – analysing photographic archives as well as painstaking archaeological excavations – her team located every bullet hole and cannon crater in the warehouse. Tang wanted these to be clearly expressed in the finished building to reveal the real horrors and heroism but also as a memorial for peace. The cultural significance of the Sihang Warehouse meant that she had to ensure the authenticity of her restoration work to warrant that these were unquestionably the real scars of war. The result

**It doesn't have to be expensive to be good**

is a triumph of heritage renewal but also a piece of thoughtful, functional public architecture.

Hers is a bold vision of heritage, but she is also not afraid to relate to technology and non-traditional and innovative practices, describing China's contemporary era as bursting with fresh ideas, materials, structures and computer power. She is clearly not opposed to new architecture and creative designs but she sees it as her 'responsibility' to preserve the vitality of historical buildings, to allow them to step into the future 'in a respectful way'.

Tang Yu'en describes her own work over thirty years, and the practice of architecture generally, in humble tones: 'We do not evaluate architecture on the basis of the money invested in it. It doesn't have to be expensive to be good. It also doesn't have to be luxurious or massive to be worthy of comment. What is important is whether the design addresses local conditions. We merely need to ask: is it dignified?'

↗ 1

**Page 131** A glass ceiling in the Peace Hotel

**Architect:** Tang Yu'en, with Jiang Weizhe and Ni Zhengying
**Project:** Peace Hotel
**Location:** Shanghai, China
**Completion:** 2010

As one of the most important art deco landmarks in Shanghai, the Peace Hotel was constructed on the Bund in 1929. Designed by Palmer and Turner, this concrete-framed building has granite facing on the lower floors and terracotta above. After many decades of alterations and structural damage, the restoration has brought the building back to its former glory with lavish interiors and careful repairs. It has redefined the hotel's original floor plans and layout, and retained as much of the original architecture and architectural features as possible.

↗ 2

↗ 3

↗ 1

↗ 2

**Architect:** Tang Yu'en, with Zhang Jiezheng and Ju Qihong
**Project:** Shanghai Library
**Location:** Shanghai
**Completion:** 1996

Shanghai Library was the first civic library in the city built for the general public, and designed at a time when China was commissioning new opera houses, galleries and other such cultural institutions. It was intentionally designed with both Chinese and Western architectural characteristics to celebrate Shanghai's mixed cultural heritage. It projects a postmodern aspect, with classical allusions in the arcade, columns and capitals, but mixed with Chinese-style carved eaves. It is still one of the ten largest libraries in the world. Tang Yu'en states that 'everything was designed by me'.

↗ 3

**Architect:** Tang Yu'en
with Zhang Jiezheng
**Project:** Shaoxing Museum
**Location:** Fu Mountain, Shaoxing, Zhejiang Province
**Completion:** 2010

Fu Mountain stretches along the west of Shaoxing, an ancient city that, thanks to its strategic location, served as a Qin stronghold some 2,500 years ago. These and other such forgotten histories have been captured in this museum. The design blends the local architecture into the mountain using traditional courtyard layouts and modern architectural vocabulary. Three staging posts are cut into the mountain to break up the route and to minimize the perception of climbing up the slope. The landscape embraces the building but the entrance to the south of the site is planned as a 'citizen square'.

↗ 1

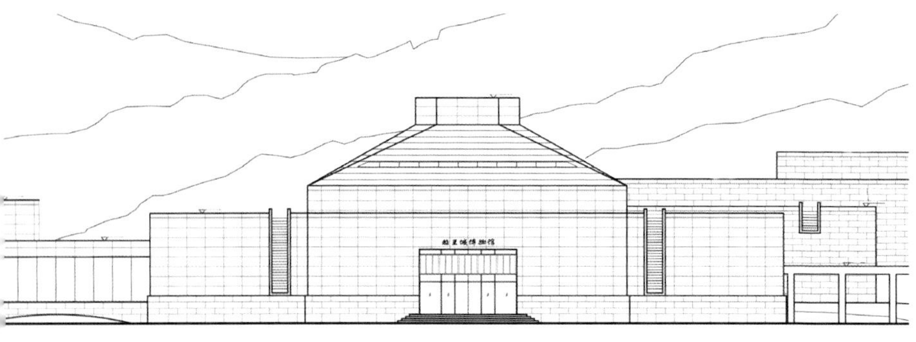

↗ 2

↗ 3

绍兴博物馆

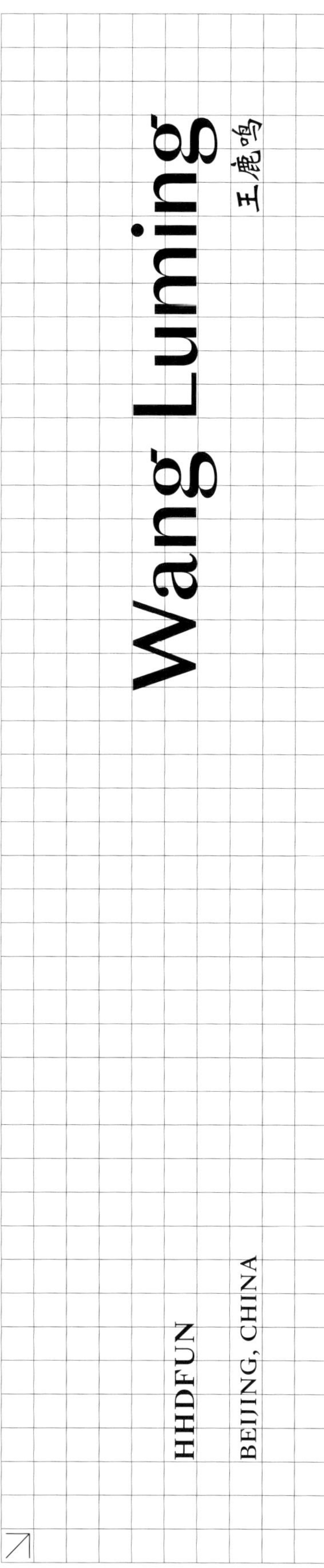

Wang Luming is a young architect who represents a new generation of architectural practitioners in China, an architect engaged in cutting-edge computer modelling and parametric design, using electronics and even artificial intelligence as part of her armoury. In 2016, the Chinese president famously called for an end to 'weird architecture' – intended to be a condemnation of political vanity projects though widely seen as an attack on algorithmic or parametric modelling – but architects such as Wang Luming and her husband, Wang Zhenfei, are pushing back to reclaim the importance of new technologies in efficient architectural form-making.

Wang Luming and Wang Zhenfei are co-founders and principals of Beijing-based design and research studio HHDFUN. This is a company that is as much at home with mathematical equations and geometric principles as it is with construction policy and urban context. Wang admits that computational abstraction is not commonly associated with the word FUN, but she delights in a complex array of computational algorithms complemented by advanced 3D software packages as their primary approach to architectural design.

The second pillar of Wang's methodology, multidisciplinary integration, is embodied in one of the software tools at her disposal. Building Information Modeling (BIM) is an automated design technique that aids information-sharing. It is a collaborative knowledge resource that HHDFUN have taken to heart so as to make synergetic working and team-building their modus vivendi. This in particular is a radical shift away from the silo mentality of most Chinese – and many global – architectural offices.

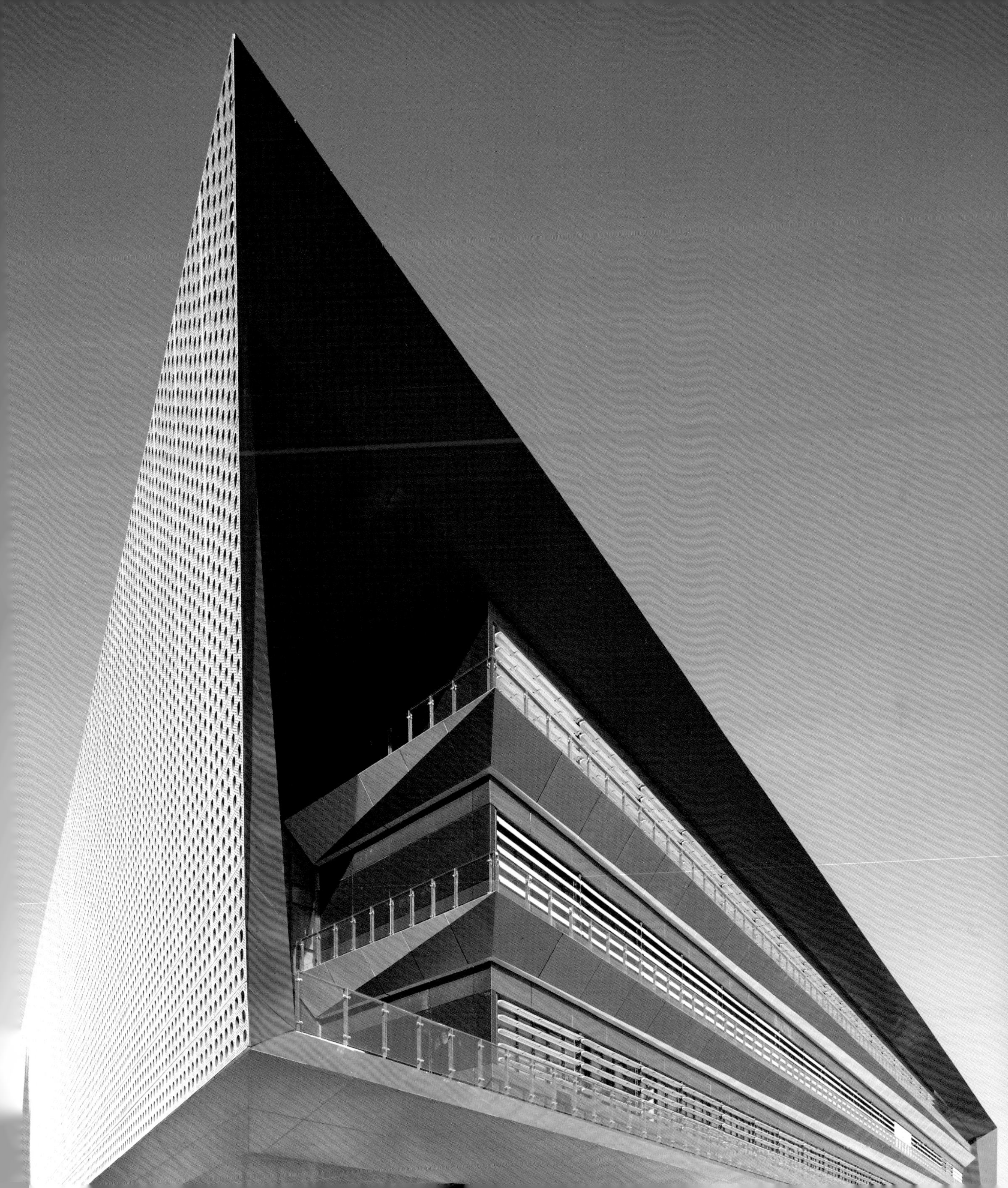

As such, Luming and Zhenfei make a point of employing people from all walks of life, including artists, fashion designers, mathematicians and engineers, to augment the design process and to provide novel critical insights. It is a Western-style 'disruptive' creative practice that HHDFUN have been engaged in for years and one that is only now beginning to be explored by others in China.

The fact that Wang describes herself as a 'cross-over architect', working with a wide range of creative collaborators, has occasionally led to a crisis of confidence in her professional path. 'Architecture in China,' she says, 'is always a fight. Sometimes I don't know what I am fighting for. The artists that we work with are more abstracted from everyday financial and practical realities. Actually, I envy the artist.'

Wang gained her undergraduate degree from Tianjin University in 2003 and then moved to the Berlage Institute in Rotterdam to take her master's in 2007, participating in the English-language Associative Design programme. It was her graduation project – applying computational modelling techniques to a real urban plot – that really inspired her to pursue a career in architecture. After university, she worked for twelve months at the offices of UNStudio in Amsterdam, an architectural practice that exemplifies the potential of collaboration across diverse design backgrounds. She then returned to China to help set up HHDFUN in Beijing in 2008.

Ironically, through her interest in high-tech computational methodology, she came to appreciate traditional Chinese architecture. Ancient Chinese settlements, she says, have an organic appearance but a structural order. 'Their paths have hierarchies, the layouts have rules,' she says, and she was awakened to the possibility of discovering governing criteria for these urban patterns. She says, 'Beijing's *hutongs* [traditional neighbourhoods] look different from modern communities but they both follow similar principles, and once these conventions have been compared and analysed, we can replicate their positive aspects using mathematical models.'

According to Wang, 'geometry is always the main principle for our design work. In the office, we never discuss aesthetics but only maths and geometry. Shapes come first and then we apply materials to the shape.'

On occasion, Wang describes these designs and the work of the practice as 'folded architecture' rather than 'parametric architecture'; a fluid, free-form design process. Indeed, she is occasionally hostile to the word 'parametric' because, she says, it has become a trend. The phrase 'folded architecture', on the other hand, references the influence of Bernard Cache, a designer who uses digital tools to produce flowing forms and dynamic experiences. For Wang, such Deleuzean European post-structuralism informs her work where the building's relationship with the wider urban context can be interpreted as 'the inside (being) nothing more than a fold of the outside'.[1]

HHDFUN is a new and relatively small office by Chinese standards. It has just fifteen staff, but has already created a creditable portfolio of experimental built work. Wang is emphatic that she does not want these to become a stylistic representation of the practice 'in the way that parametricism for many architects has become a trend'.

To try to sum up the office's ecological approach to architectural design – the third pillar of HHDFUN's metaphysical approach – Wang relates an anecdote from her student days at the Berlage when she was struggling with a design concept. 'At that time, I couldn't see the wood for the trees, but my tutor encouraged me to enjoy the forest: to allow myself to see the relationship between all things.' She continues, 'Now I view the world as complex, chaotic...and fascinating. The job of architecture is to order that chaos. To try to provide a logical explanation and coherence to it. After all, everything has a reason.'

↖ 1

**Page 139** Binhai Xiaowai High School exterior

**Architect:** Wang Luming
**Project:** Binhai Xiaowai High School
**Location:** Sino-Singapore Tianjin Eco-City, Tianjin
**Completion:** 2015

This is a showcase school building situated within the Tianjin Eco-City region. The design avails itself of passive energy-saving strategies, from solar capture to energy-efficient external wall construction, gaining a China 3-star rating. Its sustainable design includes high-performance air conditioning, water pumps, an intelligent lighting system, energy recycling, a passive ventilation system, renewable energy, and a rainwater harvesting and purification system.

↗ 2

↘ 3

↘ 4

↗ 5

↘ 6

↘ 7

**Architect:** Wang Luming
**Project:** Earthly Pond Service Centre, International Horticultural Exposition
**Location:** Qingdao, Shandong Province
**Completion:** 2014

This vast land-forming construction houses a service centre at its core, including restaurants, offices, and cultural and exhibition spaces. The architecture and landscape heights follow the natural gradients, providing multiple access points and viewing experiences at different elevations. The main architectural spaces are lower than the surrounding street levels, facing the sunken courtyard while affording views of the water and landscapes. All of the trees in the area were preserved in their entirety. A rooftop platform and green space were also created, which promotes building efficiency and helps to integrate the architecture into the landscape.

↗ 1

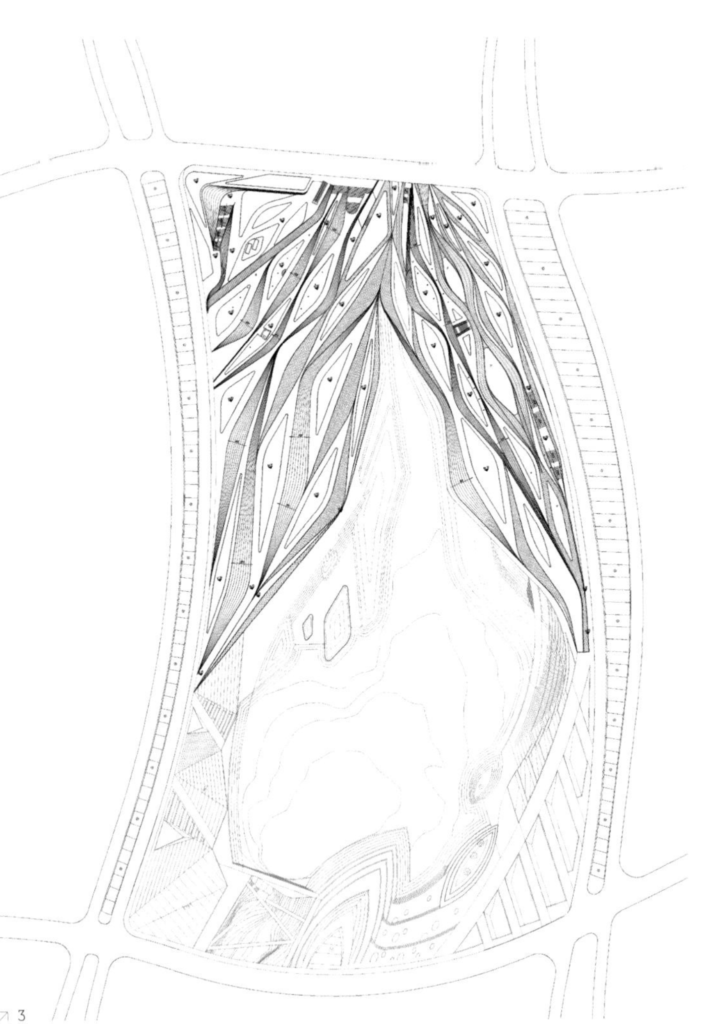

↗ 3

↗ 2

↗ 4

↘ 5

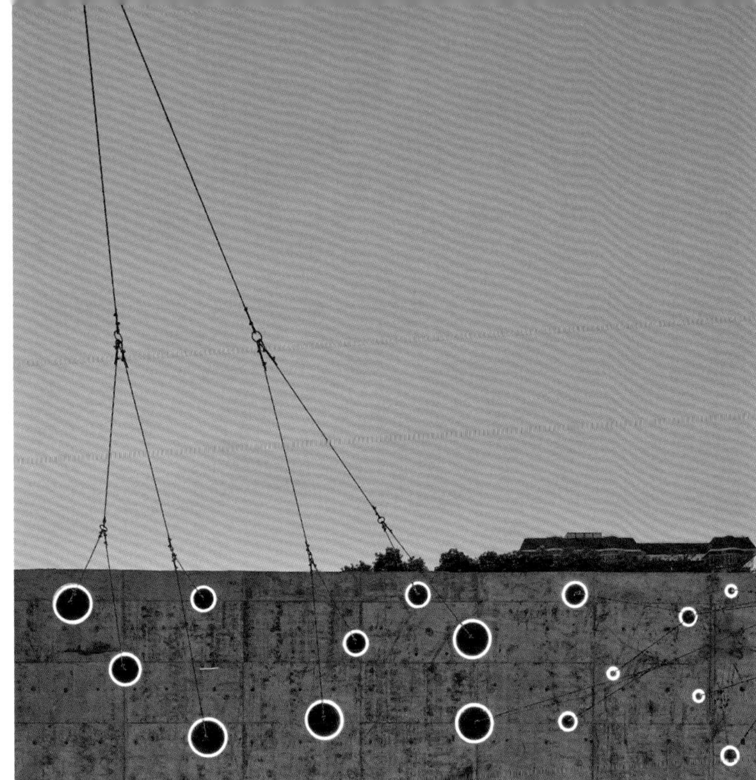

 1

↘ 3

 2

↗ 4

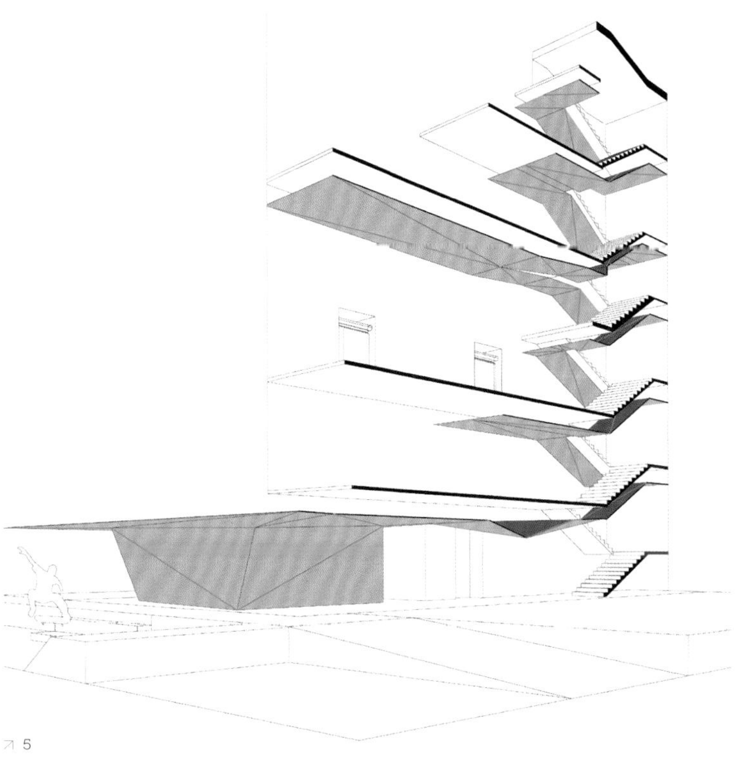

**Architect:** Wang Luming
**Project:** Freeze Factory
**Location:** Xiamen, China
**Completion:** 2014

This is a subtle and playful intervention to bring a derelict building back to life in the shadows of a rapidly growing business district development. Wang has simplified and upgraded the interiors and also transformed the exterior, rendering and modifying the building with sleek modernist character. The public space is an adaptable concrete exhibition area that doubles as a skateboard park. The parametricist intervention finds expression in a tension wire fixed to the walls and held aloft, providing a notional enclosure and literally tying the area's surfaces together.

↗ 5

↘ 6

↗ 7

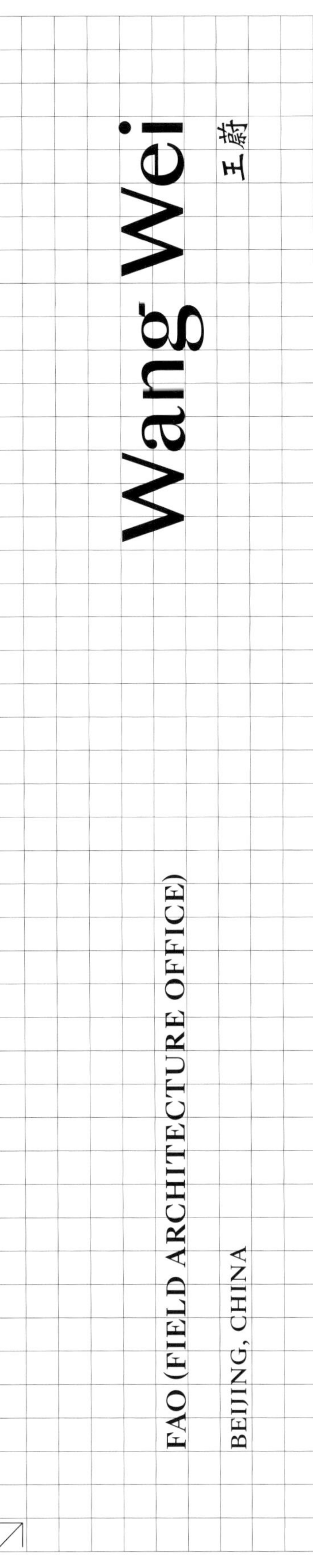

In China, it has long been common (although the situation is now changing) that getting into university is the sole aim of a schoolchild's education, and the subject that they will actually study once there is often relatively inconsequential. Every waking hour is taken up with studying for the *gaokao* (National College Entrance Examination). Parents will sometimes announce to their children on passing the exam what they will study and the exhausted student will passively accept. In Wang Wei's case, her schoolteacher suggested architecture, Wang's parents were delighted with the proposal, and the deal was done.

Wang was born in Chengdu in Sichuan province and gained both her Bachelor of Engineering and her Master of Architecture from Chongqing Architecture and Engineering Academy. From such arbitrary academic beginnings it might be unsurprising to find that she did not do too well in her early undergraduate years, but fortunately she flourished in the final year, coming top of the class and being accepted to the master's without examination. However, after qualifying she drifted into work at the China Southwest Architectural Design Institute, where she felt trapped for ten years. Wang says that she was 'always thinking about how to escape the industry'.

After a decade in the doldrums, she decided to reassess her career direction. In a bold step, she moved to New York in 2001 to study at Columbia University and New York City University as a visiting scholar, under the tutelage of leading architects and theorists Jeffrey Kipnis, Greg Lynn and Michael Sorkin. This period was a revelation that 'made me feel that architecture was meaningful again'.

Coming back to China enthused and eager, she says that 'I became a wonderwoman in many people's eyes... working at New York's pace in a cosy, relaxed city like Chengdu'. Wang was motivated by the feeling that she had lost out on ten years of her creative life, so she consciously set herself higher standards than most of her colleagues and peers. She says, 'I don't think in terms of gender. Females are equal to males, so whoever you are, if you persevere, you'll come out on top.' Within a short period, she had completed a series of urban architectural works, won a prestigious Young Architect Award, authored an academic column in an architecture magazine and become consultant to the Chengdu City Planning Commission.

She worked for seven years designing buildings in large, emerging Chinese cities but she was somewhat disillusioned by the lack of cultural integrity in those urban settings. She also became a little disillusioned by architects who sit in their offices pontificating about rural problems and proposing architectural solutions from a distance. As a result, she created a practice to confront the reality on the ground; to tackle real, urgent issues of non-urban regeneration.

Wang is the founder of Field Architecture Office (FAO), a practice that started in 2015 to specialize in rural reconstruction and local village development. As it is a young practice, many of FAO's projects are as yet unrealized, and so we have featured some of Wang's earlier urban projects here, but Wang is now determined to develop a practical approach to countryside development where, she says, the clients are not developers or financiers, but 'decades of farmers'.

Understanding Chinese vernacular architecture is central to her work, though her practice has no intention of returning to the past or recreating a conservative and one-dimensional cultural interpretation of that past. Wang is interested in the poetics of architecture, but also in the 'integrated systems' that are central to rural life. As such, she distinguishes rural architecture – the mere construction of buildings in non-urban environments – from countryside development; the latter she describes as 'a comprehensive task that ensures that rural construction becomes the carrier of vernacular culture'.

## The most important thing is to dare to do

Her buildings are not a simple replay of urban forms in a rural context but are appropriate to these complex non-urban environments. Wang sees herself as a systems designer acknowledging poverty, production standards, skills levels, indigenous materials, and the importance of long-standing traditions, users' requirements and local ambitions. All of this is considered in order to express an architecture that, she says, 'belongs to the country, and ultimately, an architecture that belongs to *this* country'.

Wang is also studying for a PhD at Tianjin University, where her supervisors are the sixty-year-old Professor Cui Kai and the eighty-year-old Professor Peng Yigang, both Chinese master architects and academicians at the China Academy of Engineering. At such an age, she says, 'they have an enthusiasm towards life, a large workload and a fast work pace – with tutors like this, how can I be lazy?'

Her febrile work ethic has evolved into a wonderfully delirious philosophy of life and professionalism. For an architect, she says, 'the most important thing is to dare to do: don't be afraid of hardship; don't be afraid of failure; don't be afraid of anything'. When asked about her greatest ambition or achievement, she says, 'my greatest ambition is that I might have a great achievement in ten or twenty years' time'.

↗ 1

**Page 151** Exterior of Yangzhou Yucai Primary School

**Architect:** Wang Wei
**Project:** Yangzhou Yucai Primary School
**Location:** Yangzhou, Jiangsu Province
**Completion:** 2012

Yucai Primary School is located on the edge of the Yangzhou Grand Canal. For this project, Wang's starting point was the children's educational needs. Assessing child psychology, she designed a school that, with its modern language and specialized architecture, was different from all other traditional primary schools at the time, creating a series of spaces that adapt to different kinds of children's activity. The colours are bright, and enhanced by large windows and rooms. The campus includes farmland to evoke a bucolic charm to benefit the children's playtime experience.

↘ 2

↘ 3

↗ 4

↗ 5

↘ 6

↗ 2

↙ 3

**Architect:** Wang Wei
**Project:** Building in Village
**Location:** Baima Village, Sichuan Province
**Completion:** 2015–16

Here, in a Chinese village, Wang has attempted to trace Chinese regional architectural precedents, including local skills and materials, to test the meeting point between modern architecture and Chinese culture. Each building expresses a lifestyle distinct from the city, designed through a consultative process with villagers and local craftspeople. Wang says: 'Even though regionalism is a complicated and dangerous word (and we shouldn't excuse it for the retreat into conservative historicism), it is actually the source of creation.'

↙ 4

↖ 1

**Architect:** Wang Wei
**Project:** Panchenggang District
**Location:** Chengdu
**Completion:** 2016

This 200-metre-long (656 ft) city complex on an old heavy industry site retains some of the memory of its past, with its alleyways, markets and bridges. It is intended to create a sense of community, featuring green space, a community centre, a gym and even a farmers' market and police station. The glass façade transitions from pink to blue, including more than 50 different colour shades. This diversity is a metaphor for the city of Chengdu, which thrives on the hybrid culture of its immigrant population.

↗ 1

↗ 2

↗ 3

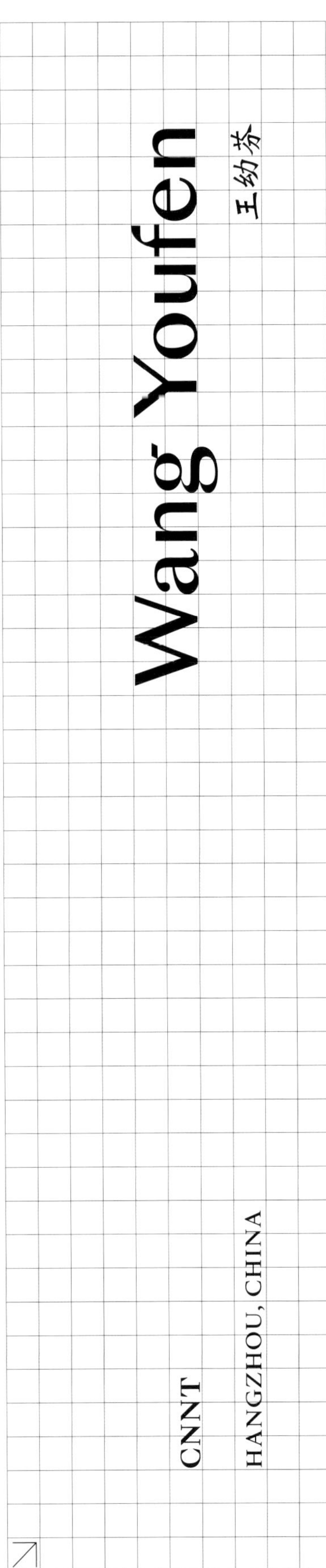

Born in Hangzhou, Wang Youfen has been involved in architecture – whether in practice or in an academic research capacity – for nearly twenty years. She perceives 'no gender difference in the construction industry nationwide' – although 'if a company is in a hurry on a project, they may tend to employ male architects in the short term because women might get married and have children. But that's about it.'

Wang is the chief architect and senior advanced engineer at CNNT (Hangzhou Zhonglian Zhujing Architecture Company), a position she has held since 2003. In 2008, she also became a professor of architecture at Southeast University's Architecture Design and Theory Research Centre in Nanjing. This is an old-established and well-regarded university whose motto is 'pursue perfection'. As the dean of the school says, it is an institution 'fully committed to the idea of open education'.

Indeed, Wang is dedicated to unfettered thinking and to broadening her students' horizons. Pointing to the tendency of Chinese architectural education in the past to focus on practical skillsets in order to create practice-ready architecture graduates, she acknowledges that this has not been particularly good for Chinese design education, although she readily admits that it was a 'historical necessity'. To kick-start the urban revolution, China needed a phalanx of proficient architectural functionaries to design and build fast. Over the past thirty years, China developed so quickly that there was little time for architectural niceties. The job was to feed the building boom. But times are changing. 'China is already slowing

检票口
Ticket Check

its pace of development,' Wang says, 'meaning that there is a very different need today. It requires a comprehensive rethink. Now we need to cultivate architects with a different mindset.'

In her teaching practice she wants to do more than simply inculcate a desire to master technique; she aims to awaken a love of learning, to help her students develop an appreciation of what is good. She advocates that her pupils acknowledge the intangible benefits that arise from reading, thinking and reflecting. 'I tell my students to read a wide variety of books – on subjects beyond architecture, such as the humanities, sociology, psychology and so on. If you have knowledge stored in your mind, you will know how to observe what is going on around you. This is an invaluable first stage in making value judgments.' She continues, 'I tell them to go out and have a cup of coffee and think because it is better than sitting indoors surfing the Internet. The benefit is unquantifiable: if you don't observe reality, how can you design for it?'

Wang is the design and project architect for many significant projects across Zhejiang province, including hotels, cultural quarters, museums, conference facilities and other civic buildings. Her latest works focus on urban renewal, a recent concept in China. She explains it – defends it, even – by saying that while some poor-quality structures should be removed, China needs to be more discerning in this current phase of development. 'City memory is relevant to all of us,' she says. 'The city is like a book. You don't just look at the last page; you read the whole story.'

It is a relatively new approach to design that has earned her plaudits at provincial and national level, including the World Chinese Architects Association Design Award, the China Architecture Design Gold Award and the National Young Architect Cup for Xiaoshan district's Commercial Street development, also known as Embroidery Square.

Her architectural design concepts come from their particular context. For her, researching the site, gaining inspiration from topography, history or memory, is essential. She notes that her projects often arise because 'the site gives birth to the idea'. The Hangzhou Wushan Museum featured on the following pages is located at the boundary between Wushan Tianfeng scenic area and Qinghefang historical area, which has been regarded as the political, cultural and business centre of this area since the Southern Song dynasty (1127–1279).

Using the slope of the Wushan Hill to derive the hierarchy of the public axis, Wang had two key considerations. Given that this is quite a 'relaxed museum dealing with folk customs', it was imperative that the experience was one of a continuous flowing space with

**City memory is relevant to all of us**

no sudden transitions. Secondly, its relationship with the mountain and the landscape dictated that it be low so as not to dominate the surroundings. After all, she says, 'the landscape is the leading actor, not a supporting player'. Here the landscape 'penetrates the museum, and resting places provide somewhere to view the trees and walk outside. At the highest point, the exhibition hall has a conversation with the forest.'

In all Wang's projects, she describes the environment as 'precious' and she aims to provide a dialogue with nature. She cites the landscape as the most crucial element in her designs, although 'citizens' satisfaction' with her work is what she enjoys most. 'I really hope that I can bring people *something* through my designs.'

**Page 161** Wuyi Railway Station façade

**Architect:** Wang Youfen
**Project:** Wuyi Railway Station
**Location:** Zhejiang Wuyi
**Completion:** 2015

Wuyi is an ancient town in south-east China that has seen tourism increase over recent years. The new station is a sleek addition to the town. Its front elevation is open to 'invite the mountain landscape inside' while also efficiently directing the crowds.

↗ 1

↗ 2

↗ 3

↗ 1

**Architect:** Wang Youfen
**Project:** Yongkang Railway Station
**Location:** Yongkang, Zhejiang Province
**Completion:** 2015

Yongkang, known as the 'Hardware City of China', is a world-class industrial area set in beautiful mountains and with rich natural resources. The design theme of the station is 'the rhythm of Yongkang'. The sweep of the interior soffits resembling sheet-metal rolls, the cuts in the entrance arch, and the folding and jointing of the exterior roof profile aim to evoke various aspects of metal forging.

↗ 1

↗ 2

**Architect:** Wang Youfen
**Project:** Zhejiang Wushan Museum
**Location:** Hangzhou, Zhejiang Province
**Completion:** 2010

This building was the winner of the World Ethnic Chinese Architecture Association Design Award. It is nestled in the foothills of Wu Mountain in Qinghefang District on a brownfield plot formerly occupied by warehouses and a temporary parking lot. The design aims to repair the mountain's natural texture, while the exhibition halls are broken down to provide a contextual scale and aesthetic to suit the neighbouring dwellings. A public mountain path connects exhibition halls to form an elevated walking trail between the museum and the mountain's historic scenic spots.

↗ 3

↘ 4

↗ 5

↗ 1

**Architect:** Wang Youfen
**Project:** Zhejiang Tourism Exhibition Centre
**Location:** Hangzhou, Zhejiang Province
**Completion:** 2015

The site is located on Wu Mountain, famous for the Chenghuang Pagoda at its summit. This building is situated further down the slopes and is surrounded by dense forestry. It is laid out on a north-south access with the entrance facing the city street. A grand entrance plaza directs visitors to the long ceremonial arcade that connects the various exhibition units, or allows visitors to break through into the surrounding hillside forest.

↗ 2

↗ 3

↘ 4

↗ 5

↗ 6

Wei Architects was founded in 2010 and in its short existence has completed more than ninety projects, ranging from large five-star hotels to small art galleries, from community kindergartens to tiny retail conversions, and from installation art to furniture design. Aside from the occasional obligatory large project, this is an unusual portfolio for a contemporary Chinese practice, comprising as it does relatively small, thoughtful designs that blend art, architecture and interior refurbishment. Wei Architects was an early proponent of minimal interventions at a time when it was less common for Chinese architects to restrain themselves. Nowadays, however, many more are tending to turn away from mega-projects and impersonal master plans and are shifting their attention to scaled-down interventions.

The founder of Wei Architects, Wei Na, was born and raised in Beijing, where her family lived in one of its many run-down residential *hutongs* (traditional alleyways). The family relocated to a modern apartment block, but Wei proudly states that she has always retained a sense of connection with native Beijingers' simple way of life. After several years away from home studying in the United States, she returned to Beijing and now works out of a refurbished industrial building, no bigger than $75m^2$ ($800ft^2$), in the centre of typically chaotic Fangjia Hutong to the north of the Forbidden City.

Wei completed her undergraduate studies at the prestigious Tsinghua University before moving to New Haven, Connecticut, to complete her master's at the Yale School of Architecture. She worked for a period

at Beyer Blinder Belle Architects in New York, a practice specializing in historical preservation, which sharpened her sensitivity to conservation as a physical and social good. She also studied for a time under Zaha Hadid at Yale, went to work for MADA s.p.a.m. in her year out, and acted as project manager for Rem Koolhaas's OMA on the Shenzhen Stock Exchange building – so she clearly has a wide range of experience at a variety of scales. But above all, it is the idea of working sympathetically with the city that inspires much of her current work.

The idea of the genius loci – the spirit of a place – is very particular in her work and she professes a keen interest in developing a sympathetic, place-based architecture. Not only is she trying to relate to a sense of a physical locality through context-driven design, but she is also exploring the emotional and abstract sense of 'placeness' itself, which is something that she believes is peculiar to Chinese culture. It is an elusive emotional intelligence that she likens to China's more spiritual cognizance of space.

Conventional architectural design – in the caricature of a Western model – envisages a building as an enclosing envelope containing a space inside. Conversely, it is said that China tends to appreciate the volume rather than the container; that without the volume, there would be no container. Wei frequently attempts to blur enclosing boundaries, to provide a transitional phase that maximizes the sense of space to heighten a user's experience.

In her unrealized project for a regional planning museum in northern China, for example, she uses light as a tectonic material, describing it as a 'solid substance'. Situated in Rizhao, a Chinese seaside resort whose name means 'sunshine', this design incorporates tracery parapets to filter the light on to the surrounding site. Visitors walk 'through' this light/shade boundary as a transitional zone of experience. This awakened in Wei a belief that design could be allied to emotion and sensitivity. It was demonstrated again in her simple refurbishment of an unloved roadside pavilion, which she transformed by use of a complex metal cloud frame, turning the original relic into a popular social space where locals come to enjoy the diffused light and cooling shade.

She calls this 'suffused space': a zone of combined physical and emotional reality that creates an atmosphere. In the refurbishment of the Shatan Courtyard house she describes how 'sunlight comes through the leaves and creates mottled shadows, so... the occupants can feel falling leaves and changing skies even from within the home'.

Wei's belief in the emotive power of architecture stems from a formative experience she had as a teenager when she visited the world-renowned Classical Gardens of Suzhou in Jiangsu Province. She says that she instinctively appreciated these man-made landscapes that manipulate small enclosed spaces to create a sense of suspense, of surprise and of deceptive perspective. 'It had the ability to maximize the potential of a space.'

Many landscape techniques are found in much of her architectural oeuvre. For example, her refurbishment of the 70m$^2$ (750ft$^2$) Song Max retail store in Beijing uses formal routes, framed views, surprise elements and ancient landscape motifs that play with perspective to maximize space. Even the changing-rooms adopt a shift in elevation and a fluid sense of enclosure, tricks traditionally used in classical Chinese gardens to create spaces of quiet contemplation.

Wei worries that too many Chinese architects lack focus because 'there are so many distractions that architects just want to finish the job and get the money, forgetting to insist on quality'. Wei believes that 'innate feminine sensibility' works to women's advantage, with enlightened clients relishing women's design sensitivity. Female architects in China still struggle to be heard, but she is optimistic that through superior results, things will change fast.

**Page 173** Xiaoxijia exterior

**Architect:** Wei Na
**Project:** Xiaoxijia (Springing Stream)
**Location:** Xiaoxi, Fujian Province
**Completion:** 2017

Wei is moving into the countryside. Originating with a range of beautifully sketchy images, this project is a remedial intervention in one of the left-behind villages of rural China. Decrepit structures (sometimes just one gable wall remains) have been restored and extended, using local labour and materials, and given a modern twist. Timber construction, raised floors and modern interiors are complemented with an undulating organic roof: a veranda-like form that extends outwards to unify the scattered village buildings. It is a modern twist on the traditional chunky timber post-and-beam architecture.

↗ 1

↗ 2

↗ 3

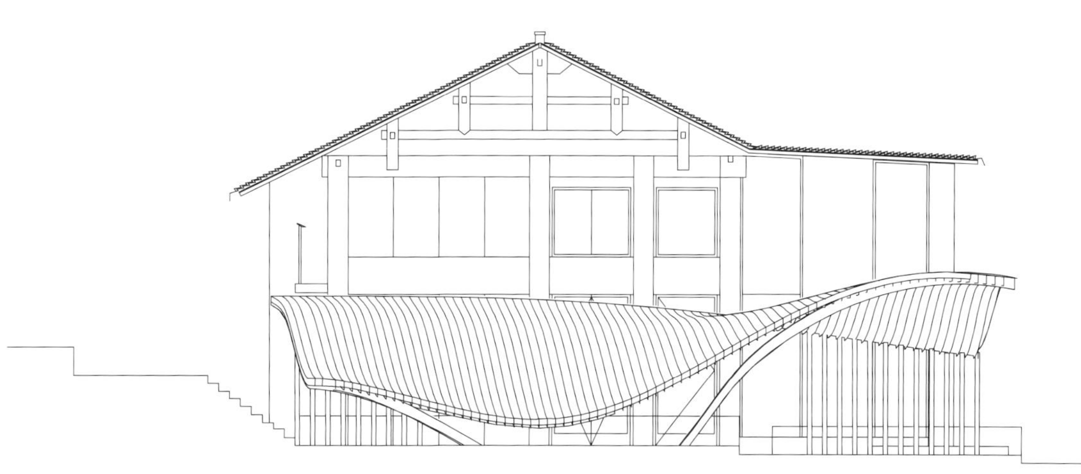

↗ 4

↗ 5

↘ 6

↗ 7

↘ 8

**Architect:** Wei Na
**Project:** WHY Hotel
**Location:** Beijing
**Completion:** 2015

In 2015, WHY Hotel was awarded the title of 'Best New Hotel', 'Hotel of the Year' and many other international and domestic awards. It is a high-end hotel complex provided with elevated walkways and winding paths, taking guests around the pool and through the bamboo groves. It is a community with a high degree of privacy. Wei's idiosyncratic sketches capture the simplicity of the design. This chic spa resort's expressive use of timber, glass and steel is deftly handled.

↗ 1

↗ 2

↗ 3

↗ 4

↗ 1

**Architect:** Wei Na
**Project:** Shatan Courtyard House
**Location:** Beijing
**Completion:** 2013

This is a residential renovation project for a small courtyard building near the northeast corner of the Forbidden City Palace Museum in Beijing. The project preserves the form of the original traditional building on the north side of the courtyard but allows it to evolve into a modern building on the east side of the yard. At the junction of old and new buildings, the roofs of modern buildings were lifted to accommodate large-scale skylights so that the morning light floods into the ground floor, down the spiral staircase and into the new underground spaces.

↗ 2

↗ 3

↗ 4

Ye Min had been poised to study electrical engineering when her mother intervened. Instead of applied sciences, she made Ye Min consider subjects that were more professional, such as medicine or accounting – subjects that her mother thought would offer more stability and a better life in the future. It was another family member, an uncle who had studied architecture at Tianjin University, who eventually inspired her choice. As her artistic skills had been encouraged in the extracurricular workshops provided by the Children's Palace (the state-run 'enrichment programme' for talented children[1]), she was nudged into enrolling in the architecture course at South China University of Technology (SCUT) in Guangdong province.

After postgraduate studies, Ye worked at the Poly Group Corporation, a state-owned enterprise that specializes in a variety of business ventures including construction and real estate, but also fishing, military hardware and entertainment.[2] (By 2005, it was the world's fifth-largest property developer.) For Ye Min, work was plentiful but dull, and she soon realized that she was poorly suited to the humdrum work of a state-management behemoth. 'I am not fond of management work,' she says simply. At the turn of the millennium, she quit to join an architectural studio in Hong Kong. Within three years, she was promoted to co-partner of that company.

Unfortunately, she found out that her new business partner did not enjoy the management side of architectural practice either, and Ye was being asked to do it. Business management 'was still beyond my capability', she admits, 'and actually design is the only thing I am

capable of. Having to become a businesswoman again led to me consider leaving architecture altogether.' However, with the fortunate intervention of a client who asked her to design a commercial office building, her design ambitions were reinvigorated, and she opened a small new architectural studio, Fei Architects, based in Haizhu, Guangzhou.

Even today, Guangzhou has far fewer independent architectural studios than Beijing or Shanghai and work is less plentiful. This is partly due to government bodies and large private developers being able to pick up many of the important architectural commissions, so that small studios find it rather hard to earn a living. 'Independent studios like mine,' Ye says, 'can only receive projects indirectly through larger institutes, making it much more difficult for small studios to survive and develop.'

A further problem stems from clients and developers, in her experience, considering female architects to be qualified only for interior finishes, decorations or furnishings – the 'feminine touches'. She explains, 'They believe that male architects share a better sense of architectural space and assume that their overall planning ability is better, regardless of the reality. Consequently, there are not many benefits to being a female architect in China, especially in independently operating design practices, while this attitude continues.'

Ye's first project, Yida Estate Plaza, was designed for a state-sponsored development company, whose only brief was that it should be 'impressive and unforgettable at first sight'. Winning several awards and featuring in the South China First Young Architects Exhibition, this early promising design was described as 'Western-styled but essentially Chinese'.

Any Western influences come from her short travels in Europe and America, trips that were predominantly organized, she says, to get away from the tedious, repetitive Chinese cityscapes. The Chinese cultural influences undoubtedly come from her tutor – and first employer – Professor He Jingtang, most famous for the Chinese Pavilion at the Shanghai Expo 2010. (He is also the architect of the rather wonderful Dachang Muslim Cultural Centre in Hebei province.) Through his aegis, Ye has developed a cultural appreciation for architecture that seeps into her practice's philosophical approach.

The name of her practice, *fei*, means 'opening' – something that illuminates the border between void and functional space. Once the border is crossed, infinite possibilities of architecture will be released. Quoting ancient Daoist philosopher Laozi, Ye says, 'When openings are cut out from the surroundings to form doors and windows, voids are turned into rooms whose function depends on the very essence of empty space.' She is convinced that architectural design does not exist for the sake of particular projects, and that instead its meaning is found in its expression of one's attitude towards life represented by those architectural spaces.

Her motto, borrowed from Eastern philosophy, is '*wu jie*' (meaning 'no boundaries'). 'Building a Chinese garden in a high-rise building, for example, is *wu jie*: having no boundary between interior and exterior; designing the space that eliminates the boundary of functions.' Ultimately, her practice philosophy rests on her invented concept of 'artecture' – believing that architecture should focus not merely on construction issues but also on those of art, culture and people's livelihoods, explored through the prism of Eastern philosophy.

Running her own practice for more than a decade, Ye Min has become less hostile to business and management practices and recognizes that quality of life and materialism are harmonious rather than contradictory. 'Humanity's continuous development,' she says, 'depends on common progress in both culture and business.'

↗ 1

**Page 187** Exterior of the Ersha Recreation and Cultural Centre

**Architect:** Ye Min
**Project:** Ersha Recreation and Cultural Centre
**Location:** Ersha Island, Guangzhou, Guangdong Province
**Completion:** 2017

The brief was launched in the autumn of 2010, with the client expecting the architect to come up with an operational plan for a huge site sufficient to yield a profit to pay for the development of the cultural centre, to generate financial support for local art and cultural industries, and contribute to the formation of a sustainable cultural industry. The exhibition halls are connected by gentle slopes of 140m (460ft) along the west- and south-facing sides. It provides a faux mountain path that not only offers river views but also serves as a most effective sun-shading for the building.

↗ 2

↘ 3

↗ 1

**Architect:** Ye Min
**Project:** Estate Plaza
**Location:** Yuexiu District, Guangzhou, Guangdong Province
**Completion:** 2006

It is rare for a private company to own an entire building in the downtown area of Guangzhou. This building for over 1,000 workers shelters behind a vegetable market and is surrounded by high-rise buildings. As such, it does not face the streets, and for such a big structure it is relatively hidden from sight. The team won several design and construction awards recognizing that it provides an environmentally friendly, convenient, fun and efficient working environment.

↗ 2

↘ 3

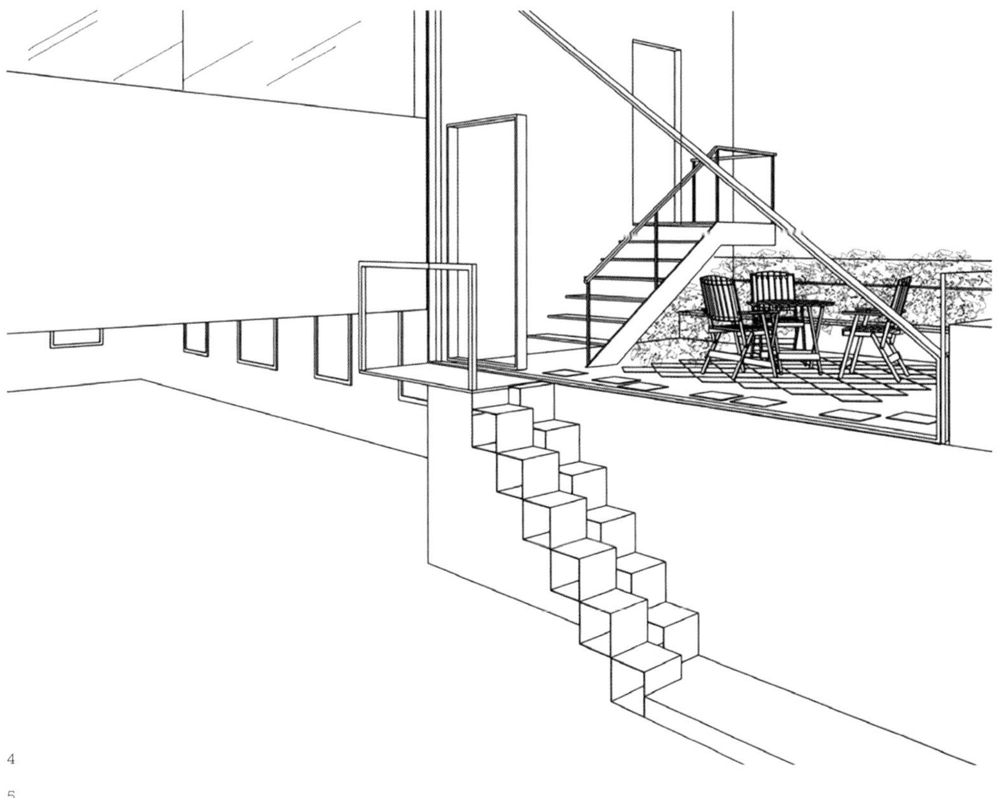

↗ 4

↘ 5

Zhang Di comes from an architectural family; it was her mother who ran the architectural practice and so, she says, it was almost a natural decision for her to become an architect.

She was born in northeastern China, but lived in many different cities as she grew up, as her family moved from place to place. At the age of seventeen she was accepted to study architecture at the University of Sheffield in the UK, and then gained her postgraduate diploma at the Bartlett School of Architecture, University College London. Here she was taught to critically engage with ideas but also to believe in possibilities. With this grounding, she is fully attuned to Westernized practices while comfortably embracing Chinese ways of working.

She recalls her first site visit, mentored by a British architect who spent three years as the project's site architect, coordinating all aspects of the built works. 'He knew the answers to any question that was asked of him and I was hugely impressed by his diligence. My mother too regularly worked on site, and I think these people have subconsciously influenced me to believe that architecture is essentially about practising.'

As a result, Zhang is less interested in teaching or writing about architecture. 'My major goal is to keep on practising,' she says; 'it is the form that I find most exciting. The making of architecture is the combination of research, creative design, implementation, execution,

communication and management. It is where all my ambitions are realized in one role.'

After her undergraduate degree, she worked for a year for RHWL Architects on London's King's Cross area master plan (one of the largest regeneration projects in Europe at the time). She qualified in 2007, and went to work at the London offices of Foster + Partners, developing the Masdar Institute in Masdar City, Abu Dhabi's new eco-city. At Foster + Partners she met her future business partner, with whom she went on to found WAA Architects in 2010. Having decided to enter the Chinese market, they set up an office in the Baiziwan district of Beijing.

WAA stands for 'we architech anonymous'. It is meant to symbolize their collaborative design ambitions, by which the architect is essential but not ostentatious and is merely one cog in the process of creating architecture. They believe in relying on others – the client, the builder, the public – to truly realize the project. Zhang says that her practice intends always to work outside the dogmatic, brand-laden world of architecture that often imposes its vision on the world. 'We hope to be flexible liberators for future inhabitants of the buildings we design.'

In some ways, this is a radical reimagining of the way that the architect in China is positioned in the construction process. As Zhang explains, 'An architect in the UK administers the building contract and coordinates and manages the realization of the project in a non-biased manner. In China, however, the architect acts more like a consultant to the client and can only advise.'

WAA engage in master planning, interiors, furniture design, art interventions and much more. Zhang even has a fashion business 'on the side', which acts as a secondary inspiration. Their interior design for Chinese retailer AnyShopStyle, for example, tries to counter the elitist conception of architecture and to establish instead 'a democratic space' that showcases the various fashion designers' work.

Zhang is fundamentally interested in how people emotionally respond to architecture. Being an architect, she says, 'is a creative job, and so I guess it attracts women by its very nature'. But she admits to not really recognizing gender differences in architecture. 'There is probably a higher percentage of female architects in China than in some Western countries,' she says. 'I think that has something to do with China's one-child policy, whereby both sexes are given equal opportunities in society. Girls from my generation have been brought up with the same high expectations as boys. Women are given equal rights in almost all careers, not just architecture.'

Zhang advocates 'human-centred architecture', but for many buildings in China this has tended not to be the case. The country, she says, has spent the past thirty years prioritizing rapid growth and mass-producing buildings. It is now time for the focus to shift to smaller-scale, user-friendly designs and a more comprehensive focus on real needs.

She has a few recommendations for the next generation of architecture students (relevant to any country's students). First, remind yourself about the basics and remember what excited (and still excites) you and inspires you. Second, 'have a little bit of social responsibility'. She wants young designers to remember that their architecture may stand for up to a hundred years and will have a direct impact on people's daily life in significant ways. 'We should always ask ourselves whether we have tried our best.' Finally, students need to realize that the practice of architecture is a long process: even in China a project programme might last for two or three years, or even decades, with the involvement of many other parties. 'Persistence,' she says, 'is one element that every architect must have to keep going through the long drawn-out development process. We must never give up experimenting and collaborating.'

↗ 1

**Page 195** A screen in AnyShopStyle

**Architect:** Zhang Di,
WAA Architects
**Project:** AnyShopStyle
**Location:** Sanlitun, Beijing
**Completion:** 2016

This is a 'democratic space in which to showcase a rotating roster of work by 300-plus designers and their micro-collections'. It comprises a series of geometric shapes, colours and materials to define the space with minimal signage. Indeed, the interior has produced a minimal intervention to allow the products, the fashion, to speak for itself.

↘ 2

↗ 3

↙ 4

↗ 5

↙ 6

↗ 1

**Architect:** Zhang Di, WAA Architects
**Project:** Yinchuan Museum of Contemporary Art (MOCA)
**Location:** Yinchuan, Ningxia Hui Autonomous Region
**Completion:** 2015

The building that first brought Zhang to global attention was the Yinchuan Museum of Contemporary Art (MOCA), which stamps a strong architectural statement onto the surrounding area. It is a 13,200m$^2$ (142,000ft$^2$) parametric building resting alongside the Yellow River, whose shape and detailing has been designed to mimic the river flow and the sedimentary accretions of the surrounding natural landform.

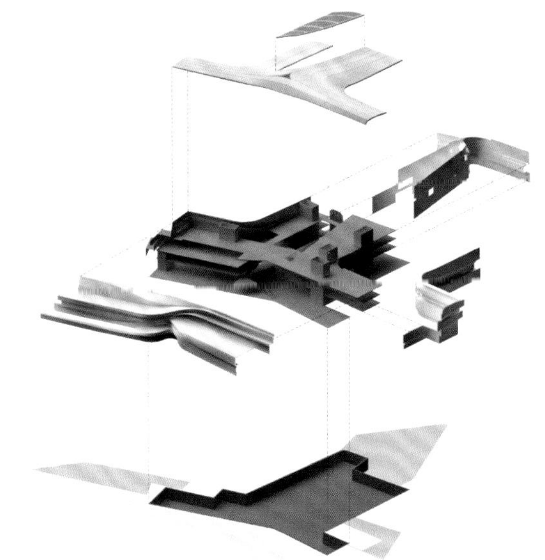

↗ 3

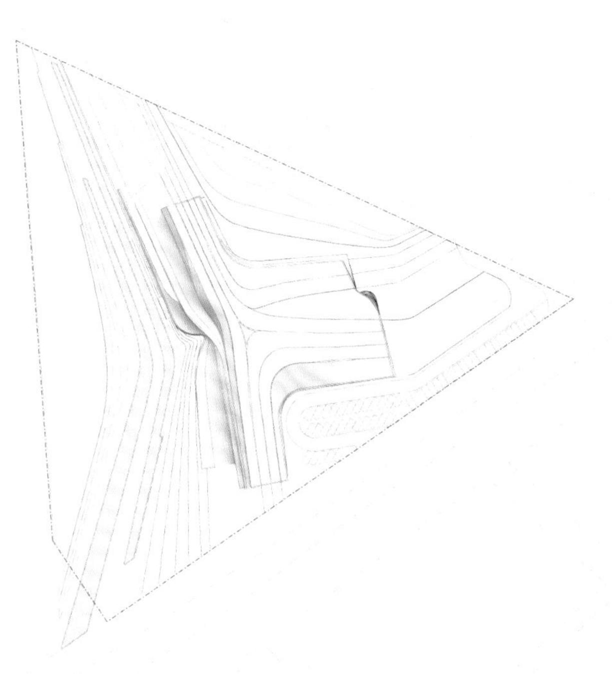

↗ 4

↗ 5

↗ 6

↘ 7

↘ 8

↗ 9

↘ 10

↘ 11

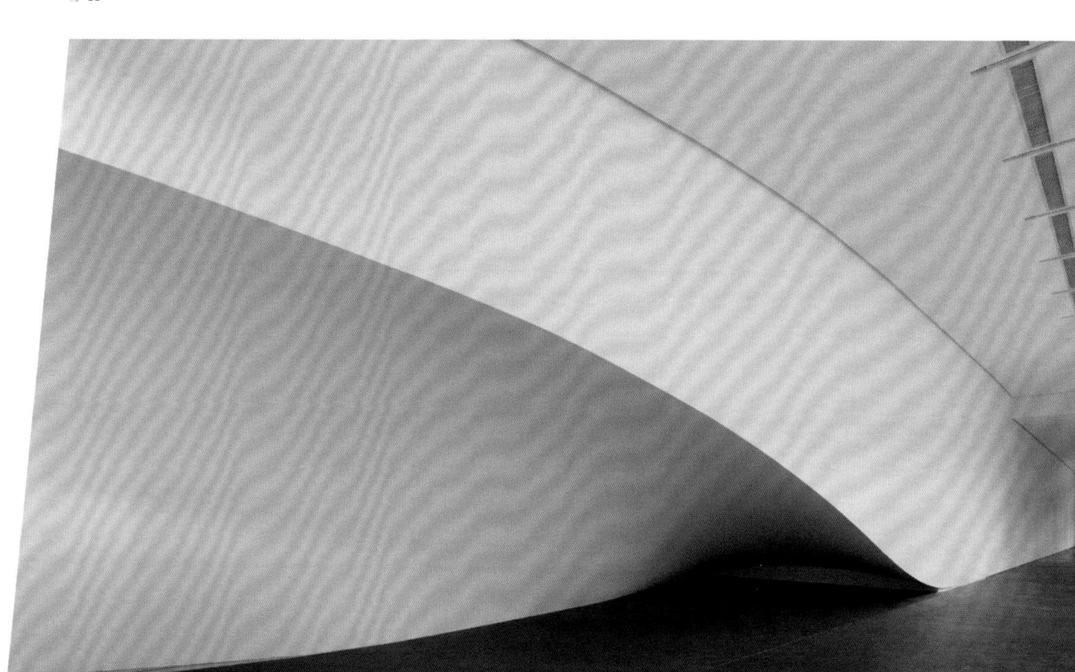

**Architect:** Zhang Di, WAA Architects
**Project:** Valley Resort, Beijing Yushan International Hot Spring Resort Hotel
**Location:** Xifeng Mountain, Changping, Beijing
**Completion:** 2014

This building has a first phase construction area of 3,000m² (32,300ft²), set in a site of 160ha (400 acres). Valley Resort is a luxury hotel organized as a series of condominiums set against the backdrop of the mountains of Changping, north of Beijing. The complex comprises low-level boxes around the perimeter of an external pool and hot springs. Concrete walls, large glazing panels and large areas of marble floors and stairs offer beautiful views and quality conditions for affluent Beijingers on retreat, just 50km (30 miles) from the capital. It provides luxurious hotel rooms, business/conference facilities, cafés and restaurants and a spa experience.

↗ 1

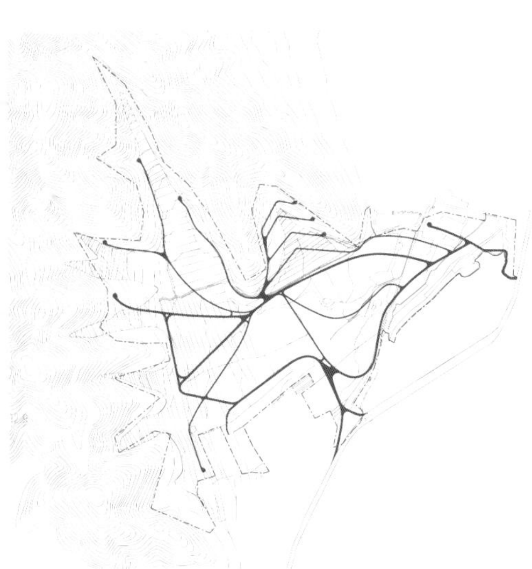

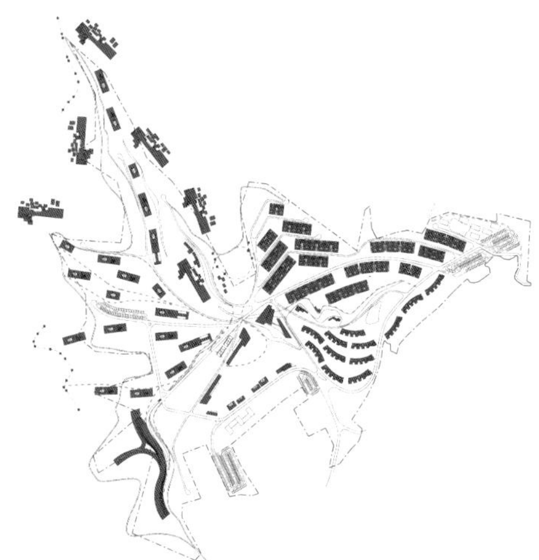

↗ 2

↗ 3

↘ 4

↗ 5

↗ 6

↗ 7

↗ 8

↗ 9

↗ 10

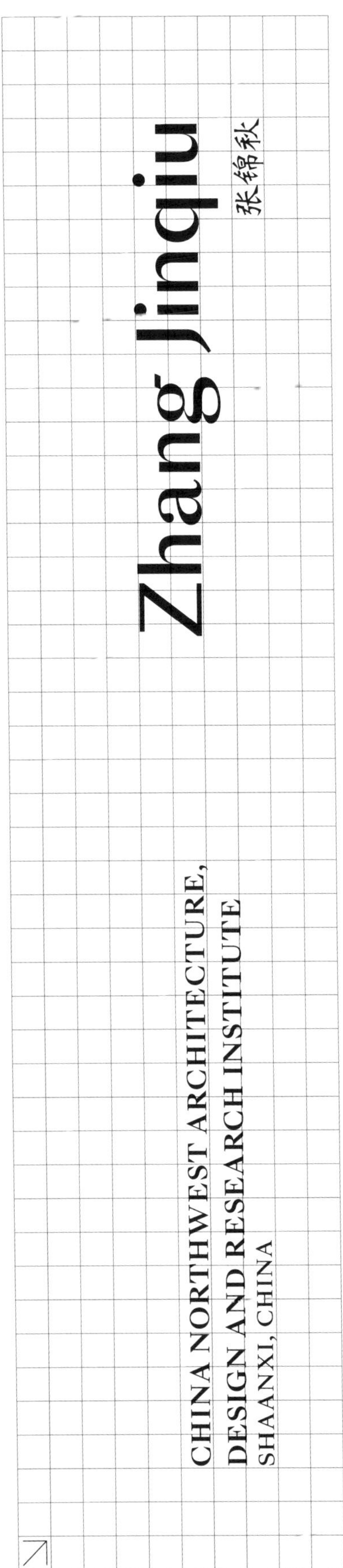

# Zhang Jinqiu 张锦秋

CHINA NORTHWEST ARCHITECTURE,
DESIGN AND RESEARCH INSTITUTE
SHAANXI, CHINA

Zhang Jinqiu was born in Chengdu, Sichuan province. In 1937, when she was one year old, the Japanese invasion forced her family to evacuate to Xipu in the remote countryside (now a Chengdu suburb). While the country suffered unbearable hardship, the young Zhang was blissfully unaware. She has nothing but happy memories. 'My life was pastoral poetry,' she says.

She wonders if the Zhang family has 'a character – or a gene – that promotes integrity and perseverance'. She was born into a family of architects, with her aunt, Zhang Yuquan, being one of the first generation of women architects in China.[1] Her family placed great importance on education, though she says that the best lesson from her parents was 'to have ambitions, to stand on my own two feet in society and not to rely on others'. She tells of Sunday walks with her father, 'where we always made judgments about what was good or bad. It was a terrific aesthetic education and I developed an ability to discriminate the merits of a scene or architecture at an early age.'

Zhang studied at Tsinghua University in Beijing, gaining a master's degree in Architectural History and Theory in 1964. She studied under the father of Chinese architecture, Liang Sicheng, and says she has 'inherited part of Liang's unfinished business, making a deep exploration of the fusion of Chinese traditional architecture and modern architecture'. After graduating, she was assigned to the China Northwest Architecture, Design and Research Institute, working in 'architectural design and theoretical pursuits', where she has remained for fifty years. She is now eighty-two years of age and still going strong.

陝西歷史博物館

During her master's thesis on Chinese gardens, which necessitated trips to Beijing's Summer Palace, she met Premier Zhou Enlai. He spoke to her about the need to 'study hard and research bravely'. She says, 'I was excited for a long time. I had no other thought than that the design of the Shaanxi History Museum (which I presided over) was the dying wish of Premier Zhou. It became a spiritual pillar to inspire me to do it well.'

Zhang's life has not been an easy journey. Tsinghua University in the mid-1960s – especially the architecture department – was regarded as a hotbed of capitalist ideas. Western and traditional Chinese architecture were roundly rejected and condemned by the Communist regime. As an academic, Zhang's father and, by association, his family had a rough time during this precarious period. In such a climate of suspicion, Zhang herself was 'sent down' to Xi'an. It was 1966, she was pregnant, and she arrived in Xi'an as the Cultural Revolution was just beginning. 'It strengthened my resolve, my willpower and my mental capacity,' she says, 'and I learned a lot.'

Her resolution ensured that she survived. She rose to be Chief Architect in China's Capital Construction Design Group in 1987 and has proved to be one of China's top professionals in the field. She is one of only two Chinese women architects to have been awarded the honorary title of 'Construction Master' by the government.

In the 1970s Zhang had begun to concentrate on Tang dynasty restoration. The Huaqing Palace was her first foray into this style, which she famously merged with her own contemporary stylistic ideals. She travelled extensively to Japan to investigate the influence of Sui and Tang dynasty techniques and to compare them with native Japanese architecture. Through this remarkable cross-cultural research, she was emboldened to combine Tang styles with modern architecture. Consequently, she is associated with popularizing the so-called neo-Tang style. Indeed, describing her role in the renewal of China's interest in traditional architecture in a modern context, American theorist Peter G. Rowe cited Zhang as a foundational influence. In 2011, at the age of seventy-five, she was elected as a member of the Chinese Academy of Engineering.

Zhang and her life's work represent a direct connection with the past. For more than half a century, she has been working in Xi'an, Shaanxi province, promoting Chinese cultural traditions, exploring the unity of science and art, tradition and modernism, and incorporating the latest scientific and technical developments to the benefit of conservation and heritage.

Her restoration of Xi'an's majestic Bell Tower and Drum Tower and their garden plaza is part of the project to restore the city to its Tang dynasty splendour. It helped Zhang branch out into the urban scale. Her work on Shaanxi Library and Art Museum, the Tang Lotus Garden, the Main Hall of the Huangdi (Yellow Emperor) Mausoleum, and Famen Temple, to name but a few, heralds an urban experience that is more than the sum of its parts, being nothing less than the reclamation of an ancient city as a historically important global destination.

Zhang looks back on her life as having three distinct phases. First there was a wide-ranging and pluralistic exploration of ideas in her early youth. Then came the consolidation of her ideas of an architecture suited to a specific historical context with an interest in cultural protection. Finally, she has settled into a specialization that focuses on the restoration of monuments and historical sites as part of an urban programme. She is neither an ancient nor a parodist. She seeks to combine tradition and modernity, to provide an architecture imbued with Chinese cultural atmosphere. She calls it architecture that is 'full of regional flavour, characterizing the spirit of the age'.

↗ 1

**Page 213** Exterior view of the Shaanxi History Museum

**Architect:** Zhang Jinqiu
**Project:** Shaanxi History Museum
**Location:** Xiao Zhai East Road, Xi'an, Shaanxi Province
**Completion:** 1991

Shaanxi History Museum was the dying wish of Premier Zhou Enlai. It was the first large-scale national museum to be built after the Cultural Revolution. In addition to the straightforward display function, the design makes allowances for cultural exchange, education services and facilities for scientific research. The architectural form reflects a strong connection to national tradition, local flavour and the distinctive liberated spirit of the age. The image that Zhang sought to convey was of an ancient capital city landmark. The concentrated layout combined with traditional Chinese palace features includes a symmetrical courtyard with a central hall. The design sought to chime with the rhythm of ancient Oriental philosophical traditions, something radical and challenging for China at the time.

↗ 2

↗ 3

↗ 4

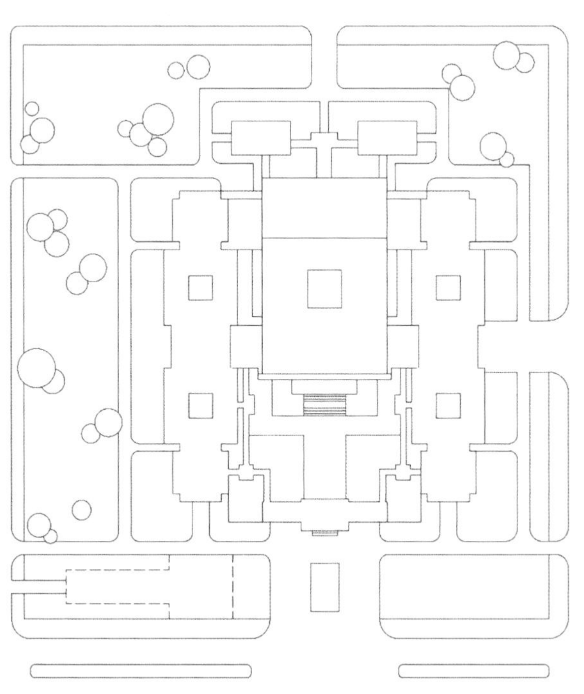

↗ 5

**Architect:** Zhang Jinqiu
**Project:** Huangdi Mausoleum
**Location:** Yan'an, Shaanxi Province
**Completion:** 2004

The Huangdi (Yellow Emperor) Mausoleum is located on a seemingly boundless plateau on the Weihe River. The project was to complete the Yellow Emperor Mausoleum Scenic Area modification and to build a new compound and sanctuary. This project adapts to new worshippers' needs, and its design draws inspiration from the mountains and rivers. It uses the classic images of heaven being represented by roundness, and earth as a square. To highlight the sanctity of a Chinese spiritual home, its pattern includes national cultural characteristics and its style combines traditional and modern.

1

↗ 2

↗ 3

↗ 4

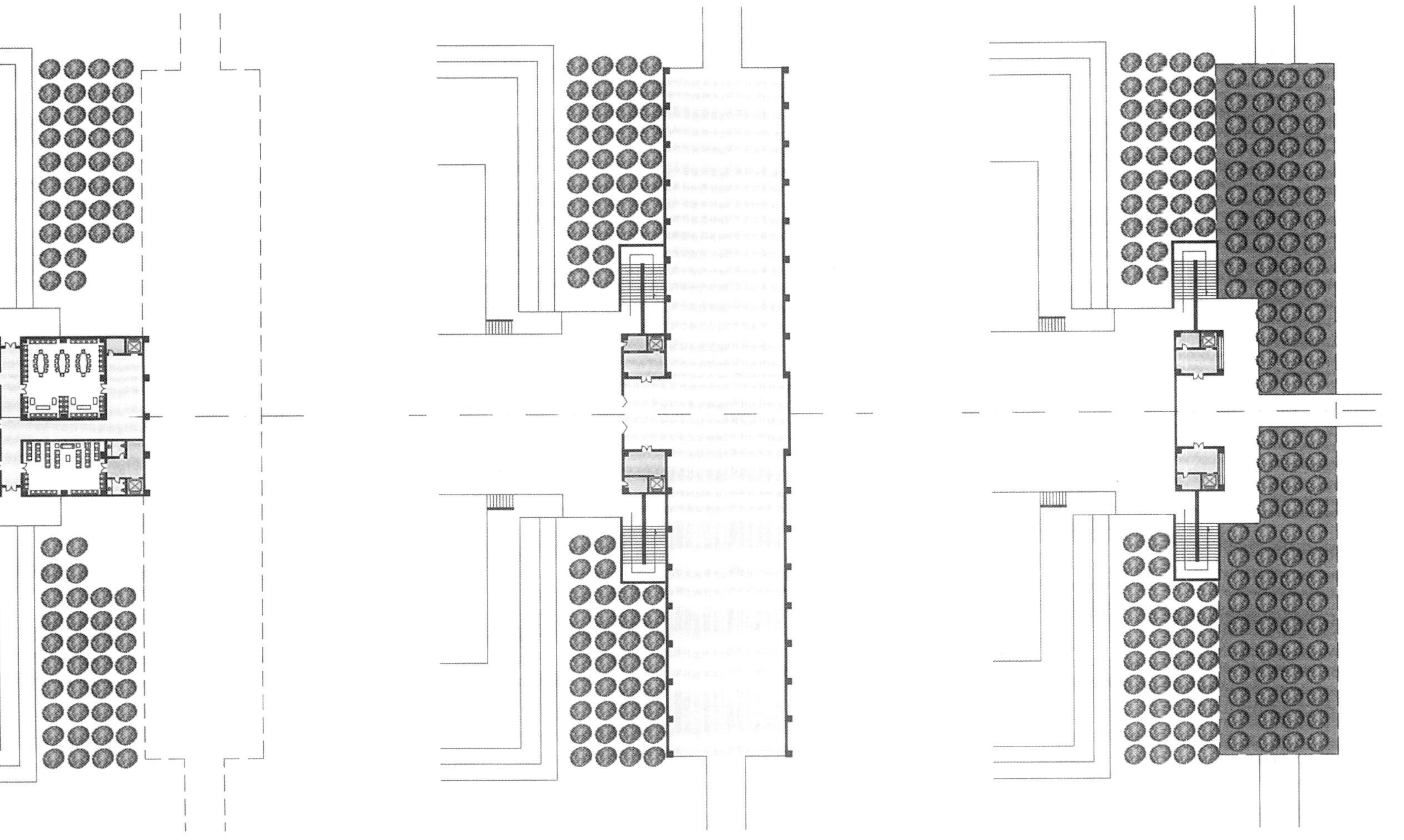

↗ 5

**Architect:** Zhang Jinqiu
**Project:** Yan'an Revolutionary Memorial Hall
**Location:** Yan'an, Shaanxi Province
**Completion:** 2009

Yan'an was the central location of the Communist Party of China for thirteen years, and the birthplace of Mao Zedong Thought. Therefore, Jinqiu says that the design of the Yan'an Revolutionary Memorial Hall 'should concentrate Yan'an spirit, its glorious revolutionary tradition as the soul and symbol of the city'. Zhang researched revolutionary pilgrimage sites like Shaoshan (Mao's birthplace) and Jinggangshan (known as 'the cradle of the Chinese revolution'). Exploring the revolutionary memorial halls, she found many common features: they are all symmetrical, dignified and solemn, but each is distinctive thanks to differences of site, context and geography.

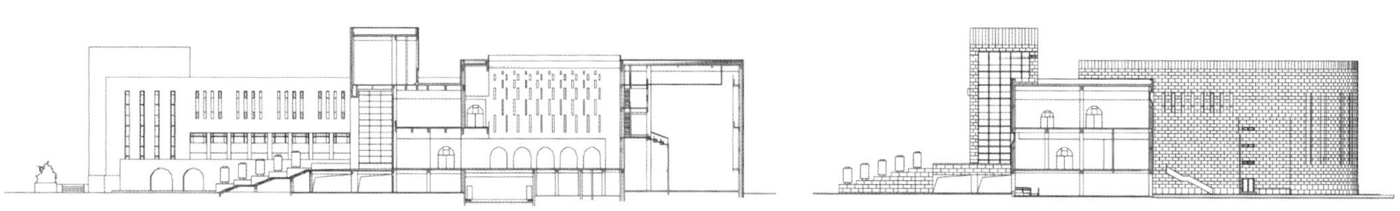

↗ 1

↗ 2

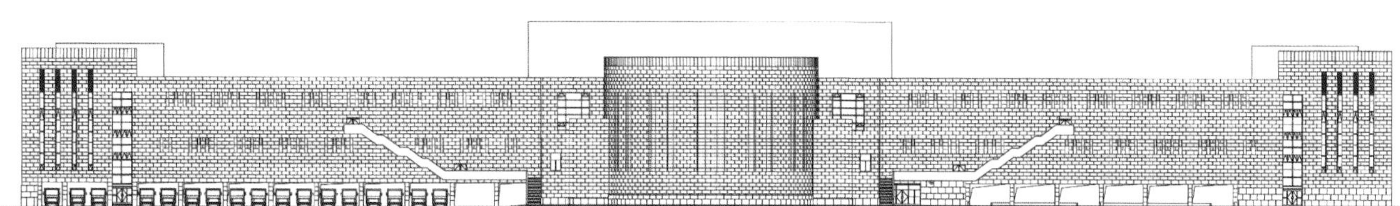

↗ 3

↗ 4

纪念馆

↗ 5

↗ 7

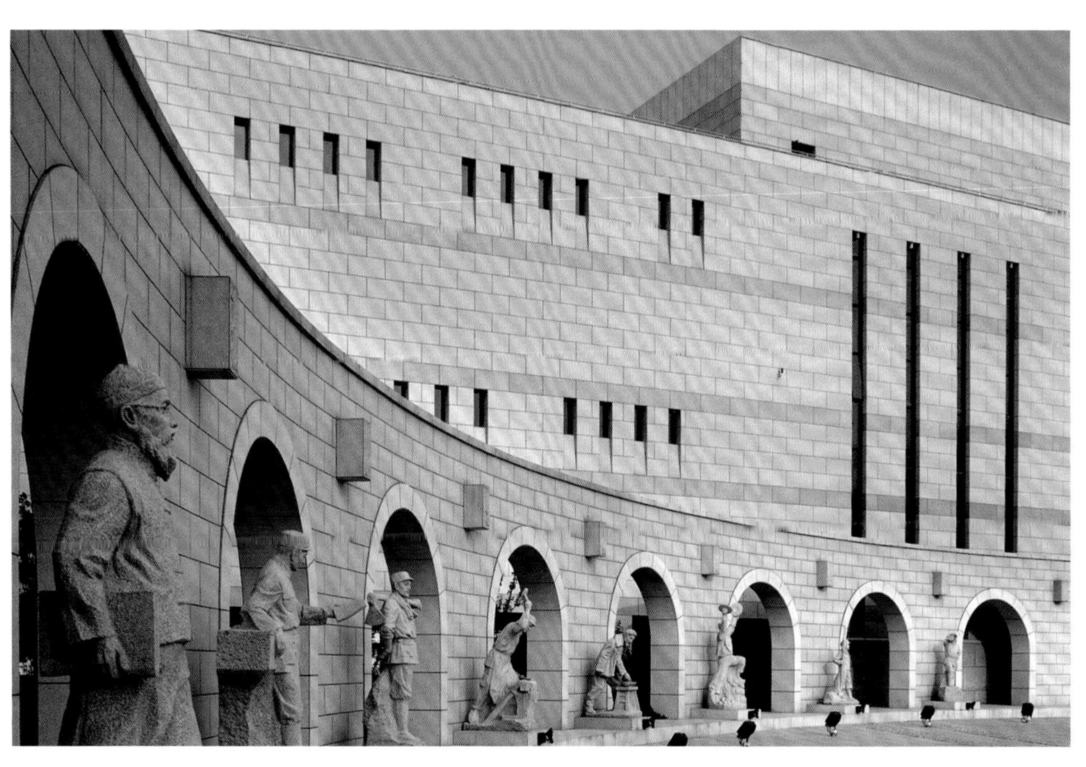

↗ 6

# Zhao Zhao

赵曌

DADA ARCHITECTS

BEIJING, CHINA

Among other things, Zhao Zhao is an architect, artist, urban planner and lead designer at Dada Architects in Beijing. In 2004 she graduated – top of her class – from the Central Academy of Fine Arts, which was a school trying out some new ideas in Chinese architectural education at the time. The course taught architecture as a core subject but also graphic design, furniture-making, typography, photography and interior design, all of which opened Zhao's mind to the broader potential of three-dimensional design.

In her second year of study, she met architect Ma Yansong (who was then still working for Zaha Hadid, a few years before he founded MAD Architects), and she had the good fortune – and talent – to spend 'most of my undergraduate years doing competition projects with him'. She says, 'I saw how he dealt with problems, failure and marginalization. He simply never gave up, and now he runs the most successful Chinese architectural office in the world.' She has clearly inherited some of that same grit and determination.

While she realizes that it would be commercially simpler and safer to conform, she is made of sterner stuff. 'There are far too many architects in this country who just follow trends. After the Bird's Nest stadium, weird buildings were all the rage; when Zaha first arrived, everyone wanted to do crazy curves; then Wang Shu won the Pritzker Prize and now everyone is looking for "Chinese characteristics".' Architects need to be more critical, individual, free, she believes. 'We have to be careful that we, as a profession, don't simply become some unscrupulous developer's accomplice.'

She recognizes that there are pressures on Chinese architects arising from the speed and instability of China's urban growth over the past twenty years or so. The burdens on architects are real, having to deal with, as they do, almost incomprehensible social changes, but she is unfazed. While acknowledging that there are many drawbacks to China's rapid development, she is quick to point out that there are also huge opportunities. The country has started to transform itself from a 'net importer of experience and capital to a net exporter', she says, adding that China is on the cusp of a production and design revolution.

Zhao co-founded Dada Architects in 2007 and over a decade she has tried to develop an approach that might inspire young designers – in China or elsewhere – to 'stop locking themselves in their own particular domain'. She simply wants them to broaden their horizons, create opportunities and seize the moment. Now is the time for Chinese designers to avoid playing safe and pigeon-holing themselves. She wants them to be bold, to experiment with a variety of design possibilities, drawing on allied disciplines such as interior design, product design or industrial design.

Zhao sets a good example. Her own interdisciplinary practice sees her networking with artificial intelligence specialists in Silicon Valley, designing giant convention centres, or exhibiting at the Milan Furniture Fair. For her, the acquisition of knowledge, risk-taking and paying attention to detail are the most important hallmarks of her work.

In 2014 she won a prestigious Cooper Hewitt National Design Award for a wearable personal health monitor; the award was presented to her by Bruce Mau, a kindred interdisciplinary practitioner. Across her portfolio of projects, her work engages with cutting-edge technology but is increasingly becoming 'grounded in nature'. It is a way of working – indeed, a way of seeing – that came as something of a eureka moment for Zhao.

## I never care much about my gender

Spending too many hours hunched over the drawing-board in her student days left her with debilitating damage to her vertebrae. She took up tai chi as a way of easing her discomfort. Working with a tai chi master alerted her to the simplicity and profundity, as she puts it, of ancient Chinese wisdom, aesthetics and culture. Tai chi awakened her to a renewed appreciation of nature and a belief in humanity's codependency with the environment.

Zhao's award-winning health monitor was designed to analyse an individual's emotional and physical state and direct him or her to a healthier life balance. Similarly, her architecture has evolved and now takes on a more subtle form. She describes the parametric sweep of her bridge designs, for example, as reflecting the imperceptible curves formed by the weight of a snowflake falling on a bamboo leaf.

Speaking of her role as a female architect, she says, 'I never care much about my gender', and notes that for her generation, growing up under the one-child policy, she experienced one of its more counterintuitive and unintended consequences. With every family having only one child, 'no matter whether it was a boy or a girl, the parents had to invest the same level of attention. The prejudices of gender have therefore tended to fade because parents have only one chance. As a result, the proportion of working females in China is much higher than in Western countries.' And as far as Zhao is concerned, she will not be giving up her hard-won freedom. She is too keen to play her part in the next phase of Chinese development.

**Page 227** Façade of the 7th Strawberry Symposium Exhibition Centre + Hotel

**Architect:** Zhao Zhao
**Project:** 7th Strawberry Symposium Exhibition Centre + Hotel
**Location:** Changping District, Beijing
**Completion:** 2011

The buildings were designed for the 7th International Strawberry Symposium. They are situated in a 60,000m² (15 acre) agricultural area on the outskirts of Beijing, with a long tradition of cultivating strawberries. Zhao says that she used parametric design to reduce the construction budget. The exterior is 3.6m x 3.6m (12ft x 12ft) reinforced composite concrete panels. The complex took just eight months to complete.

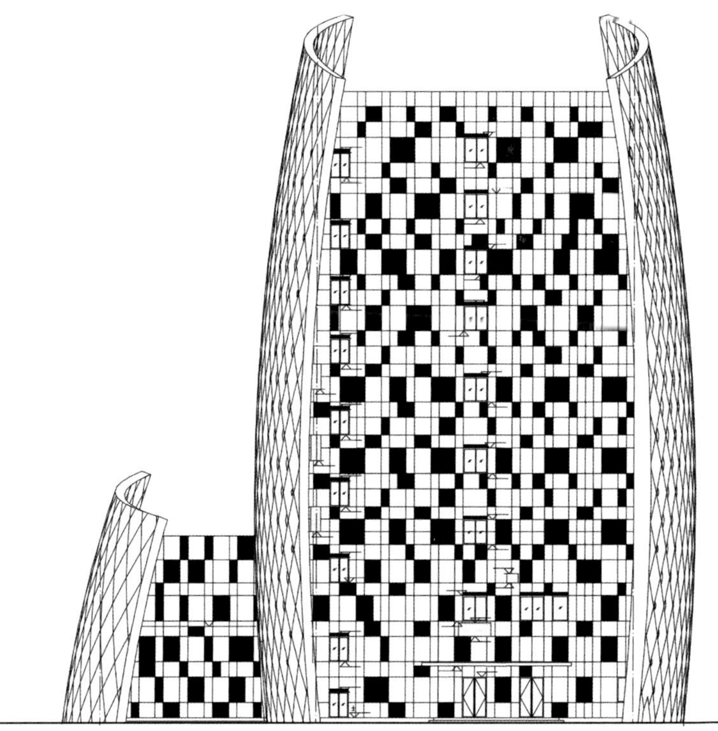

↗ 1

↘ 2

↗ 3

↘ 4

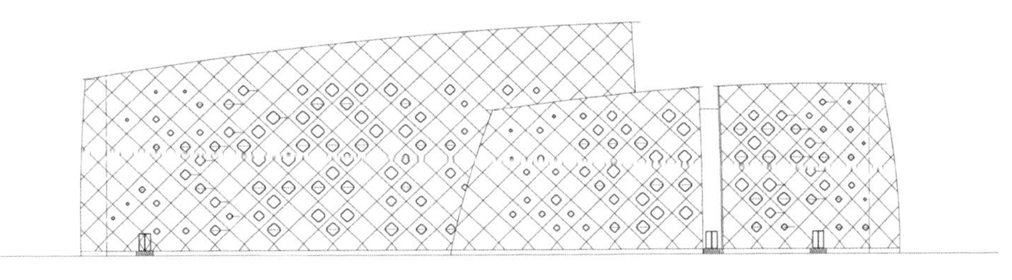

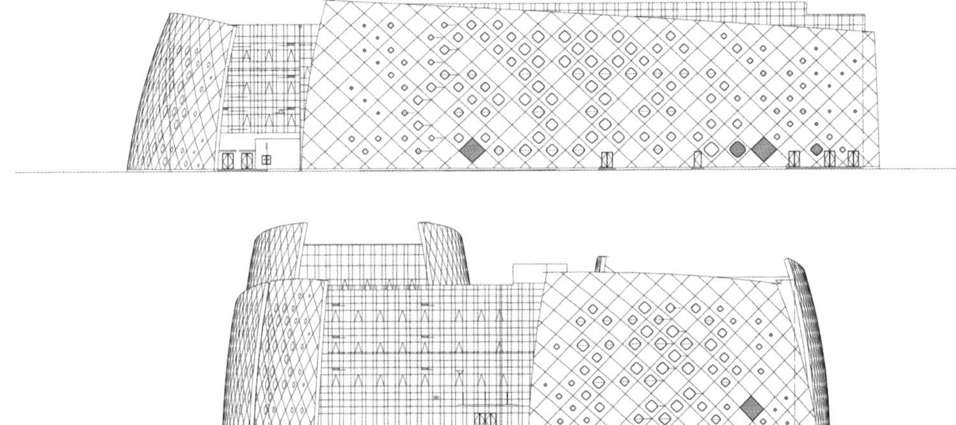

↘ 5

↗ 6

↘ 7

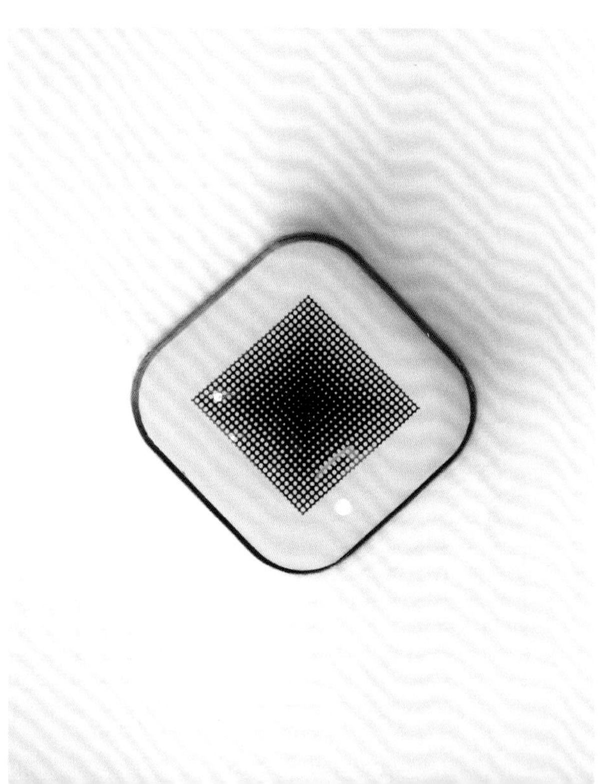

↘ 8

↗ 9

↘ 10

**Architect:** Zhao Zhao
**Project:** Wenyu River Bridge
**Location:** Changping District, Beijing
**Completion:** 2015

Zhao created the master plan for the new Changping Future Science and Technology Park, and the Wenyu River Bridge was designed to serve the surrounding commercial areas and link them together. The bridge is the first in this area. Zhao used parametric design to generate the unique form of the bridge, which sits well with the undulating nature of the surrounding landscape.

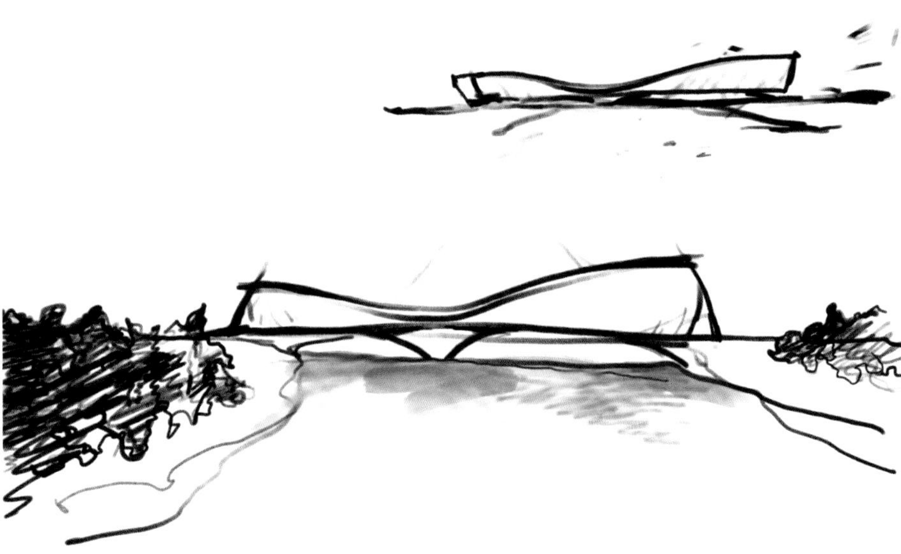

↗ 1

↗ 2

↗ 3

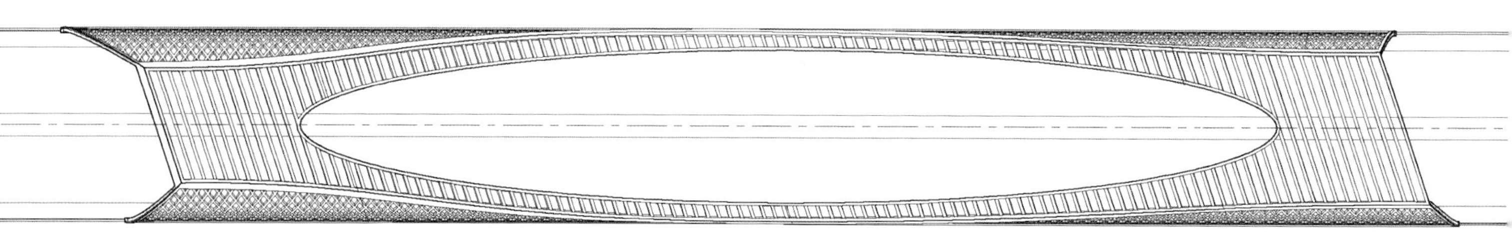

↗ 4

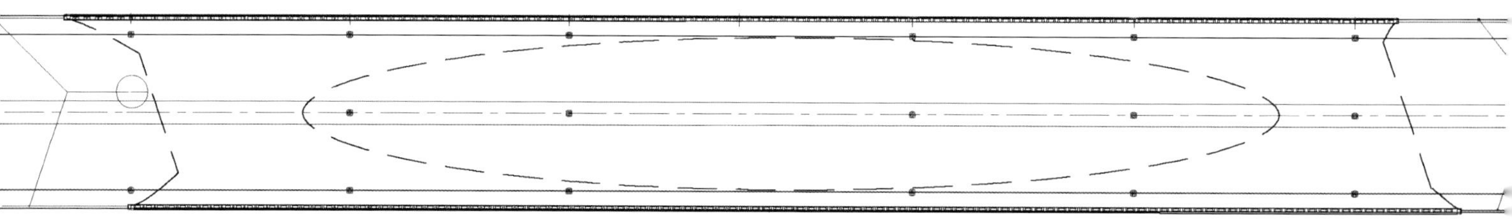

↗ 5

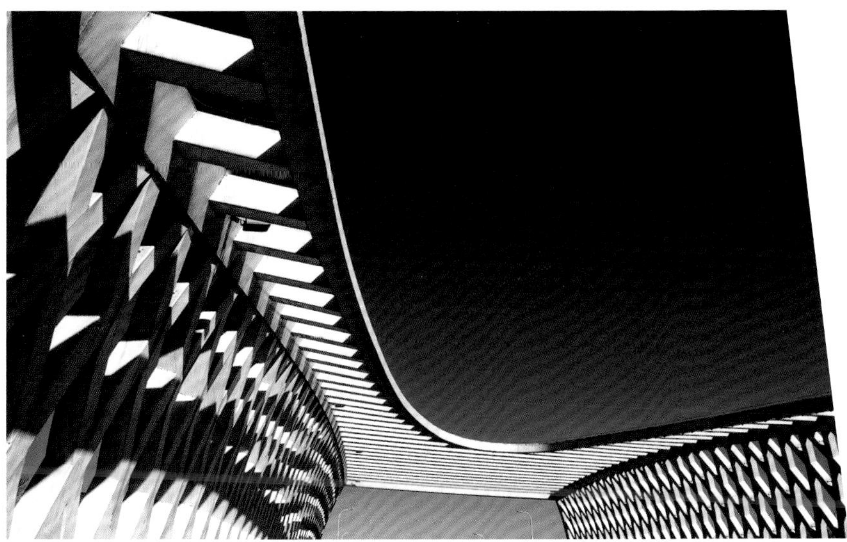

↗ 6

↘ 7

↗ 1

**Architect:** Zhao Zhao
**Project:** Chongqing Xiantao Big Data Valley
**Location:** Xiantao District, Chongqing
**Completion:** Under construction

In March 2014, the Chongqing Municipal Government finalized the planning and construction of Xiantao Big Data Valley, an industrial park that came into use in late 2017. The overall project comprises commercial areas, and 'livable city' quarters that focus on low-carbon lifestyles. Here the architect's designs emanated out of classic shan-shui (mountain and water) imagery, but within an urban context.

↘ 2

↘ 3

↘ 4

 5

**Architect:** Zhao Zhao
**Project:** Dongsha River City
**Location:** Changping District, Beijing
**Completion:** Under construction

Dongsha River faces serious environmental problems. The design of Dongsha River City is part of an exemplary project of the Eleventh Five-Year Plan (2006–10) to demonstrate the collaboration between technology and the environment. The main core of the plan is a green belt that will serve as a breathing lung for the entire district, which includes creative working areas, hotels and commercial centres, and a cultural quarter.

↗ 1

↗ 2

↘ 3

# Notes

## DEDICATION

1. Y. Ma, quoted in R.M. Poole, 'Zaha Hadid Inspires MAD Architect's Harbin Opera House', *BlouinArtinfo*, 2 April 2016: http://uk.blouinartinfo.com/news/story/1368987/zaha-hadid-inspires-mad-architects-harbin-opera-house/
2. V. Ng, quoted in O. Wong, 'How world-renowned architect Zaha Hadid influenced Hong Kong's famous skyline', *South China Morning Post*, 1 April 2016
3. E. Jiřičná, quoted in R. Kennedy and R. Pogrebin, 'Female Architects on the significance of Zaha Hadid', *New York Times*, 1 April 2016

## INTRODUCTION

1. A. Williams, *China's Urban Revolution: Understanding Chinese Eco-cities*, Bloomsbury, 2017
2. F.S. Victor, 'Soviet Influence on Urban Planning in Beijing, 1949–1991', *The Town Planning Review*, Vol. 67, No. 4, October 1996, pp.457–84
3. Y. Huang, 'Urban Development in Contemporary China', in G. Veeck, C.W. Pannell, C.J. Smith and Y. Huang, *China's Geography: Globalization and the Dynamics of Political, Economic and Social Change*, Roman & Littlefield Publishers, 2006, pp.233–62 (Chapter 9)
4. S. Chan, *Writing in(to) Architecture: China's Architectural Design and Construction since 1949*, East Slope Publishing, 2012, p.141
5. X. Qiu, *Death of a Red Heroine*, Hodder and Stoughton, 2006, p.145
6. T.M. Chen, 'Female Icons, Feminist Iconography? Socialist Rhetoric and Women's Agency in 1950s China', *Gender & History*, 15, 2003, pp.268–95
7. G. Sharp, 'Myth-Making and the "We Can Do It!" Poster', The Society Pages, 4 January 2011, https://thesocietypages.org/socimages/2011/01/04/myth-making-and-the-we-can-do-it-poster/ (accessed 6 April 2018)
8. A.C. Hu, 'Half the Sky, But Not Yet Equal: China's Feminist Movement', *Harvard International Review*, 22 August 2016
9. H. Guo, 'The Impacts of Economic Reform on Women in China' (thesis), University of Regina, Saskatchewan, August 1997, pp.1–136
10. 'Cahinese Education', Summer 1989, p.41, quoted in Guo, *op. cit.*
11. W. Ma, in S. Mow, J. Tao and B. Zheng, *Holding up Half the Sky: Chinese Women Past, Present, and Future*, The Feminist Press at CUNY, 2004, Table 1, p.111
12. L.H. Fincher, 'How Much Less than Half the Sky?' in *China Story Yearbook 2015*, The Australian National University, 2015, p.189
13. R. Kanthor, 'Holding Up Half the Sky: Women Speak Out on the Status of Feminism in China', Takepart, 29 July 2016, http://www.takepart.com/feature/2016/07/29/women-china (accessed 6 April 2018)
14. B. Larmer, 'The long march from China to the Ivies', *1843* magazine, April/May 2016
15. 'Photographer Luo Yang captures China's new generation of "Girls"', BBC News, 25 November 2016
16. D. Matthews, 'What future for women in Chinese higher education?', *Times Educational Supplement*, 21 January 2016
17. L.T. Chang, *Factory Girls: Voices from the Heart of Modern China*, Picador, 2008, pp.57–58
18. Tao Jie, Zheng Bijun and Shirley L. Mow (eds), *Holding Up Half the Sky: Chinese Women, Past, Present, and Future*, The Feminist Press, 2004, p.xiv
19. M. Wang, 'Architectural Experiments: 筑的实验', *Time + Architecture: 2*, 2000, pp.8–11
20. M. Zeiger, 'Despite the pulls of gender, there is still the work – the ideas, designs and buildings that transcend any single notion of identity', *The Architects' Journal*, 1 March 2016

## DING WOWO

1. See K.W.M. Siu and G.J. Contreras (eds), *Design Education for Fostering Creativity and Innovation in China*, IGI Global, 2016, p.14

## DU JUAN

1. Y. Wang and S. Rayer, 'Foreign In-Migration to Florida, 2005–2014', Bureau of Economic and Business Research, University of Florida, 15 April 2016: https://www.bebr.ufl.edu/population/website-article/foreign-migration-florida-2005E280932014 (accessed 20 March 2018)

## PENG LELE

1. See Guanghui Ding, 'Constructing a Place of Critical Architecture in China: Intermediate Criticality' in *Time + Architecture*, Routledge, 2016, p.100

## WANG LUMING

1. Giles Deleuze, *The Fold: Leibnitz and the Baroque*, trans. Tom Conley, University of Minnesota Press, 1988

## YE MIN

1. Edward L. Davies, *Encyclopedia of Contemporary Chinese Culture*, Taylor & Francis, 2009
2. Cain Nunns, 'China's Poly Group: The most important company you've never heard of', GlobalPost, Public Radio International (Minneapolis, MN), 25 February 2013

## ZHANG JINQIU

1. Lin Fei, *Legendary life of the first generation of Chinese woman architect Zhang Yuquan*, Tianjin University Press, 2006, p.240

# Research Team

**Austin Williams** is senior lecturer in Architecture and Professional Practice at Kingston School of Art, UK, and Honorary Research Fellow at XJTLU University, Suzhou, China. He is the director of the Future Cities Project in London, the China correspondent for *The Architectural Review*, and the author of *China's Urban Revolution: Understanding Chinese Eco-cities*.

The founder of the mantownhuman manifesto, featured in Penguin Classics' *100 Artists Manifestos*, Williams has spoken at a wide range of conferences, from New York to Ningbo and from Hawaii to Hong Kong, and is a regular media commentator on development, environmentalism and China. He directed over 200 short documentaries for NBSTV and authored and illustrated the *Shortcuts* design guides. You can find him as Future_Cities on Wechat and Twitter, or visit www.futurecities.org.uk.

**Lead Researchers**

Dai Yiqing

Kuang Wei

Di Yang

**Researchers**

Jiang Yi

Huang Yunheng

Ding Xiao

Li Yixuan

Li Yuchen

Qian Shiyu

Tang Lanke

Wei Zhuo

Xue Yuan

Yu Miao

Yu Xinning

# Acknowledgments

I would like to thank the all-female team that worked on this project: an excellent and highly dedicated group of young researchers and interviewers based at XJTLU university that comprises:

Dai Yiqing, Wei Kuang, Di Yang, Ding Xiao, Yu Miao, Jiang Yi, Yu Xinning, Huang Yunheng, Tang Lanke, Xue Yuan, Li Yuchen, Li Yixuan, Qian Shiyu and Wei Zhuo. Each one is an essential member of XJTLU's MPTF network and has played a variety of hugely important roles that have resulted in this book. It was an initial conversation with Qian Shiyu that sparked the idea and led to the formation of the research project team. All the above are the real heroes (heroines) of this book.

I would specifically like to single out Dai Yiqing, Wei Kuang and Di Yang, who have directed this project impeccably, sometimes in frustrating and stressful circumstances while still managing to keep everything on course. I cannot thank you enough. This book is dedicated to you. I look forward to watching you seize the very best opportunities ahead.

Thanks to Dong Yiping and Xi Junjie for ideas and assistance and thanks to the brilliant MPTF editorial teams – always fronted by strong women – for backing the project that eventually gave rise to this book.

Clearly, I am indebted to all the featured architects for their time, generosity and documentation, and for relating their fascinating life stories.

Each of the individual architects' portrait photographs are by Wei (Joshua) Ping and Yang (Derry) Chow of Joer Studio based in Beijing, Hangzhou and London. To achieve such beautifully understated results has involved a lot of organization, coordination and diplomacy on their part for which I am very grateful.

My thanks go to all the editors, designers, sales and marketing, and others in the Thames & Hudson production team without whom this book would not exist. But primarily I want offer my thanks to Lucas Dietrich, Fleur Jones and Bethany Wright at Thames & Hudson in London for their confidence in, support for and appreciation of this project.

# Picture Credits

All plans, drawings and photographs are courtesy of the architects, unless otherwise noted.

The portraits on the following pages are by Wei (Joshua) Ping and Yang (Derry) Chow: 14, 22, 32, 46, 56, 68, 80, 94, 102, 110, 122, 130, 138, 150, 160, 172, 186, 194, 212, 226, 245–46

**Introduction, pp. 8–13:** image 1: International Institute of Social History, Amsterdam; image 2: Photo Time Life Pictures/National Archives/The LIFE Picture Collection/Getty Images; image 3: Edward Farrell; **Di Shaohua, pp. 14–21:** Dongrun Apartment: PRAXiS d'ARCHITECTURE; Spring Art Museum and Ying Gallery: Xia Zhi; **Ding Wowo, pp. 22–31:** Ding Wowo, Jinlong Feng, Bowen Hou; **Dong Mei, pp. 32–45:** Beijing Badaling Forest Experience Centre and Ding Xiang Eco-Village: Zhang Yong; Hei Hu Primary School: 1: Biechu Koōngjiaān Architects; 5: Liu Xiaochuan; **Du Juan, pp. 46–55:** Open House: Margot Errante; Room with a Changing View: Denice Hough/IDU; House with a Borrowed Landscape: Leon Suen/IDU; **Fan Beilei, pp. 56–67:** Baggy Treehouse: Hou Bowen and Jason Hu; Original Homestay and Shangsi'an Retreat: Hou Bowen; **Rossana Hu, pp. 68–79:** Rachel's Burger: Dirk Weiblen; The Waterhouse, Sulwhasoo Flagship Store and Le Méridien Zhengzhou: © Pegenaute (www.pedropegenaute.es); **Jiang Ying, pp. 80–93:** Silo Reconversion: Kelvan Dong; Youth Hotel in iD Town: Chaos.Z; Z Gallery: Liky Foto; **Doreen Heng Liu, pp. 94–101:** NODE; **Lu Wenyu, pp. 102–9:** Ningbo Contemporary Art Museum: Lv Hengzhong; Renovation of Wencun Village: Lv Hengxhong and Lu Wenyu; **Peng Lele, pp. 110–21:** G-Dot Art Space: page 111 and images 1–2: Tong Huiyi, images 3–6: Atelier 100s+1; Songzhuang Town: Atelier 100s+1; S+Q Sculpture Studio: Zeng Renzhen; **Qi Shanshan, pp. 122–29:** Shen-photo c/o Studio Qi; **Tang Yu'en, pp. 130–37:** Shanghai Library: Chen Borong; **Wang Luming, pp. 138–49:** Binhai Xiaowai High School and Freeze Factory: Wang Zhenfei; Earthly Pond Service Centre: Wang Zhenfei (images 1–2, 5) and DuoCai (image 4); **Wang Wei, pp. 150–59:** Yangzhou Yucai Primary School: FAO; Building in Village and Panchenggang District: Gao Wenzhong; **Wang Youfen, pp. 160–71:** CNNT; **Wei Na, pp. 172–85:** Springing Stream: Jin Wei-Qi; WHY Hotel: Zhi Xia; Shatan Courtyard House: Shen Yanlei; **Ye Min, pp. 186–93:** Fei Architects; **Zhang Di, pp. 194–211:** AnyShopStyle: WAA (image 1); NAARO (page 195 and images 2–6); Yinchuan Museum of Contemporary Art (MOCA): NAARO; Valley Resort: WAA; **Zhang Jinqiu, pp. 212–25:** China Northwest Architecture Design and Research Institute; **Zhao Zhao, pp. 226–43:** Dada Architects

# Index

Page numbers in *italic* refer to the illustrations

## C



## D

# E



# F



# G



# H

# I



# J



# K



# L



# M



# N

## O



## P



## Q



## R



## S

# T

## U



## V



## W



## X



## Y

## Z